Today's ISMS

Works by William Ebenstein

Today's Isms: *Communism, Fascism, Capitalism, Socialism (Fifth Edition)*
Totalitarianism: *New Perspectives*
Two Ways of Life: *The Communist Challenge to Democracy (Second Edition)*
Communism in Theory and Practice
Great Political Thinkers: *Plato to the Present (Third Edition)*
Modern Political Thought: *The Great Issues (Second Edition)*
Man and the State: *Modern Political Ideas*
The Nazi State
The German Record: *A Political Portrait*
Introduction to Political Philosophy
Political Thought in Perspective
Fascist Italy
Church and State in Franco Spain
The Pure Theory of Law
The Law of Public Housing
American Democracy in World Perspective *(co-author)*

Fifth Edition

Communism

Fascism

Capitalism

Socialism

William Ebenstein
University of California, Santa Barbara

Prentice-Hall, Inc., Englewood Cliffs, New Jersey

Library of Congress Catalog Card Number: 67-17373

Printed in the United States of America

Current printing (last digit):

10 9 8 7 6 5 4 3 2

Prentice-Hall International, Inc., London
Prentice-Hall of Australia, Pty. Ltd., Sydney
Prentice-Hall of Canada, Ltd., Toronto
Prentice-Hall of India (Private) Ltd., New Delhi
Prentice-Hall of Japan, Inc., Tokyo

To the memory of Joy

Preface

The major conflict of our age is the struggle between aggressive totalitarianism and the free way of life. Not long ago the chief threat to liberty was fascism; today it is communism. The violence and terror of totalitarian communism and fascism, ranging from slave labor camps to genocide, reflect a fanatical ideology that brooks no compromise.

This book is a discussion of the main representatives of each side—communism and fascism on the totalitarian side, capitalism and socialism on the democratic. In a short book, it has seemed advisable to concentrate on the isms that shape the fate of the world rather than to discuss in detail the numerous other isms that are important, but that have not been decisive, in the struggle for men's minds. These lesser isms, whether philosophical, political, social, or economic, are therefore dealt with in this book only to the extent that they are related to the four major isms. The psychological roots of totalitarianism and democracy are given particularly close attention, since it is difficult to understand either system without understanding both the personality traits and psychological motivations to which each system appeals.

The key approach in this book is through the *way of life* concept rather than through one particular aspect, such as government or economics. Totalitarianism and democracy are more than specific social, political, or economic systems: they are two diametrically opposed ways of life, with contradicting beliefs and values, based on distinct and opposite conceptions of the nature of man. The scope and gravity of the present world crisis can therefore be fully grasped only by perceiving it, not as the mere result of conflicting political or economic ideas and practices, but as a conflict between two ways of thought and action encompassing the totality of social life.

William Ebenstein

University of California
Santa Barbara

Contents

The Totalitarian Way of Life

1

1. Totalitarian Communism, 3

2. Totalitarian Fascism, 105

The Democratic Way of Life

2

3. Democratic Capitalism, 139

4. Democratic Socialism, 211

Index, 263

Today's ISMS

The Totalitarian Way of Life

1

1. Totalitarian Communism
2. Totalitarian Fascism

Totalitarian Communism

The economic interpretation of history

Before Marx, history was interpreted in several typical fashions. Some interpreters sought the key to history in the working of divine providence and conceived of human development as but part of the unfolding of God's design of the whole universe. The main difficulty of this *religious* interpretation of history lies in the fact that God's will is unknown and unknowable to man's direct experience and that whereas there is only one God, there are many contrasting human conceptions of God and his plans for mankind.

A second dominant pre-Marxist approach to the understanding of human history was *political:* great emperors, kings, legislators, and soldiers were viewed as the decisive forces in history; and historical writing was largely the record of kings, parliaments, wars, and peace treaties.

This political emphasis in human affairs has one main shortcoming: it tends to exaggerate the relative role that most people assign to government and politics in the total setting of their lives. It is natural that statesmen, politicians, and political philosophers consider politics the most important single element in human relations, and political remedies the most important answer to human troubles. But human nature and human problems are more intricate than politics; politics is only one approach—and not always the most penetrating one—among many others.

A third major approach, the *hero interpretation of history* (popularized in modern times by Carlyle), is closely related to the political one, inasmuch as most heroes in world history are conventionally chosen from great kings, emperors, generals, legislators, founders of new states, pioneering reformers, and revolutionaries. The main weakness of the hero interpretation is that it overstresses the role of individuals at the expense of larger cultural, religious, social, and economic circumstances that form the background without which there can be no meaningful exercise of leadership. Although it is undoubtedly true that leaders mold events, it is no less true that events mold leaders.

The fourth pre-Marxist approach to the understanding of history was through the impact of *ideas:* ideas were conceived (by Hegel, for example) to be the principal causes of the historical process, and the material conditions (social, economic, technological, military) of society were thought of as essentially derived from, and caused by, the great motivating ideas. This emphasis on ideas often also implied that history was progressively evolving toward the realization of key ideas, such as freedom and democracy.

While undoubtedly containing—like the other interpretations—much that is valid, the exclusive emphasis on ideas as the main driving force in history overlooks the fact that ideas not only generate events but also reflect them. Therefore, to isolate ideas as the chief agent of human action is to neglect the framework of circumstances; circumstances, after all, make some ideas possible and others not, and it is circumstances from which ideas derive their vitality and practical impact.

The study of history may also be focused on *war:* the phenomenon of conflict is present in all phases of human development, and the birth, rise, and decline of states are often directly connected with warfare. The shortcoming of the military interpretation of history lies in its failure to recognize war as the result, rather than as the cause, of events. There is no doubt that war often marks a turning point in the life of nations and civilizations; yet the dramatic swiftness and decisiveness of war should not draw our attention from the multitude of psychological, ideological and material factors that lead to war and contribute to its complexity.

Marx's analysis of society was set forth through his *economic interpretation of history:* the production of the goods and services that support human life, and the exchange of those goods and services, are the bases of all social processes and institutions. Marx does not claim that the economic factor is the only one that goes into the making of history; he does claim that it is the most important one, the *foundation* upon which is erected the *superstructure* of culture, law, and government, buttressed by corresponding political, social, religious, literary, and artistic ideologies.

In a general way, Marx describes the relations between men's material conditions of life and their ideas by saying that "*it is not the consciousness of men which determines their existence, but, on the contrary, it is their social existence which determines their consciousness.*"

In a nomadic society, for example, horses might be considered the principal means of acquiring and accumulating wealth. From Marx's viewpoint, this foundation of nomadic life is the clue to its superstructure of law, government, and dominant ideas. Thus, Marx would say that those who are the owners of the greatest number of horses in such a nomadic society would also be the political chieftains who make and interpret the law; they are also likely to receive the highest respect and deference from the tribe's members who own no horses. In the realm of ideas, the predominant social and cultural concepts would reflect the dominant economic position of the owners of horses. Even in religion the impact would not be missing: God might, for instance, be represented in the image of a swift and powerful rider, and the concept of divine justice and rule would be, in a sense, an extension and magnification of human justice as determined by the horse-owning chiefs.

In a settled agricultural society, the ownership of land would provide the clue to the political, social, legal and cultural institutions and conceptions. In such a society, according to Marx, the landowning class is the real ruler of state and society, regardless of any divergent formal organization of authority. Similarly, the landowning class would also set the predominant social standards and values.

Finally, according to Marx, *in the modern industrial society of the last two hundred years the ownership of the means of industrial production is the master key:* the capitalists not only determine the economic destiny of society, but also rule it politically (regardless of formal and legal façades to the contrary) and set its social standards and values. The ultimate purpose of the law, education, the press, and artistic and literary creation is to maintain an ideology that is imbued with the sanctity and justice of capitalist property ownership.

Our understanding of history has gained immensely from Marx's economic interpretation. It is virtually impossible to write history today without some attention at least to the relation of economic forces and conflicts to political, military, and international issues.

In pointing out Marx's overemphasis on economics, however, one must not go to the other extreme of denying that economic interests play an important part in human affairs. The Marxian theory reduces man to an earth-bound beast with no spark of the lofty and divine; some anti-Marxian theories, on the other hand, have raised man to the level of an angelic being, having no contact with the earth, nearly divine in his goodness. Men are only too often inclined to dress up their selfish and material aims and actions in high-sounding moral or religious phrases.

Marx's economic interpretation suffers from the same defect which afflicts all theories that pretend to supply the master key to history: *excessive generalization and simplification.* Whenever a single factor (be it the hero, war, religion, climate, race, geography, and so forth *ad infinitum*) is required to do the work of explanation and illumination that can only be properly done by several factors, its burden proves too heavy. No single factor has been predominant throughout history, and which factor is the most important in a particular situation is a question of empirical inquiry.

In any event or series of events there is always a complicated pattern of many factors, and it is none too easy to disentangle them. It is difficult enough to identify precisely the component motivations of an action of one person, because these actions are often mutually contradictory and logically inconsistent. It is even more difficult to isolate the determinant components in a single action of a small group; and it is virtually impossible to generalize about large-scale collective actions and processes throughout the whole of history.

To take one practical illustration: the Marxist interpretation holds that *imperialism* is caused primarily by economic interests and rivalries and that war in the capitalist era is the culmination of such imperialist rivalries. There have undoubtedly been manifestations of imperialism in history, ancient as well as modern, whose origins can be traced to economic factors—some of the classical imperialist expansion of advanced capitalist nations like Holland, England, and France in the eighteenth and early nineteenth centuries can be attributed chiefly to economic forces. It is also possible to set forth examples of minors wars, in antiquity as in more recent times, that have been primarily motivated by economic interests and conflicts.

The economic interpretation, nevertheless, misses the core of the great and vital conflicts of history.

The Greeks who fought the Persians 2500 years ago did so, not primarily to protect Athenian investments and trade interests in Asia Minor, but because they knew that the victory of Persia would mean the end of Greek civilization. Persian victory would undoubtedly have entailed serious economic and financial losses for the Greeks, but the main effect would have been the destruction of the Greek way of life, its devotion to the search for truth, and its appreciation of human values. Because the whole fabric of Western civilization is unthinkable without its Greek source, Persian victory over Greece would have meant the spiritual and intellectual "Asianization" of Europe.

To take more recent illustrations, the core of the conflict in World Wars I and II was not the protection of British investments in Africa or of American loans to Britain and France, but the more fundamental issue of whether freedom—religious, intellectual, political, racial—was to survive, or whether totalitarian militarism was to rule the world. Again, there is no doubt that a German victory in World War I or II would have entailed profound economic losses for the vanquished, but the economic effects would have been relatively minor compared with the effects of forced reversion to a way of life based on a denial of the Western tradition.

Finally, the present conflict between communist imperialism and the free world cannot be explained in Marxian economic terms, according to which imperialism is the last phase of an advanced and mature economy with an abundance of capital that it seeks to invest in less developed areas. From the economic viewpoint, the Soviet Union and Red China are hungry for capital, suffering from its scarcity rather than abundance. Their imperialism is motivated by noneconomic drives: the *political* aim of world domination.

What makes communist imperialism so serious a concern to the rest of the world is precisely—contrary to Marxist logic—its noneconomic character: the fact that its main weapons are tanks and subversion. The Hungarian Revolution of 1956 clearly showed that Soviet imperialism can ultimately rely only on tanks and guns, and not on economic or ideological penetration. The repression of the Tibetan rebellion by Red China in 1959 and her conquest of Indian border areas in 1959–1962 showed that Red China, too, ultimately relies on armed force as the primary instrument of imperialist expansion.

What the Marxist-communist interpretation misses in the analyses of major conflicts, is, first, the element of *power* (which is often the cause rather than the effect of economic advantage) and, second, the clash of *value systems,* which are frequently more important to people than economic interests, regardless of whether the values concerned are specifically political, religious, intellectual, or—in a wider sense—the symbolic expression of a whole way of life.

In fact, where conflicts of interest are primarily economic, compromise will usually be relatively easy. It is where more deeply felt values are at stake, such as individual liberty, freedom of religion, or national independence, that compromise becomes more difficult.

Dynamics of social change

Before Marx, basic social change was thought to be the result of the work of great political leaders, legislators, and pioneering reformers. Marx rejects the traditional emphasis on the force of personality as the principal agent of important social change and looks for an explanation in impersonal economic causes. The two key concepts that he uses in approaching the problem of basic social change are, first, the *forces of production* and, second, the *relations of production.* The clash between these two is the deeper cause of basic social change, as expressed by Marx in his *Critique of Political Economy* (1859): "At a certain stage of their development the material productive forces of society come into contradiction with the existing productive relationships, or, what is but a legal expression for these, with the property relationships within which they have moved before. From forms of development of the productive forces these relationships are transformed into their fetters. Then an epoch of social revolution opens. With the change in the economic foundation the whole vast superstructure is more or less rapidly transformed."

The Marxist conception of the *forces of production* expresses *man's relation to nature* and is essentially what we would call today technological and scientific *know-how.* Marx's notion of the *relations of production* expresses *man's relation to man* and encompasses all that we would include today under the term *social institutions.* Seen in these more modern terms, what Marx roughly suggests is that in every social-economic system there is at first a balance between knowledge and social organization, but gradually a disequilibrium or lag develops between available scientific knowledge and existent social institutions. *Our scientific knowledge grows faster than our social wisdom.*

This lag is the more modern, and broader, version of Marx's more specific lag between the forces of production and the relations of production. Since the economic aspects of society are for Marx its chief determining factor, it is not surprising that he reduces the general phenomenon of the lag between knowledge and wisdom to the more specific lag between forces of production and relations of production.

Thus, to provide an illustration in line with the Marxist pattern, when new productive forces developed within the productive relations of the feudal system, social revolution was, according to Marx, inevitable because the productive relations of feudalism (property relations, market controls, internal customs and tariffs, monetary instability) did not permit the utilization of the newly developing productive forces of industrial capitalism.

The capitalist system, having run its cycle, now shows the same tendency to rigidity, Marx holds, and it is due to meet the same fate when its productive forces (the capacity to produce) have outstripped its productive relations (law of private property, production for private profit). Like the social systems preceding it, capitalism thus will eventually stand in the way of scientific knowledge and will not permit technological resources to be fully employed.

What has doomed all historically known forms of economic organization, according to Marx, is the fact that when new productive forces develop, the existing productive relations—i.e., the existing social institutions—stand in the way of their proper utilization. Each system thus eventually becomes wasteful in terms of the creative potentialities that have developed in its womb but are not permitted to be born and to grow. Only public ownership of the means of production can, according to Marx, bring into existence a new system of productive relations based on production for common use rather than for private profit that will match the tremendous forces of production actually or potentially known to man. In other words, man's capacity to produce will find full expression only in a social system in which production is limited by scarce resources and incomplete knowledge, and not by such faulty social institutions as production for private profit based on the private ownership of the means of production.

Marx's insight that man's knowledge of physical nature ("forces of production") grows faster than his wisdom in creating social institutions ("relations of production") is highly important in understanding a vital source of social tension and conflict both within and between nations.

What distinguishes Marx from non-Marxists is his insistence that *basic social change*—caused by the excessive lag between advanced scientific knowledge and retrograde social institutions—can be brought about *only by revolution;* whereas non-Marxists affirm that the necessary changes can be effected by peaceful means.

Revolution the only way out

In the *Communist Manifesto,* Marx explains why revolution is the only method of basic social transformation. When technological know-how ("forces of production") begins to outstrip the existing social, legal, and political institutions ("relations of production"), the owners of the means of production do not politely step aside to allow history to run its inevitable course. Since the ideology of the ruling class reflects the existing economic system, the owners of the means of production sincerely believe that the existing system is economically the most efficient, socially the most equitable, and philosophically the most harmonious with the laws of nature and the will of whatever god they venerate.

Marx penetratingly denies that the individual feudal landowner or industrial capitalist obstructs social change out of selfish greed: the resistance of the ruling class to change is so obstinate—making revolution finally inevitable—precisely because it identifies its own values with universally valid ones. The ruling class will, therefore, mobilize all the instruments of the legal, political, and ideological superstructure to block the growth of the forces that represent the potentially more progressive economic system. For this reason, Marx states early in the *Communist Manifesto,* the "history of all hitherto existing society is the history of class struggles."

Marx could find no instance in history in which a major social and economic system freely abdicated to its successor. On the assumption that the future will resemble the past, the communists, as the *Communist Manifesto* says, "openly declare that their ends can be attained only by the forcible overthrow of all existing social conditions."

This is the crucial tenet of Marxism-Leninism and is the one that most clearly and irreconcilably distinguishes it from democracy.

Marx had no clear-cut notion of how the political transformation from capitalism to communism would come about. Though in the *Communist Manifesto,* as throughout most of his other statements on the problem, he believed in the need for revolution, he was occasionally less dogmatic. Speaking in 1872 at a public meeting in Amsterdam following the Congress of the International, Marx conceded that the working class can travel on different roads in its quest for power: "We know that we must take into consideration the institutions, the habits and customs of different regions, and we do not deny that there are countries like America, England, and—if I knew your institutions better I would perhaps add Holland—where the workers can attain their objective by peaceful means. But such is not the case in all other countries."

Marx never fully pursued the implications of this distinction, and the orthodox opinion of Marxism-communism has remained that fundamental social and economic change is impossible except by class war, violence, and revolution.

In the early 1830's there occurred two major revolutions that Marx failed to appraise properly. In 1832, the passage of the Reform Act in England meant that the government of the nation would thenceforth be shared by the aristocracy and the middle classes, with the weight constantly shifting in favor of the latter.

At about the same time, the Jacksonian revolution in the United States effected a similar peaceful shift in class power, by bringing the men from the backwoods into American politics and successfully challenging the supremacy of the gentlemen from Virginia and New England who had treated the government of the United States as their God-given preserve.

These changes in Britain and the United States were more than just political victories: they inaugurated a permanent shift in the distribution of social and economic power in both nations, the kind of basic change that Marx had in mind. When revolution swept all over Europe in 1848, England was spared because the aims of the revolution of 1848—winning for the middle class its proper share of social and political power—had already been peacefully obtained by the British middle class in 1832.

If Marx had accorded the political factor its due weight, if he had fully grasped the importance of the Reform Act in England and of the Jacksonian revolution in the United States, he might have realized that socialism, too, might be accomplished without violence in countries that possessed democratic traditions strong enough to absorb far-reaching social and economic changes without resorting to civil war. A recognition of the cultural and political factors in the equation of social change would have amounted, however, to a virtual abandonment of the central position of Marx: that history is the history of class wars and that ruling classes always defend their positions to the bitter end.

When Marx allowed, occasionally, that in countries like England, the United States, or Holland, violent revolution would be unnecessary in transforming capitalism into the classless proletarian society, it was obvious that what the three countries had in common was *political democracy*, supported by democratic habits and institutions in all kinds of human relations, whether political or not. Whether the range of Marx's exceptions should now be enlarged or not thus depends on whether democracy has spread in the world since his death.

In any case, Marx's concession that in a few politically advanced countries revolution might be unnecessary has always caused the communists a good deal of headache. Lenin took up the question in *State and Revolution* (1918), his best known and most influential political tract, claiming that by 1917 "this exception made by Marx is no longer valid" because England and the United States had developed bureaucratic institutions "to which everything is subordinated and which trample everything under foot." Between 1872 and 1917, both England and the United States broadened the suffrage and moved steadily in the direction of more political and social reform. In 1884, only one year after Marx's death, a British Liberal leader, Sir William Harcourt, stated, "We are all socialists now," indicating the acceptance of basic social and economic reform by all parties.

Since the plain historical record of the years 1872–1917 seemed to contradict Lenin's dogma, it was necessary to rewrite history. Far from admitting that England and the United States had moved toward more political and social democracy since 1872,

Lenin maintained that both countries had become more repressive, authoritarian, and plutocratic. To Sir William Harcourt's "We are all socialists now," Lenin would have replied, "You are all bloodthirsty, militaristic lackeys of Wall Street."

Since 1917, the communist case has become progressively weaker. In the United States, there has been the peaceful revolution of social reform, which started early in the century with Theodore Roosevelt's Square Deal, was continued by Woodrow Wilson's New Freedom, and culminated in Franklin D. Roosevelt's New Deal.

In Britain, Lloyd George's "People's Budget" of 1909 gave the propertied classes a foretaste of things to come. In 1945, the victory of the Labor Party at the polls was more than a mere electoral triumph. Just as 1832 meant the incorporation of the middle classes into the government of the nation, 1945 meant the same thing for the working classes in Britain. Whether the Labor Party is henceforth in office or in opposition, the British working class will remain an active partner in the business of governing the nation.

In the light of these facts, the only way left open to communist interpretation is to rewrite history. In the communist mythology, the New Deal was not the revolt of the little man against Big Business, but a clever plot of Big Business to keep itself in power. Similarly, the communists deny that the British Labor Party is socialist and claim that it is actually a front for the propertied classes.

The relentless communist insistence on revolution as the only way of basic social change violates Marxist doctrine at one central point. According to Marx, the conditions of man's existence determine his consciousness, and social change is, therefore, not the product of mere will and free choice. Where the conditions of society permit peaceful change from private to public ownership of the means of production, the use of force and subversion is, in a deeply Marxian sense, un-Marxian.

The communist dogma of universal revolution and dictatorship is in harmony with Marx's theory of consciousness only in societies in which the conditions of social and political life have created a general distrust in the possibility of peaceful change; it is out of harmony in nations whose democratic consciousness is the result, not of paper constitutions, but of the conditions of their existence. By insisting on universal revolution and dictatorship as the one and only method of change, communists in fact proclaim the un-Marxian doctrine that, regardless of historical, cultural, social, economic, and political conditions, a uniform consciousness—the creed of communism—can be imposed everywhere by sheer force.

There is a similar, reverse dogmatism maintained by anticommunist adherents of free enterprise, who would like to see it practiced in the whole world. They, too, violate elementary common sense and historical experience. Whether a society is likely to operate a capitalist economy is not a matter of pure logic and choice, but the result of historical environment, cultural heritage, social institutions, and political ideologies. Thus, in 1900 it would have been easy to predict that basic changes in Britain or the United States would occur without revolution and that such changes would be accompanied by violence and revolution in countries like Russia or China.

At present, it is often possible to predict whether change will be possible with or without violence. Yet there are countries, such as Brazil or India, where prediction is difficult because the balance of democratic versus undemocratic habits and traditions is not easy to define. Clearly, in view of the fact that such borderline countries exist, no general prediction based on dogma—be it communist or anticommunist dogma—is likely to be accurate. Every prediction is a question of investigating each particular situation rather than of applying preconceived universal laws of development.

Usually, correct theory is a guide to effective policy, and faulty theory is punished by practical failure. Where the communist concept of revolutionary change is supported by the underlying facts of social and cultural development—as in the economically and politically backward areas of Europe, Asia, Africa, and South America—either communist revolution has succeeded or communist spearheads have penetrated the body politic in preparation for the conquest of power. Where the anticommunist position has been theoretically sound, where democratic conditions of existence make revolutionary change unappealing and unnecessary—as in northwestern Europe, North America, Australia, New Zealand, Uruguay, and Israel—anticommunist policy has been successful.

If the world today is divided, with one major orbit led by the United States and the other by the Soviet Union and Red China, this political division generally follows the division into two ways of life: in one orbit, social change can be transacted more or less peacefully; in the other, human relations are not yet established on a basis of consent. Where these internal conditions are not clearly defined, the external political commitment is uncertain also. The economic aid program is the indirect method of the United States to counteract communism by helping economically retarded nations so that they do not have to look to communist revolution as the way out.

Economic contradictions of capitalism

The end of capitalism will be brought about, Marx argues, not by "subversive conspiracies" of professional revolutionaries, but by the same inexorable laws of social development and change that destroyed previous systems. Marx uses, first, the "grave-digger" theory: the more capitalism succeeds, the more capitalist enterprise is organized in *large-scale* units and the more it inevitably creates its own grave-digger, a class-conscious proletariat. Big Labor inevitably follows Big Business.

The capitalist class has no way of escaping the dilemma of rearing its own destroyer as it goes along: the *law of the falling profit rate* (which is not to be confused with the absolute amount of profit) makes such escape impossible. Marx's prediction of the declining profit rate was based on the assumption that, under the capitalist system of production, the entrepreneurial class would steadily accumulate more and more capital; the lessened scarcity of capital would then inevitably be reflected in the decline of the price (interest) and return (profit) of capital.

There can be no disagreement—because the facts speak too plainly—that the absolute amount of profits has risen immensely since Marx and is constantly rising.

What about Marx's prediction that the *rate* of profit (and of interest) would go down because capital would become more abundant?

Here, too, the prediction has not come true. During the depression of the 1930's, the rates of profit and interest were low and seemed to confirm Marx's forecast. Yet in the 1950's and 1960's, as in earlier periods of prosperity, the rates of interest and profit again reached new highs, thus disproving Marx.

Contrary to Marx, the facts of economic history do not support his "law of the falling profit rate." Marx made his erroneous prediction because he looked primarily at the *supply* side of capital: more and more capital is constantly created and accumulated in the capitalist system, and increased supply of a good leads to a lower price—provided the demand remains the same. Yet this is exactly what did not happen. The reason for the high interest rates (price of capital) in the 1950's and 1960's is that, despite an all-time high in the supply of capital, the *demand for capital has grown even faster* since too many companies simultaneously want fresh capital for the improvement, expansion, and building of productive facilities.

The price of capital (interest) or return of capital (profit) are subject to the classical economic law of supply and demand and not to any predetermined Marxian law of constant decline. Whenever the demand for capital outruns the supply, the rate of interest goes up, and the price of capital behaves like any other price.

The reason Marx overlooked the importance of the demand side in the capital market was his expectation (and hope) that the capitalist system would gradually lose its vitality and growth, thus requiring less new capital for investment. This, however, has not happened.

Finally, Marx also underestimated the role of technological progress. Capitalism constantly produces not only more capital, but *more efficient capital.* More available capital need not lead to lower rates of profit if the capital is more efficient.

In a stationary economy in which there is little or no technological innovation, more capital might automatically lead to lower rates of profit and interest. In a progressive economy in which the productivity of capital is constantly raised, profits and the rate of profit may go up although the absolute amount of available capital is also rising.

Moreover, technological innovation strengthens the demand side in the capital market because new technologies require large capital investments, thus counterbalancing the effects of increased capital on the supply side. The current capital investment needed to create a new job in the average American industry is well over $20,000, and it is much higher in electronics, chemicals, and petroleum. Therefore, as long as capitalism continues to progress technologically, the effects of increased capital resources will not, as Marx assumed, depress either the absolute volume of profit or the rate of profit.

Marx's main objection to capitalism was its inefficiency as well as its injustice. Here again, experience has contradicted his forecasts. The per capita consumption in the United States is still about 4-5 times higher than in the Soviet Union. As to technological innovation, the capitalist countries still are in most cases the creators, and the communist, the borrowers and imitators.

Marx also stated that capitalists would seek to stem the impact of the law of the falling profit rate in two ways: first, they would constantly seek to "rationalize" industry, or make it technologically more efficient. This would eliminate the less efficient enterprises and would lead to concentration of economic power, large-scale industrial organization, and increasing proletarianization. Second, they would invest capital in underdeveloped countries, where the return for capital (profit) is still very high. This device, Marx points out, only delays, but does not avert, the inevitable doom. In the colonial country, too, capital becomes increasingly more abundant, a native capitalist class develops, threatened by its own proletariat, and the law of the falling profit rate makes the imperialist solution of the capitalist dilemma at home unfeasible.

Contrary to Marx, the flow of private investments from industrially advanced nations has not been guided primarily by the economic consideration of high profits, but by the political consideration of safety and stability. In 1966, American investments abroad were over $50 billion. The Western Hemisphere, in which American capital has traditionally felt safest, accounts for about one half, and Western Europe accounts for over one quarter. In Asia and the Pacific, the trend of American investments has been toward Australia, Japan, and the Philippines rather than toward more underdeveloped nations like India and Indonesia. This is a typical illustration of Marx's underestimation of the political factor in economics.

Another source of tension that undermines the vitality of the capitalist system, according to Marx, is *unemployment*. In Marx's own time, industry expanded at an enormous rate, and there was a chronic shortage of labor. Yet Marx foresaw that the maldistribution of wealth and income under capitalism would lead to periodic crises of unemployment. The depression decade of 1929–1939 seemed to confirm his prediction; there was severe unemployment right up to 1939, when the preparation for war gradually eliminated it.

After World War II, the growth of welfare state policies in the major capitalist countries led to the recognition of full employment as a primary social objective. Among the major Western economies, only the United States has had a serious unemployment problem, averaging about 6 per cent in the decade of 1954–1963 but dropping to considerably lower levels in subsequent years. Other Western nations, such as France, West Germany, Sweden, and Switzerland, have for years had a labor shortage and have imported large numbers of workers from Italy, Spain, Greece, and Turkey. Oddly—and contrary to Marx's predictions—communist states like Poland and Yugoslavia have suffered from chronic unemployment for many years, and since the middle 1960's even the Soviet Union has publicly admitted the existence of unemployment.

Marx also predicted that two other developments would disintegrate the capitalist system: the *concentration of economic power* and, as a direct result, the *increasing proletarianization* of society. There is little doubt that, compared with earlier stages of industrial development, the contemporary capitalist economy shows impressive features of concentration. Yet it is doubtful that the tendency toward concentration in the capitalist system keeps on forever; at a later stage of industrial development the forces of competition begin to catch up with excessive concentration. Also, antimonopolistic public policies play an important part in strengthening competition.

Marx did not foresee that in highly advanced capitalist nations concentration of management might be mitigated by important counterforces: the spreading ownership of industry among large numbers of persons through the holding of shares of corporate businesses and the growing control of business managements by government, public opinion, and labor unions.

The role of the salariat

Marx's prediction of the inevitable proletarianization of society in a capitalist economy has been very largely disproved by events.

In the initial phases of industrial development, under capitalism or any other system, the industrial working class, Marx's "proletariat," constantly increases at the expense of artisans, landless peasants, and other social groups whose members seek employment in the expanding factories and mines. In a later and more advanced phase of industrial development, however, the industrial working class begins to decline in proportion to the total population, though it still continues to increase in absolute numbers. What Marx did not foresee was the enormous growth in an advanced economy that would create employment, but not of the proletarian type.

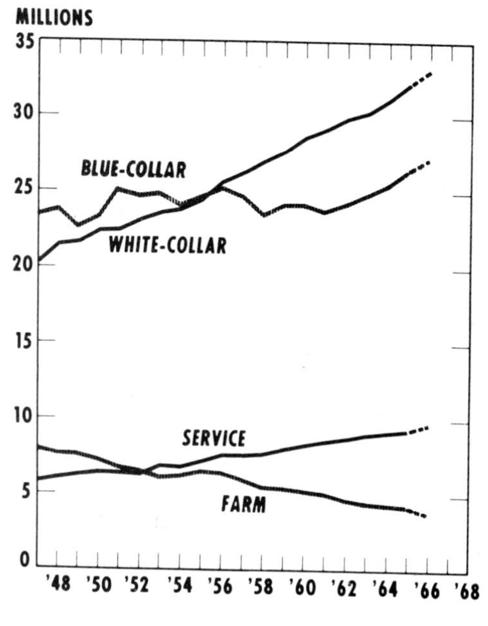

Reprinted from First National City Bank of New York, *Monthly Economic Letter* (October, 1966).

Occupational shifts in civilian employment.

In the United States, for example, the volume of industrial production and the number of persons employed in industry have increased tremendously since 1900, yet the proportion of the industrial working class in the total work force has consistently declined, for two reasons.

First, within industry itself, there has been an increasing shift of employment from blue-collar workers (Marx's "proletariat") to white-collar workers. In 1947, the percentage of white-collar personnel, or "salariat" (professional and executive employees, sales personnel, office workers), in manufacturing was 16 per cent of all employees; in 1965 white-collar personnel had risen to 26 per cent of all employees in manufacturing. The proportion of blue-collar workers in manufacturing in 1947–1965 thus sharply declined and barely kept its absolute size, although production more than doubled. The increase of total employment in manufacturing in the period of 1947–1965 from 15.5 million to 18 million has been almost entirely due to an increase of non-production personnel—that is, white-collar workers and professional, technical, and managerial personnel. Both technological progress and automation have reduced the number of workers needed to produce a given quantity of goods, such as coal, steel, or automobiles.

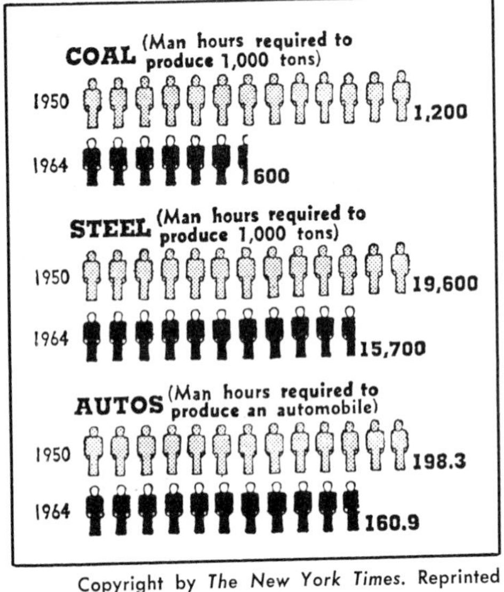

Copyright by *The New York Times*. Reprinted by permission.

The effects of automation.

The second reason for the relative growth of white-collar workers, or the salariat, is the rapid growth of employment in enterprises that produce services rather than physical goods, such as the government, motion pictures, radio and television, journalism, education, advertising, and the thousand and one new forms of service and entertainment made possible by the worker's increase in income and leisure.

This new type of economy is called *service economy* to distinguish it from the industrial economy that preceded it. Marx foresaw the transition from the agrarian to the industrial economy, but in all his writings there is not an inkling of the service economy that follows the industrial economy.

In 1870, about 75 per cent of all American workers were in

industries that were producing goods. This percentage has gone down steadily over the years, until in 1965 only about 40 per cent of all workers were engaged in such industries. As the American economy becomes more productive, more and more people are engaged in service industries, providing for the amenities and luxuries of life rather than for its bare necessities.

By contrast, in 1965, about 70 per cent of the Soviet labor force were producing goods, and the rest, services—the relative composition of the American labor force in 1870. Yet the same trend operates in the Soviet Union, too, and as her economy progresses, the proportion of persons employed in the service industries is rising.

The intensity of the shift from blue-collar to white-collar employment in the United States becomes even more striking if we look at the entire nonagricultural labor force. Between 1947 and 1965, the number of blue-collar workers rose by only 11 per cent, or from 23.6 million to 26.4 million. During the same period, the number of white-collar employees rose by nearly 60 per cent, or from 20.2 million to 32.2 million. Thus, of the total increase of about 15 million in both categories, the white-collar workers accounted for 80 per cent of the new jobs.

In addition to white-collar and blue-collar workers, there are two other groups that fit into neither—farm workers and service workers (cooks, waiters, janitors, barbers, hospital attendants). These two groups are numerically not as important as blue-collar and white-collar workers, but they show the same over-all trend from goods-producing to service-producing employment as living standards rise. In 1953, service workers for the first time exceeded the number of farm workers and are consistently increasing in relative and absolute strength, whereas farm workers have gone down in both absolute and relative strength.

The following figures illustrate the growth of the salariat and other changes in the composition of the American labor force in the years 1910–1965. Most striking are the proportionate growth of clerical and sales persons from 10.2 per cent of the total labor force in 1910 to 22 per cent in 1965, the sharp drop of the combined total of farm laborers and unskilled industrial laborers from 29.2 per cent to 8.2 per cent, and the increase of the proportion of semiskilled and skilled workers from 26.4 per cent to 31.4 per cent. Politically, the latter is very important because the skilled workers and the foremen generally look upon themselves as middle class and tend to be more conservative in their political outlook.

The year 1956 was a milestone in American economic development; for the first time in American history, or in that of any nation, *the number of persons engaged in the production of goods was smaller than the number of persons employed in the performance of services.* Subsequently, the same changes occurred in the Swedish and British economies where more people now produce services than goods.

If we assume that leisure time will continue to expand, that government activity is going to stay on a high plateau and probably will increase, that people will earn more and spend more, then it may be safely predicted that the changes in the American economy from 1965 to 2000 will be along similar lines as in the years 1910–1965. In that case, Marx's prediction about the proletarianization of the labor force will be even more emphatically shown to be false since an increasingly larger proportion of the American labor force will be engaged in the performance of services rather than in the production of goods.

By contrast, where capitalism exists only in a rudimentary stage, as in the underdeveloped countries of Asia and Africa, the salariat is numerically and politically very weak, and communist infiltration stands a much better chance of achieving its objectives, as has been proved in the past.

What is politically important in this development is that *the salaried person tends to identify himself with the middle and upper classes rather than with the working class,* even if his income is below that of the worker. This is wholly contrary to Marx's expectations and predictions. Marx assumed—necessarily, from his interpretation of human action—that the transformation of the independent middle class into a dependent salaried class would automatically change the outlook of the old middle class from bourgeois to proletarian. Yet the new middle class of the salariat has generally refused to join the ranks of organized labor. Whereas about one-half of workers in goods-producing industries are in labor unions, only seven per cent of white-collar and service employees are unionized. This difference also shows up regularly in elections. Salaried persons, more often than not, vote Republican, whereas members of labor unions typically vote Democratic.

This attitude has been particularly marked in societies with rigid class lines; but even in the United States, with its more fluid class lines, the salaried man (or woman) who earns $500 a month is generally politically more conservative than the wage earner who earns $150 a week or more. Because salary earners have failed to identify themselves psychologically with the working class, they have very largely remained outside the ranks of organized labor. In the United States, the labor movement has been able to organize the workers in industry and to a lesser extent in agriculture but has found it very difficult to organize teachers, clerks, civil servants, and other groups of white-collar employees.

The political problems posed by the rise of the salariat are not confined to industrial development under capitalism; they also appear under communism. In its first phase of industrialization, Russia witnessed a tremendous growth of her industrial proletariat. But as the Soviet Union entered a second phase of industrialization, a new salariat began to develop, with a way of life of its own and with its own ideas, different from those of the working class. Because under communism the state has been so much more responsible for developing industry than under capitalism, the number of government workers and white-collar employees has increased proportionately faster than the number of factory workers.

Despite communist denials, class lines are beginning to crystallize in communist Russia and the other communist states. One important line of differentiation is that between white-collar and factory worker, a distinction not necessarily based on differences of income. The influence of the white-collar group—"intelligentsia" in Russia—is constantly rising at the expense of the working class, as can be seen in the changing social composition of Soviet political bodies, university students, and other key groups of social importance.

As long as the Soviet leaders adhere to Marxist-Leninist propaganda, they will find that time works against them and that the slogans of Marxism-Leninism will not fit a society in which the white-collar class rather than the proletariat sets the style of life and thought. Thus, a class struggle along orthodox lines is beginning to take shape in communist societies undergoing industrialization, and—as in capitalist countries—proletariat and salariat do not generally find themselves on the same side of the barricades.

The first explosions in the communist world took place in Czechoslovakia and Poland in the spring of 1953; they were followed by the major rebellion in East Germany of June 17, 1953, the uprising of Polish workers in Poznan in June, 1956, the Hungarian Revolution of October-November, 1956, and the victory of "national communism" in Poland late in 1956.

The driving force of rebellion in all these instances was not the bourgeois middle class, as might have been expected from the prophecies of Marxism-Leninism, but the industrial workers, who could no longer bear the ruthless exploitation by the communist bosses in the party and government.

This kind of class war—proletariat against salariat—was never foreseen by Marx and Lenin, and communists today cannot deal with it intelligently and effectively; they must deny its very existence as incompatible with their dogma.

Lenin's contribution to the theory of communism

The nature and deeper meaning of philosophical ideas can frequently be inferred from their appeal and impact. In the countries of Western Europe and the United States, the inevitability of revolution as preached by Karl Marx has had little impact; the liberal tradition in those countries keeps the door open for peaceful change. Although many social reformers have agreed with some of Marx's indictments of capitalism, they have refused to embrace a philosophy of class hatred and war to remedy social injustices. Where democratic habits and institutions prevail, the underlying psychological tie in social relations is one of sympathy and affection; in such a climate, men and women are unwilling to accept a philosophy of hatred and violence.

Particularly in the United States, Marxism has proved itself a failure as far as wide popular appeal is concerned. In the last century the frontier seemed to many to offer utopia here and now, whereas the Marxian utopia lay in the distant future, separated from the present by a sea of blood. Also, Marxism has made little progress in the United States because it attacks not only the economic foundations of capitalism, but also the constitutional foundations of American democracy.

In only two major countries did the ideas of Marx take root in the nineteenth century: Germany and Russia. Despite the façade of representative institutions, imperial Germany was in fact an autocracy that did not permit genuine government by the people. The Germans followed the philosophy of Hegel (although Marx claimed that he had turned Hegel upside down). Hegel had asserted that the *state* was an objective reality and that its laws, like those of nature, were susceptible of being *understood,* but not *changed,* by man. Marx followed the cast of Hegel's thought by claiming that the laws of *society*, in respect to its nature and evolution, have the same scientific validity that Hegel had claimed for those of the state.

By contrast, the liberal philosophical tradition of the West rejects the Hegel-Marx conception that human reason can only understand the laws of the state and society and affirms the possibility of rational control and creative change of social and political institutions. The experience of free government is the psychological background for this affirmative, activist philosophy, whereas the experience of autocratic government in Germany provided the psychological background for the determinism of Hegel and Marx. In an environment of mental and political enslavement, man is prone to think of himself as being small and helpless, and his emotional pattern will find philosophical expression in determinism. Such a philosophy assures him that his own helplessness is not a personal misfortune, but a principle of world order.

In nineteenth-century Russia, conditions for the acceptance of Marxian ideas were even more favorable than in imperial Germany. Whereas the latter paid homage to virtue by at least adopting the forms and formalities of representative institutions, Russian tsarism long recoiled from such hypocrisy on the ground that pretenses, if practiced long enough, might easily turn into second nature.

Of all the major states in Europe, Russia was first in illiteracy, economic backwardness, religious obscurantism, oppression of minorities, political despotism, and social inequality. Marx's prophecy, clothed in the language of scientific magic, of the eventual liberation of man from bondage and oppression through revolutionary action made a strong impression on Russian radicals. *Das Kapital*, Marx's *magnum opus*, was translated into Russian before any other language; oddly enough, the tsarist censorship permitted the publication of the work on the ground that it would not be read by many because of its difficult style.

Among the Russian followers of Marx, Lenin (1870–1924) was both the leading theoretician and the most agile and effective practical politician.

Lenin's contribution to the theory of communism, perhaps the only one he made, is to be found in his pamphlet *What Is To Be Done?* (1902).

Just as Hitler openly revealed his intentions to the world in *Mein Kampf* (and was not believed until it was too late), Lenin has left in his writings an accurate blueprint of communist goals and the strategy and tactics to achieve them. Much discomfort and sorrow could have been spared the world if his basic ideas had been more widely known and accepted at their face value.

Lenin's most important single contribution to the theory of Marxism is his concept of the *professional revolutionary.*

Marx, tinged by nineteenth-century respect for man's capacity to think for himself, had assumed that the working class would *spontaneously* develop its class-consciousness in the daily struggle for economic existence and that its leadership would largely come from its own ranks. Lenin had much less confidence in man, even if he belonged to the select class, the proletariat. Communist activity, said Lenin, is to be carried on along two lines. First, work-

"Fellow-comrades and undercover agents of the F.B.I. . . ."

ers are to form labor organizations with primarily economic objectives, operating openly, legally, and as publicly as conditions allow.

Side by side with such organizations, there are to be small groups of professional revolutionaries, patterned after the army and the police, highly select and entirely secret. Lenin did not care whether the professional revolutionary was of proletarian origin or not, as long as he did his job well. The organizations of the professional revolutionaries must be highly centralized, he went on, and must constantly guide and supervise the open communist-led economic associations—the labor unions, the cooperatives, and the rest.

In particular, Lenin advised the professional revolutionaries to *infiltrate* and form cells in all existing social, political, educational, and economic bodies in society, be they schools, churches, labor unions, or political parties. Above all, he advised infiltration of the *armed forces*, the *police*, and the *government*.

Lenin also made it perfectly clear that communists should engage in *illegal* work even where legal Communist parties are permitted. He thought that legal opportunities should be utilized to the fullest extent, but he specifically advised communist activists to work through *front organizations*, constantly changing names and officers of organizations and always keeping the ultimate objective in mind: revolutionary seizure of power.

In particular, the secret nucleus of professional revolutionaries is responsible for the recruitment and training of spies, saboteurs, and agents for all other activities relating to intelligence, foreign and domestic. From the testimony of former communist agents it is evident that one of the first things a recruit into the inner ring of communist leaders has to do is to break all connection with overt Communist party or front groups, stop reading the party press, and lead the life of a solid, respectable bourgeois. There are bridges between the legal Communist parties and the inner rings of spies and agents of the professional revolutionaries since necessity often compels the choice of such agents from party ranks; ideally, however, the two sets of organizations are to be kept separate. Therefore what appears as the overt leadership of Communist parties is but a front for the real bosses, men who are unknown to the public and even to the ostensible communist leaders in many cases and who report directly to Moscow.

Outlawing the Communist party is therefore no answer to the problem of how to deal with communism; the hard core of communist leadership and activity is always underground, even when the law permits Communist parties to operate above ground. Since there are always some links between the legal party and the inner nucleus of the professional revolutionaries, a legally functioning party is an asset, small as it may be, to counterespionage. It is probably for this reason that J. Edgar Hoover, director of the Federal Bureau of Investigation, has not advocated the outlawing of the Communist Party of the United States.

The Leninist approach to communist theory and strategy has been most effective in underdeveloped countries. Marx thought that communist revolution would first occur in economically advanced countries like Germany and England, where capitalism was mature—with one foot already in the grave, as it were. Lenin agreed with Marx that communist revolution was inevitable, but he asked: Why wait until capitalism has matured? Why not smash it where it is weakest—that is, in economically backward areas like Russia and Asian or African nations? It is a tribute to Lenin's political genius that he saw the importance of underdeveloped countries over half a century ago, whereas today many people in the West still do not grasp the crucial role of the underdeveloped areas in the balance of world power.

Thinking about the spread of communism in military terms, Lenin argued that Western capitalism had to be attacked in its "soft underbelly" of Asia, Africa, and Latin America if a frontal attack on Western Europe and North America were not practical. It is a matter of record that communism has not spread significantly in the "mature capitalist societies" of Western Europe and North America but has achieved its greatest successes of conquest of power or penetration in countries like China, Cuba, Vietnam, North Korea, and Laos. In such underdeveloped areas society is very poorly organized. Even the strongest organization—the government—generally rests on shaky foundations. The mass of the populations consists of poor peasants, living in isolated villages, with inadequate means of communication. There are few or no independent labor unions and practically no urban middle class—the backbone of anticommunist resistance in more advanced countries.

Where society lacks cohesion, the Leninist concept of the professional revolutionary is of strategic importance in the communist aim of conquest. All that is necessary for successful communist infiltration and conquest is a comparatively small force of well-organized revolutionaries who can deal skillfully with an unorganized mass. A small but disciplined army unit can control a numerically larger but undisciplined and unorganized civilian population. So, too, the communists believe that in the underdeveloped areas they can take control with a relatively small force, provided it is well organized and disciplined.

Communist doctrine and policy today

Since Lenin's death in 1924, there has been no new addition or modification of basic Marxist-Leninist thought. Stalin and Khrushchev, who ruled Russia from 1924 to 1964, were stronger in practical administration than in theorizing. Most of the post-Leninist communist writings are but a rehash of Marx and Lenin, adapted to the momentary needs of the dictatorship. The core of communist long-term strategy, largely followed by the communist leaders today, consists in the concept of the *four basic tensions* underlying our present-day world:

(1) The tension between capitalists and proletarians everywhere
(2) The tension between imperialist states and colonies
(3) The tension between rival imperialist states
(4) The tension between communist states and capitalist states

This conception of the four basic tensions, far from being a mere exercise in semantic classification, provides a clear blueprint for communist strategy and tactics. It is virtually impossible to open a newspaper without seeing some evidence of communist application of these concepts to practical issues and policies.

(1) The *tension between capitalists and proletarians* is the classical conception of Marxism and goes back to Marx's belief in the contradiction between forces of production and relations of production. Capitalism today represents in communist propaganda the forces of production, the technological and scientific know-how, which cannot be fully utilized under the capitalist system of production for profit. The proletariat represents symbolically the relations of production, a new set of social institutions to be fully established after the overthrow of capitalism, allowing for the fullest use of all available knowledge and resources in a communist economic system, in which social institutions will aid, and not hamper, the productive process.

The great depression of 1929–1939 convinced the communists that capitalism is in a state of hopeless decay and that the tension between actual production under capitalism and productive capacity under a communist organization of the economy must ultimately lead to a revolutionary solution. When after World War II a major economic crisis failed to materialize in the capitalist world, particularly in the United States, communists began to doctor facts and figures to prove that the prevailing prosperity was actually a depression and that a really big depression was around the corner.

Communist propagandists have been even more disappointed by the phenomenal economic expansion of some leading capitalist countries, such as West Germany and Japan, that, in the 1950's and 1960's, grew faster than both the Soviet Union and the United States. Communist opposition to the unification of Western Europe is based not only on politics and diplomacy but also on economics; the Common Market countries (France, Germany, Italy, Belgium, Holland, and Luxembourg) have shown that rapid economic progress can be reconciled with individual liberty and international cooperation—a contagious example to the enslaved peoples in Eastern Europe. COMECON, the Council of Mutual Economic Aid of the Soviet Union and the East European communist states, cannot match the Common Market for economic and political reasons. Economically, COMECON was intended from the beginning as an instrument of centralized planning primarily for the benefit of the Soviet Union. Politically, COMECON is an organization of totalitarian *governments,* not of free *peoples.* The existence of COMECON has not removed the iron curtain between the Soviet Union and its communist neighbors. By contrast, the 180 million people of the Common Market can move as freely among their six countries as within one nation.

The main concern of communists with the tension between capitalists and workers is *political rather than economic.*

Thus, in formulating a policy for a strike, a communist will ask himself one primary question: Will it aid the cause of the communist revolution? The welfare of the particular group of workers involved is secondary to the over-all objective of serving communism.

When Russia was a friendly nonbelligerent on the side of Nazi Germany in 1939–1941, the communists fomented strikes in Britain and the United States, not to help British or American workers, but to paralyze production in Britain and the United States, the two main opponents of Nazi Germany. The moment Russia was drawn into World War II by the German attack on June 22, 1941, communists everywhere opposed strikes as treason, exhorted workers to work sixty, seventy, and eighty hours a week, and called everybody a fascist who sought to protect the rights of the workers against the demand for all-out production.

Some trade unions in Britain and the United States for a long time failed to understand that communist zeal and devotion to unions had little to do with genuine concern for the workers' welfare but was primarily a vehicle to further communist objectives.

Unions have fought for over two generations against company unions; they now refuse to be dominated by a new type of company union boss—the communist union leader who represents the Soviet Union rather than the workers in his own country. As a result, there has been a thorough housecleaning of communists in most labor unions in this country and in Britain in the last few years.

In communist states, the nature of labor unions as company unions is most clearly evident: their official task is not to defend the interests of the workers against their employer, the state, but to impose the decisions of the boss, the state, on the workers. Strikes are, of course, illegal.

(2) The *tension between imperialist states and colonies,* although mentioned by Marx, was more clearly elaborated by Lenin, who lived in an age of colonial rebellion. Whereas Marx predicted the proletarian revolution in the most advanced industrial nations of the West, Lenin concentrated on the backward areas of the world as the most fertile soil for communist propaganda and eventual conquest.

When communists speak of colonies, they refer not only to territories legally dependent upon another state—the number of such dependencies had in any case approached the vanishing point by 1967—but also to small, weak states that are in fact in the sphere of influence of the leading Western states. From the communist viewpoint, most states in Latin America or Africa are colonial although they are legally independent and sovereign. The communist strategy is alway to help the colonial or weaker state against the West.

All over the globe, communists take up the cause of anti-imperialism, as long as the imperialists are British, French, or American rather than Russian or Chinese. Thus, Cuba under Fidel Castro has been hailed by Moscow and Peking as being truly independent because on both domestic and international issues the Castro regime rapidly moved into the communist camp. Similarly, when the Belgian Congo became independent in 1960, the Soviet Union quickly tried to turn it into a communist satellite. Pro-

Western nationalist forces in the Congo, Ghana, or Indonesia are, in Moscow's and Peking's eyes, nothing but "colonial lackeys of Wall Street imperialism." The suppression of a major communist rebellion in Indonesia in 1965 and the ouster of the procommunist dictator of Ghana, Nkrumah, in 1966 were particularly unpleasant news to Moscow and Peking.

Also, communists approach colonial tensions from a long-range viewpoint rather than in the light of the immediate interests of local Communist parties. Thus, in Iran the ultranationalist dictatorship of Mossadegh was supported by Moscow until his downfall in 1953, despite his anticommunism, because he sought to oust Britain and the United States from any sphere of influence in that oil-rich country. In Argentina, the fascist dictatorship of General Perón was also endorsed by the Kremlin until his overthrow in 1955 because he was anti-British and anti-American.

Finally, in more recent years the Soviet Union has showered President Nasser, the militarist dictator of Egypt, with arms and all forms of diplomatic support although the Communist party is outlawed in Egypt. This is a minor consideration to the Soviet government, compared with the fact that Nasser is bent on wiping out Western influence not only in Egypt but in the whole Near and Middle East.

The communist line in all these cases is simple: whatever hurts the influence or prestige of the Western powers is good for world communism although local communists may have to take this long-term view from prison cells. An ultranationalist, anticommunist regime in a backward or weak state is looked upon by Moscow as but a prelude to communization, provided American or British influence can be kept out of the picture. Communist support for anticommunist regimes in weak states makes perfect sense in the light of long-range communist objectives.

It would be unwise, however, to underestimate the weapon the communists have in their hand when they exploit the slogan of anti-imperialism for their purposes. In Asia and Africa, the two main areas of imperialist domination and spheres of influence, imperialism has been traditionally identified with the West (Britain, France, Holland, and the United States); although the Western nations have been recently repenting and reforming, granting independence to their colonies, such repentance and reform have come at a late date in the eyes of impatient Asians or Africans. The communist propagandists harp on the sins of the past, and the colonial peoples have a longer memory of their sufferings than do those who have perpetrated them. Also, a major asset of communist anti-imperialist propaganda is the fact that Western imperialism is a matter of experience, often bitter experience, to colonial peoples, whereas Russian or Chinese imperialism is unknown to them.

Paradoxically, as communist power spreads in Asia and other backward areas, it carries in itself a virus of immunization because communist reality so patently belies communist words. Thus, many Indians were rudely jarred from their neutralist feelings about communism when Tibet, a state bordering on India, was occupied by Red China in 1950. In 1959, China invaded Indian border territory and annexed it despite Indian protests. India discovered the hard way that "coexistence" with communism requires more than paper agreements, and she began to look to the West for more diplomatic and economic help.

India and China now lead the struggle for the soul of Asia, and indirectly of all backward countries. China is following the communist totalitarian system, whereas India is trying to combine political democracy with a program of rapid economic development.

If India succeeds, world communism will lose a decisive battle. If India bogs down in a quagmire of lassitude, corruption, and economic stagnation, the field may well be clear for communism in India to sweep from there to the rest of Asia. During the 1950's, Red China's economy grew by an average annual rate of 8 per cent, as compared with India's average annual growth rate of 3.7 per cent during the same period. In the 1960's, both nations have been unable to sustain impressive growth records. The catastrophic effects of the "Great Leap Forward" of 1959–1961 substantially slowed up Red China's economic progress in the early 1960's, but since then she has shown again remarkable economic and technological progress—without receiving economic aid from either the United States or the Soviet Union. By contrast, India's economy has been stagnant throughout the 1960's. She suffered from near-famine conditions in 1964–1966 and was saved only by massive economic aid by the United States and other Western nations. Yet in spite of this large economic aid—in addition to military aid which she receives from both the United States and the Soviet Union—India has been barely able to keep her output in line with her annual population increase of about 12 million. If over the next 20 or 30 years India should only hold her own while continuing to receive large foreign economic aid, whereas Red China is able to move ahead by its own effort in economic, technological, and scientific development, India can hardly hope to do well in her race with Red China for leadership in Asia.

If India, with a population of about 500 million, should ever become communist, the balance of world power might gradually shift to communism. In the general elections of 1952, the Indian Communist Party polled only 3.3 per cent of the popular vote; in the elections of 1957, this figure rose to an alarming high of 8.9 per cent, and the Communist party was able to take over control of one state, Kerala, with a population of 14 million. In 1959, the President of India dismissed the communist state government of Kerala, on the ground that it was unable to govern peacefully in accordance with the Indian Constitution, and in 1960 an anticommunist coalition government was elected to office. In the general elections of 1962, the communists managed again to increase their share of the popular vote—to 10 per cent of the total vote. This increase in electoral strength occurred despite the large-scale invasion and conquest of Indian border territories by the Red Chinese armies in 1959–1962.

(3) The *tension between rival imperialist states* goes back to Marx's theory of the decay of capitalism. When the rate of profit falls because of large accumulation of capital relative to the labor force, the capitalist looks for profitable employment of capital outside of his own country and finds such opportunities in backward countries, countries in which capital is very scarce and labor abundantly available. However, as time goes on, investment opportunities in backward areas constantly shrink, and capitalists then look to their governments for aid. According to the Marxist-communist doctrine, the capitalist state is but the executive committee of the propertied classes, and therefore the flag willingly and eagerly follows trade. As capitalists from several countries collide in the same zone of influence and expansion, their governments become involved in a struggle for power.

War under capitalism is thus viewed by communists as a clash between rival imperialist forces motivated by the quest for economic expansion. World Wars I and II are interpreted by communists in this fashion, although if England was so anxious to preserve her commercial position in 1914, the communists have never explained why she did not go to war with the United States, which by 1914 had attained first place in industrial—and inevitably political and military—power. In 1939, American supremacy in industry, finance, and the resulting ability to wage war had become even more obvious, and communists again find it difficult to explain on Marxist grounds why England and France chose to fight Germany rather than the United States.

The new (1961) Program of the Communist Party of the Soviet Union states that "the contradictions between the principal imperialist powers are growing deeper," and then specifies what the main sources of conflict in the noncommunist world are: "The Anglo-American, Franco-American, Franco-West German, American-West German, Japanese-American, and other contradictions are becoming especially acute. Fresh contradictions will inevitably arise and grow in the imperialist camp."

Although this assumption may seem unrealistic to noncommunists, communists not only believe in it but base their policy on it. Because they do not believe that capitalist states can work together peacefully and amicably, communists exploit existing tensions and create new tensions between capitalist states. Thus in Britain the main communist propaganda slogan is that America will fight to the last Englishman. In France, the communists have managed to exploit the issue of wine versus Coca-Cola as one of French national independence versus American imperialism; if the communists find themselves unable to promote military conflict between the capitalist nations, at least they are trying their best to create dissension and confusion.

The successful creation of NATO (North Atlantic Treaty Organization) in 1949 was a blow against world communism not only because of its military value against aggression but also because the very existence of NATO belies the communist myth that capitalist states cannot collaborate for common objectives. By contrast, the disunity between the United States and her French and British allies over the Suez issue and the whole problem of peace in the Middle East was one of the great successes of Soviet diplomacy, starting with the seizure of the Suez Canal by dictator Nasser in July, 1956. The disunity between the United States and her Western European allies enabled Russia to become firmly entrenched in the Middle East for the first time in her history.

Later, in 1963, the Soviet Union scored another success when France vetoed the entry of Great Britain into the Common Market. While General de Gaulle is staunchly anticommunist, his opposition to British entry removed a major source of anxiety in the Soviet leadership for the time being. With Britain in, the Common Market nations would surpass the Soviet Union in population and economic strength, not to speak of the dynamic psychological effects of such a community based on freedom. Without Britain, a united Western Europe is a source of constant concern, but not a fatal blow, to communist goals.

In 1966, the Soviet Union scored an even greater triumph: the French government ordered NATO headquarters to leave France and for all practical purposes withdrew from any military participation in NATO. General de Gaulle based this policy on his concept—or dream—of a closely cooperating Europe from the Channel to the Urals, in which France and Russia are to be the two leaders, with Britain and the United States being excluded from the Continent. While the Soviets realistically appraise France's limited power that no grandiose schemes can conceal, they naturally welcome and support every move that, under de Gaulle, has weakened the Atlantic community.

(4) The *tension between communist and capitalist states* is increasingly recognized by communists to be the most important of all four tensions. Marx had never given much thought to the question of coexistence between capitalist and communist states. He thought in terms of conflict as the vehicle of social development, but his concept of conflict related to domestic class struggles. Being steeped in nineteenth-century economic optimism, Marx may have hoped that tensions between states would eventually be resolved through economic means. Lenin and his successors, however, faced with the realities of governing the first communist state and spearheading what they considered to be a world revolution, gave a great deal of thought to the question of how communist and capitalist states can get along in one world.

As far back as 1924, when Russia was still on the defensive and struggling for her very existence, communist leaders developed a doctrine that was not taken seriously in the West but that accurately anticipated future policies. In his *Foundations of Leninism* (1924), Stalin says that the world is divided into two hostile camps, "the world front of imperialism" and the "common front of the revolutionary movement in all countries." In particular, Stalin affirms that in the present stage of capitalism "wars cannot be averted," and he urges a *coalition between communist states in Europe and colonial revolutionaries in Asia,* such as the Soviet Union later practiced in China, Laos, Korea, and Vietnam.

In 1924, Stalin considered the Soviet Union as the "base for the overthrow of imperialism in all countries," and this idea of the *Soviet Union as the first phase of the inevitable communization of the world* has since then guided Soviet long-term strategy. In *Problems of Leninism* (1926) Stalin quoted with enthusiastic approval the following statement by Lenin: "We are living not merely in a state, but in a *system of states;* and it is inconceivable that the Soviet Republic should continue to exist for a long period side by side with imperialist states. *Ultimately one or the other must conquer.*" Stalin also frequently quotes the Leninist statement that the Soviet Union should "attract to itself the oppressed classes of other countries, raising revolts in those countries against the capitalists, and in the event of necessity coming out even with armed force against the exploiting classes and their governments."

With a slight dash of humor, Stalin held out one hope for the capitalist states. War is not inevitable if the capitalist countries are willing to surrender voluntarily without resisting communization. Stalin wrote that communism may spread to so many countries that the remaining capitalist states will realize the hopelessness of resistance, and this "encirclement" by communist states will make voluntary surrender "expedient." Put another way, the alternative to enforced slavery is voluntary slavery.

Before World War II was over, the Soviet government betrayed every pledge it had made to establish democracy in Eastern and Southeastern Europe. With the help of the Red Army, communist regimes were set up in Rumania, Bulgaria, Hungary, Poland, and East Germany. Leaders of proven democratic background and loyalty were imprisoned, exiled, or killed. In China and Indochina, communist revolutions were supported, with complete success in the former, and with partial success in the latter. In Greece, the communists started a civil war in December, 1944, which ended in communist defeat after Yugoslavia broke with Moscow in 1948. In Malaya and the Philippines, communist guerrilla forces fought for years against the established regimes, causing much bloodshed and devastation. In France and Italy, the communists tried to stage general strikes on several occasions, presumably with the ultimate intent of transforming industrial strife into civil war.

In the Balkans and Eastern Europe, the communists argued that there had never been political democracy and that the real choice lay between fascist totalitarianism and communist dictatorship. If such flimsy propaganda did have an effect on noncommunists for a time, its value was completely destroyed in Czechoslovakia in February, 1948. Although the Soviet Union used the Czechoslovakian Communist Party as its tool, this was the first case of the subjugation of a truly democratic nation to communist dictatorship by armed force, represented by the threat of the Red Army standing on the borders of Czechoslovakia ready to intervene. The communist seizure of Czechoslovakia gave the prime impulse to the formation of the North Atlantic Treaty Organization and speeded up tremendously the rate of rearmament in the Western nations, particularly in the United States.

Above all, the communist aggression in Czechoslovakia showed that the only argument the communists respected was force. It was partly because of the Czechoslovakian experience that the United States, joined by many other members of the United Nations, determined to resist armed communist aggression in Korea in 1950 by force.

After the death of Stalin in 1953, Nikita Khrushchev gradually emerged as Stalin's successor. In a major address before the Twentieth Congress of the Soviet Communist Party on February 14, 1956, Khrushchev stated that Soviet foreign policy was guided by the following five principles: peaceful coexistence; nonaggression; noninterference in internal affairs of other nations; mutual respect for territorial integrity and sovereignty; and equality and mutual benefit. In addition, Khrushchev declared that communization of noncommunist nations need *not always* be carried out *by force,* particularly where this could be done by parliamentary majorities. Significantly, no country has ever gone communist as a result of free elections.

Soviet acceptance of the principle of peaceful coexistence suggested to many that communism had abandoned its objective of world revolution and world conquest, and that post-Stalin communism would be different from Stalin's foreign policy. Some optimists in the West went even so far as to hail the "dawn of liberalism" in the Soviet Union. Yet only nine months later, in October and November of 1956, the dawn of Soviet liberalism turned into the nightmare of the Hungarian tragedy.

Immediately after the Hungarian Revolution was suppressed, Khrushchev had this to say to a group of Western diplomats at a diplomatic reception in Moscow on November 18, 1956: "Whether you like it or not, history is on our side. *We will bury you.*"

In spite of all the talk of coexistence by Stalin's successors—Khrushchev, Brezhnev, and Kosygin—Soviet foreign policy has been more daring and ambitious than in Stalin's days. Stalin, following the tradition of the tsars, concentrated on the expansion of Soviet power in areas in which Soviet land armies could be the decisive factor. His successors have discarded such limitations. In 1956, ignoring geographical frontiers, Soviet influence was firmly established in the Near and Middle East through deals with Egypt.

Between 1955 and 1966, Egypt received about $1 billion in economic aid from the Soviet Union, or one-fifth of all Soviet foreign economic aid. During the same period, Egypt also received over $1 billion of Soviet military aid, or nearly one-third of all Soviet military assistance given to other states. Soviet military equipment given to Egypt included the most modern tanks, jets, and submarines. Since 1966, Egypt has also received considerable quantities of Soviet missiles of all types, publicly paraded in Cairo on several occasions. After his visit to Egypt in 1966, Premier Kosygin referred to Egypt as an "important stronghold of national liberation and progressive development throughout the vast area of the Near East and Africa" (June 10, 1966). The Soviet government under Brezhnev and Kosygin is courting Nasser even more than Khrushchev had done. Since the overthrow of Ben Bella of Algeria in 1965 and of Kwame Nkrumah of Ghana in 1966—two of the most ardent supporters of Moscow in Africa—Nasser's pro-Soviet orientation has proportionately become more valuable in Soviet eyes.

Since 1959, Soviet power has also become firmly entrenched in the Western Hemisphere through the establishment of Fidel Castro's communist regime. Cuba has been the number one center of propaganda, infiltration, sabotage, and subversion in the Western Hemisphere. Emboldened by the inaction of the United States, the Soviets introduced large numbers of aircraft capable of carrying atomic bombs as well as large quantities of missiles into Cuba in 1962. On October 22, 1962, the President of the United States announced that Cuba would be subjected to a blockade and that the Soviet missiles would have to be removed from Cuba—or else. After first denying that there were any Soviet missiles in Cuba, the Soviet government realized that the United States meant business. As a result, the missiles were shipped back to Russia, but thousands of Soviet "technicians" were left behind in Cuba, as well as large quantities of Soviet weapons other than missiles. Thus, the threat of force by the United States saved peace and the existing balance of power between the communist and noncommunist world, temporarily at least. This was one of the rare and momentous occasions in the relations between democratic and totalitarian states when a leading democracy took the initiative in resisting the spread of aggressive imperialism before it was too late rather than travel the endless (and hopeless) road of appeasement.

The Soviet defeat in the Cuban missile crisis was probably one of the factors that contributed to Khrushchev's ouster in 1964. Subsequently, the new Soviet leadership intensified Soviet economic and political links with Cuba. Guerrillas trained in Cuba were sent to various Latin American countries to foment revolution and civil war; such activities assumed alarming proportions in Guatemala, Venezuela, Colombia, and Peru. In 1966, the first "Tricontinental Conference" was held in Havana, attended by representatives of 83 communist organizations in Africa, Asia, and Latin America. The Tricontinental Conference, a direct outgrowth of the Afro-Asian Solidarity Conference held in Cairo in 1957, established a permanent organization, the Afro-Asian-Latin American Peoples' Solidarity Organization, headquartered in Havana. Behind the long name of this organization lies a short goal: to communize Africa, Asia, and Latin America through "wars of national liberation." While the Russians and the Chinese squabbled at Havana over who would run the tricontinental organization of subversion (the Russians won), there was agreement among Russians and Chinese regarding the objective of communist expansion through "wars of national liberation."

The meaning of the communist concept of "coexistence" was authoritatively defined at an international gathering of leaders of 81 Communist parties assembled in Moscow on December 6, 1960. In a major policy statement, the leaders of international communism approved of "peaceful coexistence" for several reasons. First, it provides "favorable opportunities for the development of the class struggle in the capitalist countries and the national-liberation movements of the colonial and dependent countries." This means that, according to the communist concept of peaceful coexistence, communists are free to propagandize and subvert both advanced and underdeveloped countries without hindrance, whereas an Iron Curtain prevents democratic nations from doing the same in communist countries. Second, the communist leaders emphasized in the "December Declaration of 1960" that "peaceful coexistence of countries with different social systems does not mean conciliation" between communism and democracy, but an "intensification of the struggle" of all Communist parties for the "triumph" of communism. Almost the same language was used to describe peaceful coexistence in the new (1961) Program of the Communist Party of the Soviet Union.

In sum, in the communist version of the phrase, peaceful coexistence means all forms of war short of nuclear war: local limited wars, guerrilla fighting in underdeveloped countries, and infiltration by subversion, propaganda, and espionage. In the communist view of world affairs, peaceful coexistence becomes an umbrella that permits communist imperialism to conquer the world by minor wars and subversion, particularly in the underdeveloped countries, whose "sacred struggle" and "just anti-imperialist wars of liberation" are promised full support in the 1961 Program of the Communist Party of the Soviet Union. By contrast, in this same communist interpretation of peaceful coexistence, the United States is supposed to refrain from any interference—however nonmilitary—in communist states. A communist take-over of a country in Asia, Latin America, or Africa by armed force or political subversion is called "national liberation," whereas American aid to any people enslaved by communism to regain their freedom would be "capitalist imperialism" that would have to be stopped by force, as Soviet leaders have publicly stated on numerous occasions.

The limited nuclear test ban agreement of 1963 between the United States, Great Britain, and the Soviet Union fits the overall Soviet strategy of expanding communist power and influence throughout the world by all means short of nuclear war. Should the best of possible results of the test ban agreement ever come about, that is, gradual nuclear disarmament, the Soviet Union would then be provided with a shelter of nuclear security under which it could continue to spread its power by propaganda, infiltration, sabotage, and limited local wars fought with conventional weapons.

In his address to the 23rd Congress of the Soviet Communist Party on March 29, 1966, Leonid I. Brezhnev, its General Secretary and top Soviet leader, clearly showed the continuity of communist thought and policy. First, Brezhnev expressed the orthodox communist conviction that "the doom of capitalism" is "becoming more and more obvious." However, he warned that the capitalists, unmindful of the historical law of their doom, "will never give up their domination by their own free will. It is only through tenacious class battles that the working class and the rest of the working people will achieve victory." Brezhnev also promised that the Communist Party of the Soviet Union "will do everything in its power for the world socialist system to become ever mightier and to advance from victory to victory." With respect to the issue of spreading communism in underdeveloped countries, Brezhnev fully stood by the policy objectives of the 1961 Program of the Communist Party of the Soviet Union. He stated that the CPSU "regards it as its internationalist duty to continue to do everything to support the struggle of the peoples for final liberation from colonial and neo-colonial oppression." In Vietnam, for example, the Soviet

Union supplied the bulk of foreign military aid for the Viet Cong and the North Vietnamese forces. Red China talked much more belligerently but aided the communist side in South Vietnam much less than did the Soviet Union.

Social-economic changes under communism

The first major attack in this century against the established social order occurred in Russia toward the end of World War I. The tsarist regime was overthrown in a bloodless revolution in March, 1917, and it seemed as if Russia would have the opportunity to develop democratic institutions for the first time in her history.

The majority of the Russians wanted political liberty as well as fundamental social change. Inexperienced in the conduct of public affairs, however, and failing to understand the true nature and goals of communism, the new, democratic government of Alexander Kerensky allowed the Bolsheviks, led by Lenin and Trotsky, to subvert and quickly destroy the new democratic state.

Between March and November, 1917, the Bolsheviks (the party was not known as the Communist Party until 1919) used three classical methods of gaining power, methods they were to repeat later in almost identical fashion in other countries.

First, they presented themselves in their propaganda as a people's party, dedicated to liberty, democracy, and social justice and opposed to all forms of reaction and social injustice. In an agrarian country like Russia, the communists emphasized the need for agrarian land reform and encouraged the seizure of land by the peasants even before they were in control of the government. A generation later the Chinese communists proclaimed themselves (and were believed by many to be) no more than *agrarian reformers,* thus following the pattern of propaganda established by the Russian communists in 1917.

The second technique the Bolsheviks employed was *infiltration* of other political parties, trade unions, soldiers' councils, and local government authorities. In particular, the communists managed to infiltrate and gradually disrupt the Social Revolutionaries, the largest party in Russia, dedicated to political democracy and social reform and especially concerned with the question of the peasants. This technique of infiltration was again employed by the communists during and after World War II when they tried to take over socialist parties in a number of countries.

The third method used by the Bolsheviks in their revolution was *force*. In free elections in the summer and fall of 1917, the Bolsheviks polled about one-quarter of the total vote. Though this represented a far from negligible proportion, considering their fanaticism and frenzied activity, the Bolsheviks accepted the fact that in a free election they could not hope to win. In November, 1917, therefore, the Bolsheviks seized the key positions of power in Moscow, and from there the revolution quickly spread all over Russia. Opposition to communist revolution sprang up spontaneously in various parts of the country, and a civil war ensued that lasted until 1921.

The ravages of World War I, followed by the devastations of the civil war, made immediate social reform impracticable. Lenin was realistic enough to see that the Russian people would starve to death if communist principles were imposed at that time. As a result, he inaugurated in 1921 the New Economic Policy, which permitted limited private ownership; this policy's main objective was to maintain and increase production on the farms and in the workshops and factories by retaining the old capitalist incentives of efficiency and profit. The application of the NEP for about seven years gave Russia a breathing spell, allowing the communist rulers to consolidate their power more effectively and giving the Russian people the temporary illusion that the bark of communism was worse than its bite.

But in 1928 Stalin decided that the time had come to put communist principles into practice, and he withdrew the temporary concessions earlier made by Lenin (who died in 1924). The First Five Year Plan, starting in 1928, aimed primarily at the rapid industrialization of Russia and secondarily at the collectivization of farming. In 1917 many peasants had sympathized with Bolshevism, not for reasons of theory or ideology, but because the Bolsheviks promised them the land they and their ancestors had tilled and coveted for centuries.

The reasons that motivated Stalin to force collectivization on the peasants were manifold. First, the communist rulers felt that agricultural production would be raised by mechanization and that this could be more easily effected in large-scale, collectivized farms than on small, individually owned ones. Second, individual ownership and operation of farms was a basic denial of a key principle of communism, namely, that all means of production be transferred to public ownership. Collectivization would bring agriculture in line with industry, which was developed from the start on the basis of state ownership and operation. Third, the communist rulers saw in continued individual farm ownership a direct political and psychological threat to the acceptance of totalitarian political direction from the center.

The independent peasant had to be transformed into a dependent agricultural proletarian; as a member of a collective farm, the peasant was constantly working with others, talking to others, eating with others, and could thus be more easily supervised and regimented.

Another reason behind collectivization was the need for labor for the newly developing industries in the cities. The required labor force could be obtained only by mechanizing agriculture and thus saving human labor. Finally, collectivization had an important military objective: in case of war, the collectives were to provide the nucleus for organized resistance behind the lines. In World War II, these military expectations were largely fulfilled: the Germans were never completely able to suppress Russian guerrilla activities behind their lines.

The cost of fundamental social and economic change in Russia was heavy. In the process of collectivizing the farms in the years 1929–1933 between four and five million peasants lost their lives or were uprooted from their homes and deported to slave labor camps in Siberia or the Arctic. To show their resistance to collectivization, the peasants slaughtered as much livestock as they could, so that by the time collectivization was accomplished, the number of livestock had greatly decreased. The number of cattle in the Soviet Union was 67 million in 1928, 34 million in 1934, 48 million in 1940, 58 million in 1950, and 87 million in 1965. Cows numbered 33 million in 1928, 19 million in 1934, 23 million in 1940, 25 million in 1950, and 39 million in 1965. During the same period the Soviet population increased by 80 million, from 150 to 230 million. The human population thus increased at a much faster rate than the number of cattle and cows.

By contrast with Soviet figures for livestock, there were 57 million cattle in the United States in 1928, and 107 million in 1965; there were 31 million cows in 1928, and 50 million in 1965. During the same period the population of the United States increased from 121 to 195 million, or by 74 million. Cattle and cows thus increased faster than the human population. The rate of increase of cattle and cows in the United States could have been much greater still, were it not for the fact that the problem is one of overproduction rather than of scarcity, as in the Soviet Union.

During the four decades of 1913–1953, Russia was one of the few countries in the world in which standards of food consumption dropped. The per capita consumption of grain, potatoes, and beets rose during that period, whereas that of eggs, milk, and meat declined. Advancing living standards invariably show a shift from bread, potatoes, and beets to high-quality foods like milk, butter, meat, and eggs. This is exactly what happened in the United States during the same period: the per capita consumption of wheat and potatoes dropped considerably, whereas that of meat, milk, and eggs rose sharply.

From 1953–1958, Soviet farm output increased by 50 per cent. This sharp rise was accomplished by putting new lands in Central Asia and Siberia under cultivation and by granting the peasants greater incentives for higher production. However, after 1958, farm output remained virtually stagnant, and in 1965 the per capita farm output was at best equal to 1958, and possibly slightly below the 1958 level. By comparison with all other major economies in the world, and with nearly all lesser ones, Soviet farming performed very poorly in 1958–1965.

Even in 1958, the peak of the "fat years" of 1953–1958, Soviet per capita consumption of better-grade foods was not only way behind American consumption in 1958 but was still trailing American consumption in 1890, as can be seen from the table below:

Yearly Consumption of Better-Grade Foods Per Person

	Soviet Union in 1958	United States in 1890	United States Consumption as Percentage of Soviet Consumption
Meat, poultry, and lard (kilograms)	38	89	234%
Milk (kilograms)	224	350	156%
Eggs (number)	105	293	279%

Source: Rand Corporation, 1961

More recent figures on per capita supply of six basic foods in the United States and the Soviet Union show the following:

Estimated Per Capita Food Supplies

	Kilograms Per Year	
	United States, 1963	USSR, 1963–64
Grains and pulses (as flour)	65	175
Potatoes	48	125
Sugar (refined)	42	27
Meat and poultry	100	30
Eggs	18	4
Fats	21	9

Source: Joint Economic Committee, Congress of the United States, *New Directions in the Soviet Economy* (1966), and Food and Agriculture Organization of the United Nations, *Production Yearbook 1964* (1965).

One crop, however, shows a remarkable expansion under communism. From 1925 to 1929, Soviet production of potatoes was 4.5 times that of the United States. From 1955 to 1965, the Soviet Union produced about 7-8 times as many potatoes as the United States did.

Any visitor to the Soviet Union can verify the fact of bread and potatoes being the basic foods of people living under communism. Even in luxury restaurants (luxury by Soviet standards) catering primarily to visiting foreigners, huge quantities of bread and potatoes are served with every meal. Starches—mostly bread and potatoes—make up over 60 per cent of the average Soviet diet, as compared with 20-25 per cent in the average American diet. Yet, in spite of the inferior quality of its food consumption the Soviet family spends one-half of its total income on food, whereas the American family spends less than 20 per cent of take-home pay for food of superior quality.

As can be seen from the chart on the worktime required to purchase selected commodities in Moscow and New York in 1966, the Moscow worker has to work 400 per cent of the New York worktime for white bread, 300 per cent for potatoes, but 800 per cent for eggs, 1000 per cent for butter, and 1500 per cent for sugar. The Soviet worker must work seven to ten times as long as the American worker for basic articles like shoes, dresses, suits, and shirts. Moreover, food prices in the chart refer to state-fixed prices in government stores. Foods sold by collective farmers in the open market are considerably higher. The worktime ratios in the chart are therefore slanted in favor of the Moscow worktimes required to buy basic foods.

Moscow Worktime as a Percentage of New York Worktime, 1966

If New York Worktime = 100%, Moscow Worktime =	
Foods	
White bread, 1 pound	400%
Potatoes, 1 pound	300%
Beef, rib roast, 1 pound	350%
Butter, salted, 1 pound	1000%
Sugar, 1 pound	1500%
Milk, at grocery, 1 quart	500%
Eggs, 2nd grade, 1 dozen	800%
Tea, 1¾ ounces	1200%
Men's Clothing	
Shirt, cotton	750%
Suit, wool, middle of price range	800%
Shoes, leather oxfords, pair	600%
Women's Clothing	
Dress, street, rayon	1000%
Shoes, leather oxfords, middle of price range	700%
Stockings, nylon	1000%
Other Commodities	
Soap, toilet, 3½ ounces	800%
Cigarettes, package of 20	250%
Vodka, fifth	400%

Source: Joint Economic Committee, Congress of the United States, *New Directions in the Soviet Economy* (1966).

Looking at the farm picture as a whole, one discovers that the contrast between Soviet and American agriculture is the most striking of all segments of the two economies. In the United States, out of a total civilian labor force of 72 million in 1965, 4 million were employed in agriculture. In the Soviet Union, out of a total labor force of about 100 million, almost 40 million depend on agriculture for their livelihood, or the proportion that existed in the United States in 1890. This figure does not include millions of urban dwellers who produce vegetables and potatoes on individual or collective garden plots outside many Soviet cities. In the United States, therefore, one person employed in agriculture feeds himself and seventeen other workers and their families on the highest standard in the world, and vast surpluses still accumulate which are given away or sold to the rest of the world. In the Soviet Union, nearly one-half of the population depending on agriculture for a living can barely feed itself and the other half of the people. The staple diet still heavily emphasizes bread, potatoes, and beets, while there is still a relative scarcity of better-grade foods. Items like coffee and chocolate, part of the ordinary diet of workers in Western countries, are still luxuries in the Soviet Union. Before 1914 Russia was one of the world's leading exporters of farm products; the collectivization of agriculture has turned her into an importer. In 1963–1966, the Soviet Union bought over seven million tons of grain annually, and in 1966 she contracted to buy nine million tons of wheat from Canada in the following three years. One reason for such advance purchases of food by the Soviet Union was the fact that Red China also has been unable to feed its people and has therefore been competing with Russia for available food surpluses in capitalist nations.

In the early years of Soviet collectivization of farming, government-imposed low prices induced many peasants to grow as little as possible and to slaughter much of the livestock for their own consumption. As a result, there was widespread famine in the early 1930's, particularly in the Ukraine, where peasant resistance was strengthened by the force of nationalism.

After World War II, the Soviet government decided to intensify collectivization. Between 1950 and 1964, the 250,000 collective farms were amalgamated into 38,000. The objective was to raise production and at the same time reduce the individuality of the peasant. In addition to these 38,000 collective farms (*kolkhozy*), there are 10,000 state farms (*sovkhozy*) in which the peasant works on a strict wage basis, just as in a Soviet factory. The peasant in the collective farm still has some share in the success or failure of the whole farm.

The absolute numbers of collective farms and state farms do not give an accurate picture of Soviet farming, for the average state farm employs about twice as many workers as the collective farm, has four times as much land, and its crop area is about three times as large as on the average collective farm. From the viewpoint of communist ideology, the state farms represent the highest possible form of agricultural organization and production because the peasant has been completely turned into a proletarian dependent on the state for his wage. Communist leaders hope that someday all collective farms will be transformed into state farms,

Photograph by Robert S. Ebenstein.

The author in line to buy fresh fruit in the center of Moscow.

but the Soviet government has not yet dared, for reasons of practicality, to go to such an extreme, although the amalgamation of collective farms into giant units clearly shows the ultimate goal in Soviet farm policy.

After more than thirty years of farm collectivism, the Russian peasant is still deeply opposed to communism in agriculture. Peasant pressure has forced the government to allow the member of the collective farm to devote part of his time to a small plot of land under his own personal management; he may then sell the products of his own effort on the open market at higher prices than are paid by the government (which is able to buy farm products at artificially low prices bearing little relation to the natural forces of supply and demand).

Although the peasant's own piece of land only amounts to an acre or so, it supplies him with nearly half of his income, and these dwarf holdings, amounting to only 3 per cent of all Soviet farm land, account for about one-third of total farm output and one-half of all Soviet milk, meat, green vegetables, and eggs. The peasants sell their personal produce in the regular "farmers' markets" found in most Soviet cities. It is not uncommon, however, to see individual peasants, more often women, arrive in the center of Leningrad or Moscow with a basket of fresh tomatoes or fruit and sell the produce in a few minutes to an eager crowd of buyers who are always on the lookout for items that are scarce or unavailable in government stores.

The superior efficiency of private farming over communist collective farming has also been amply demonstrated in the other communist states of Eastern Europe. In Hungary, for example, private farming on only 10.5 per cent of all farm land accounted for over one-half of total farm output in 1961. Even in the citadel of hard-line communism, Red China, private plots, covering only 7 per cent of the cultivated land, account for 80 per cent of pigs and 90 per cent of poultry raised, and supply the peasants with over one-half of their incomes (*The Economist*, July 2, 1966).

The Soviet rulers know that as long as this remnant of private agriculture is permitted, the peasant will know from his daily experience that private farming is more efficient than collectivized communist agriculture. Yet so far the Soviet rulers have not dared to abolish this private element in farming because it contributes an important share to total farm production. In fact, after Khrushchev's ouster in 1964, the new leaders sought to encourage private farming. "Unwarranted limitations have been imposed in this sphere in recent years, despite the fact that economic conditions have not been ripe for such a step," Brezhnev declared on November 6, 1964, in one of his first major policy statements. Since then, the new Soviet leadership has removed discriminatory taxes previously levied on private farming, and has even supplied funds for the construction and modernization of free farmers' markets. Also, administrative price-fixing in these markets has been discontinued. Time will tell to what extent these concessions will counteract the basic defect of Soviet farming—forced collectivization. For the time being, it appears that Soviet farming will continue to be "the most expensive food producer in the world." (Joint Economic Committee, *New Directions in the Soviet Economy*, 1966, Part II-B, p. 429.)

Psychologically, the Russian peasant has not been transformed into the proletarian that the communist rulers planned him to be. In the years after World War II, thousands of Russian peasants who had been deported to Germany as forced laborers during the war refused to go back home after having seen life outside the Soviet Union. Almost to a man, these peasants are opposed to collectivization and hope to own their own farms after communism is gone.

This sentiment of the peasants has been confirmed by events in Yugoslavia and Poland. After his break with Moscow in 1948, Tito allowed the peasants to decide whether they wanted to continue farm collectives or return to individual farming. The farm collectives rapidly disappeared, and Yugoslav farm output has more than doubled since 1952. In Poland, the Gomulka brand of national communism, brought into power by the October Revolution of 1956, also allowed the peasants to choose between individual and collective farming. Less than 1 per cent of arable land is held by collective farms, 12 per cent by state farms, and 87 per cent by private peasants. The small number of collective and state farms have done poorly, whereas private farming has prospered since 1956.

Yet all these peasants—whether in the Soviet Union or in other communist states—are not fanatical individualists. While irreconcilably opposed to collective farms, they eagerly accept cooperative farm institutions, such as Canadian, Danish, and New Zealand farmers have developed. There is a world of difference between collectivism and cooperation: the purpose of *collectivism* is to *destroy the individuality* of the farmer; the aim of *cooperation* is to *strengthen the individual farm.*

Interestingly enough, workers and professional people who have escaped from Russia have indicated in interviews that they wish to maintain public ownership in only the key industries after communism is gone, but want to return to private ownership in light industry, retailing, and some of the professions. These attitudes indicate the failure of completely dogmatizing the people in a generation of one-sided propaganda. Where economic activity—as in agriculture, light industry, and retailing—can be performed in the classical pattern of the individual owner-manager-worker, what little uncensored Russian opinion we have is opposed to the economic changes of communism. Only where ownership, work, and management are technologically not feasible in one individual unit—as in heavy industry and some public services—does public ownership seem to meet with approval.

In the field of industrialization, progress under Soviet communism has been immense, as was first proved by Russia's ability to withstand the onslaught of Germany in World War II. Though Russia received some strategic supplies from the United States during the war, the bulk of the industrial production needed to defeat Germany came from Russian workshops and factories. Russian industrialization, from the First Five Year Plan, was conceived primarily as a means of increasing, not the material welfare of the people, but the power of the state. For this reason, the government consistently emphasized heavy industry as especially vital to the production of armaments and showed less concern for the development of consumer goods industries.

Proportion of Soviet Industrial Investment in Producer Goods and Consumer Goods Industries
(Per Cent)

	1918–1958	1959–1964	1966–1970 (PLAN)
Producer goods	88.3	86.9	88.1
Consumer goods	11.7	13.1	11.9

Source: *Foreign Affairs*, July, 1966.

The net result of economic change in Russia over a generation is not so much economic communism as a totalitarian state economy. In terms of sheer industrial power, Russia now ranks second in the world, preceded only by the United States. But this ranking is significant only in appraising the *power of the state to wage war* and not in reflecting the opportunity of the people to live the good life. Viewed from the latter angle, living standards in Russia are still way behind North America, most countries of Europe, Australia and New Zealand, and numerous other nations throughout the world.

Until recently, appliances common in the American home were generally unknown in the Soviet Union; the government was too busy producing steel, tanks, military planes, missiles, and sputniks. In the last few years a start has been made toward producing some of the basic appliances. Yet, as the table below shows, the Soviet family is still a long way from the standard of ownership of appliances that the American family takes for granted.

Radios are the only item that is available fairly easily at a moderate price in the Soviet Union because radios are considered by the government as an important means of propaganda. The other appliances are high priced and often hard to get; consumers must usually wait several months or years before they can obtain them. In 1964, the waiting period for good-quality refrigerators was 3-4 years.

In the 1950's, Soviet annual production of automobiles hovered around 100,000. Production was stepped up in the 1960's, until it reached an all-time Soviet record of 200,000 in 1965—as compared with 9.3 million cars sold in the United States in 1965. Of the small number of cars produced in the Soviet Union, about one-quarter are sold abroad to earn hard currency. Most of what is left over for domestic use is assigned to government officials, taxicab transportation, and other nonprivate uses. Waiting periods for private

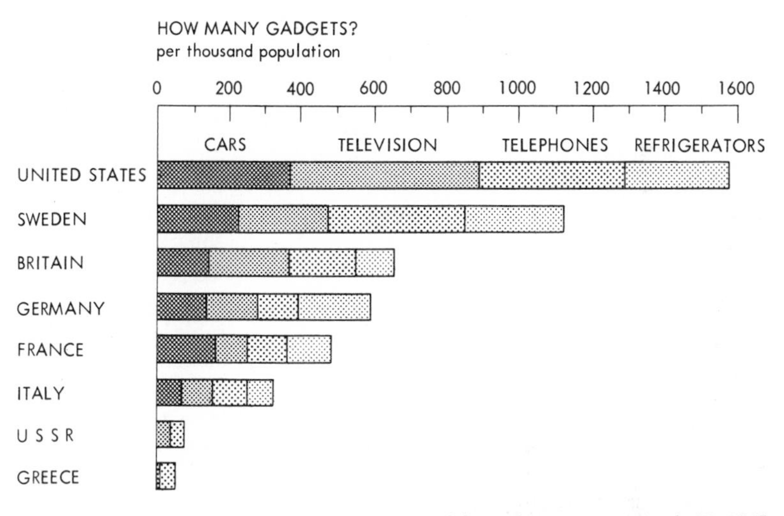

Reprinted from *The Economist*, March 27, 1965.

buyers have ranged from 3-7 years, and waiting lists have often been closed altogether. Yet, as can be seen in the chart, the price of a Soviet car equals five years' pay of the average worker, as compared with five months' pay for a similar car in the case of the American worker. Under both Stalin and Khrushchev, low levels of Soviet automobile production were the result of economic policy and of communist ideology. When Khrushchev visited the United States in 1959, he candidly stated the reason for not allocating resources and manpower to automobile production: "We could do it tomorrow, but that means freezing capital. You go ahead and do all that foolishness. It's for our benefit." Ideologically, both Stalin and Khrushchev looked upon the automobile as a typical expression of capitalist frivolity and licentious individualism which did not fit communist austerity in the era of building a powerful Soviet state and economy.

The decision of the new leadership under Brezhnev and Kosygin to introduce Russia into the automobile age is one of the most important turning points in the history of Soviet communism since 1917. It will not happen overnight, but the foundations have been laid. In 1966, the Soviet government contracted with Italy's Fiat

The Automobile in Russia and the United States

	In Russia	In United States
Cars in use	900,000	71 million
Cars relative to population	1 per 260 persons	1 per 3 persons
Auto production	200,000	9.3 million
Bus and truck production	420,000	1.8 million
Car models available	4	More than 360
Paved highways	71,000 miles in area of 8.7 million square miles	2.3 million miles in area of 3.6 million square miles
Gasoline stations	1,250	212,000
Price of auto	$6,000 for medium-sized sedan—about 5 years' pay for average worker	$2,500 for comparable car—about 5 months' pay for average factory worker

Source: Adapted from U. S. NEWS & WORLD REPORT, June 6, 1966.

Automobile Company to build a huge plant in the Soviet Union which will eventually produce about 500,000 cars a year. In the same year, the Soviets also made an agreement with France's biggest automobile company, Renault, to enlarge existing facilities of Russia's leading automobile plant in Moscow, in order to increase its annual production of cars from 80,000 to about 300,000. The announced goal was total Soviet production of about 800,000 cars by 1970. This will still be much less than one-tenth of American output, and much less than what the Soviet consumer would like to see produced, but it is a beginning that will have more than economic effects. The Soviet rulers of the 1970's and 1980's may discover that Stalin and Khrushchev were perhaps ideologically not wrong after all and that the sense of individual mobility and independence fostered by car ownership may pose some puzzling problems to a totalitarian system. Moreover, once the Soviet consumer has tasted the pleasures of car ownership, he may demand more and better consumer goods of other types—and such demands may not always be compatible with the requirements of a planned economy in which the power of the state is given precedence over the welfare of the individual.

Since the middle 1960's, the Soviet government has experimented with a measure of consumer choice. Until that time, central planners determined what each plant had to produce, how much labor had to be employed, and at what prices the goods were to be sold. Gradually, after the worst shortages of consumer goods abated, the Soviet government found that an increasing number of items (cameras, bicycles, lamp shades, sewing machines) remained unsold on store shelves and in warehouses, because they were either overpriced, defective, or poorly designed. The reforms began on a small scale before Khrushchev's ouster but were vigorously pushed by Kosygin from 1965 on. Consumer goods industries were the first affected by the "Kosygin reforms." This was done on the basis of the traditional low concern for consumer goods, so that if the reforms did not work out, Soviet production of heavy machinery and military hardware would not be disrupted. After the consumer industries, the Kosygin reforms were gradually applied to light industries, and the intention of the government is to apply them eventually to most of the economy.

As the reforms have been applied to consumer industries, performance in sales rather than in gross output has become the main criterion of enterprise efficiency and profitability. Management now directly contracts with suppliers for materials and also sells directly to wholesale and retail outlets. The size and composition of the labor force are now also determined primarily by management rather than by central planners. However, central planners still determine the volume of sales to be met as well as the rate of profit in terms of invested capital. If management can fulfill or exceed the planned sales volume, plant managers may receive bonuses of up to 50 per cent of basic salary, and production workers, too, receive bonuses. Profits of individual enterprises will thus be substantially determined by the orders they receive from stores, and their orders will in turn be largely determined by the preferences of consumers.

While these reforms will give the consumer more choice than in the past, they should not be exaggerated as a recognition of the free market and of consumer sovereignty or as a return to capitalism. In the free market economy of capitalism, the consumer determines not only which make of car he will buy but also *how many* cars will be produced. In the Soviet Union, the government will continue to determine how many resources in capital and labor will be allocated to automobile production. Similarly, the volume of construction in the free market of capitalism is determined by relative consumer preferences in relation to residential buildings, supermarkets and shopping centers (both virtually nonexistent in the Soviet Union), restaurants, and hotels and motels. In the Soviet Union, the government will continue to determine how much of available materials and manpower will be allocated to construction of heavy industry or military installations rather than of restaurants and supermarkets. The main effect of the Kosygin reforms—and by no means an unimportant one—is thus likely to be the reduction of waste through stronger incentives for increased efficiency and profitability rather than the abandonment of the key principle of communist totalitarian economics. For the government will continue to decide how, for what purposes, and in what relative proportions available capital resources and manpower are to be allocated.

Of all the segments of the Soviet economy, services and housing have been the most neglected—not as the result of providential mishaps, but of deliberate government policy. As to services, complaints in the Soviet press reveal that it takes three to four months to have shoes repaired, even longer to have a radio or television set repaired, and that it is next to impossible to get any laundering or drycleaning done. Perpetual shortages of restaurant and hotel facilities not only limit domestic Soviet tourism but also deprive the government of the eagerly sought hard currencies of foreign tourists. Lack of adequate public transportation is another constant topic of public complaint. Shops and stores of all types are in conspicuously short supply. "Why are there queues in our food stores?" *Pravda* asked (January 23, 1966)—as if it didn't know. In 1965, 16 persons per 1,000 of population were working in Soviet trade establishments, as compared with 76 in the United States. According to Soviet studies, Soviet citizens spend about 70 per cent of their leisure time on routine chores, such as shopping in numerous stores for specific products, cooking, laundering, repairing clothes, or waiting for buses.

The Soviet record in housing is even more dismal than in services. In the precommunist Russia of 1914, available per capita living space for the urban population was 7 square meters (1 square meter is equal to 10.76 square feet). In 1923, this figure had only slightly dropped to 6.45 square meters. In 1940, after a decade of communist industrialization and planning, per capita living space dropped more sharply to 4.34 square meters. Until 1957, the figure still stood under 5 square meters. From 1958 on, the Soviet government made a determined effort to improve housing conditions, but so far, progress has not been very significant. In 1965, urban per capita living space was still only 6.42

square meters, or less than in 1914. The Soviet government itself defines 9 square meters per person as the minimum "health norm," but at the rate of building in recent years this health standard will not be reached for many years to come. Current living space per person in the Soviet Union is less than half the available per capita space in Austria and West Germany, and less than one-fourth the available per capita space in the United States.

Housing standards can also be measured by the density of occupancy of space, that is, the number of occupants per room. Density in the Soviet Union was 2.60 persons per room in 1923, 3.46 persons in 1940, and 2.33 persons per room in 1965, or exactly four times the density in the United States (0.63 persons per room). The typical four-room apartment in a Soviet city houses four families, all sharing the kitchen and toilet facilities. Bathrooms of the American type are still a rarity. Even most new apartments built in the 1950's were designed for two to four families per apartment, each family occupying one room. The most recent apartment buildings have some single-family tiny apartments, but such luxury is still a dream for the great majority of the Soviet urban population. Although the government has sought to improve housing conditions since the late 1950's, the rate of progress has been very slow, and the gap between Soviet and Western housing standards has not been appreciably narrowed. The conclusion of a student of Soviet housing therefore seems justified that "among industrial nations there is none with housing conditions so bad as those of the U.S.S.R." (*New Directions in the Soviet Economy,* 1966, Part II-B, p. 553.)

Conveniences in the Soviet home supplied by public utilities are still very meager by Western standards. Only a minority of urban housing units enjoys gas or hot water, and rural housing still largely lacks electric lighting, while running water and proper sewage facilities are still the exception rather than the rule. Even the telephone is still a luxury. The Soviet Union has about 7 million telephones for a population of over 235 million, as compared with about 100 million telephones in the United States with a population of about 200 million. In one year alone, between 1964 and 1965, the number of American telephones increased by about 5 million, or about three-quarters of all Soviet telephones. Canada, with a population of under 20 million, has more telephones than the Soviet Union. Telephone books, too, are not readily available in the Soviet Union, and trying to find a telephone number is a major adventure in red tape.

The Soviet emphasis on production rather than welfare or consumption is also illustrated by the attitudes toward the unemployed, the aged, and the women in the total setting of the economy. The Soviet policy on unemployment relief is one of the few instances in which a Biblical teaching is practiced: "He who does not work shall not eat." Soviet logic maintains that a person who loses a job can always find work if he is willing to take any job at any wage; therefore, there is no unemployment relief. The Soviets do not worry about the loss of pride and emotional disequilibrium a person might suffer if he has to take a lower-paying job of less prestige in an entirely different part of the country. Similarly, the pension for the aged is kept deliberately so low that many old people keep on working as long as they are able. This is in sharp contrast to the outlook in the United States and other capitalist countries that penalize the recipients of old-age pensions if their earnings exceed relatively moderate amounts.

Female Percentage of the Labor Force
Soviet Union and United States, 1960

	Soviet Union	United States
Total	53.7	32.8
Major types of employment:		
Industry	45	20.9
Construction	29	3.7
Agriculture	61.5	9.8
Transport	29	8.6
Commerce	69	37.7
Services	64.3	51.3

Source: Joint Economic Committee, Congress of the United States, *New Directions in the Soviet Economy* (1966).

With respect to the role of women in the labor force, the above table speaks for itself. Women compose 32.8 per cent of the labor force in the United States, as contrasted with the female percentage of 53.7 in the Soviet Union. The most conspicuous contrast of percentages is in construction; women constitute 29 per cent of the Soviet labor force, with 3.7 per cent of women employed in construction in the United States. The visitor to the Soviet Union is struck by the large number of women that can be seen digging ditches, repairing roads, and building houses and factories. In numerous cases, one can see entire gangs of road workers composed of women.

The high percentage of women in the Soviet labor force is probably due to three factors. First, the husband generally earns too little to support his wife and family on his wage alone. Second, since entire families generally share one room, and four, five, or six families share one kitchen, there is not much incentive for women to stay at home. Third, the Soviet rulers deliberately encourage and cajole women to do any kind of work rather than to worry about dishpan hands or about how a woman of forty can look like a girl of twenty.

Although the Soviet national product is only about 40 per cent of that of the United States, Soviet annual investment in heavy industry and national defense is about equal to that of the United States. As a result, per capita consumption of the Soviet citizen runs to only about 20-25 per cent of American per capita consumption. Annual investment in new housing is twice as high in the United States as in the Soviet Union, although the available living space per person is already four times as high in the United States.

The Soviet bias in favor of industrial and military power can also be seen in the uneven differentials of productivity in the Soviet economy. In agriculture, Soviet productivity (or the output per man in an hour) is only about 10 per cent of American productivity; in steel, about 50 per cent; and in electronics, about 66 per cent.

The price for this rapid industrialization has been steep. Millions of Soviet subjects have been employed for years in slave labor camps to provide cheap labor. The number of slave laborers in the two decades from the middle thirties to the middle fifties ranges from a conservative low estimate of five million to the more likely figure of about ten million. Since 1957 slave labor camps have been closed, but, never having admitted their existence, the Soviet government has not divulged how many persons are still employed in "correctional labor" camps.

The Soviet worker is subjected to managerial authority such as has not been known in capitalist countries for over two generations. The communist promise of liberating the worker from capitalist oppression has turned into the reality of complete subjection to management, the direct representative of the all-powerful state.

The labor unions are no more than "company unions," since their purpose is to push the interests of the employer, the state, at the expense of the interests of the workers.

Economic change in the Soviet Union has failed to solve the problem of social justice, for the sake of which the change was ostensibly undertaken in the first place.

During the first 15 years of the Soviet regime, an attempt was made to limit inequalities of income to a moderate range of differential; from the middle of the 1930's on, however, with the inauguration of the era of purges, the last vestiges of equalitarianism were wiped out and an entirely new policy was brought into being. Wages based on performance rather than on fixed hourly rates became the policy, a policy that labor unions in free nations had opposed for two generations as a system of exploitation.

The old-fashioned capitalist appeal for higher production compensated by higher incomes was covered up with slogans like "socialist competition," and workers were driven on to greater production efforts by the policy of Stakhanovism, inspired by the alleged feats of a coal miner named Stakhanov. Whereas the original concern in communist theory had been with problems of just distribution, Soviet policy has in practice concentrated on maximum production. The *incentive of higher income* rather than service to the community has become the main appeal of Soviet social and economic policy, and the philosophy of equality has been derided as "petty-bourgeois prejudice."

In line with Soviet anti-equalitarian policy, personal income taxes are among the lowest in the world. The Soviet government derives 90 per cent of its revenue from *sales taxes* and other indirect levies that proportionately hit the lowest income groups hardest. Only 10 per cent of the Soviet government revenue comes from income taxes. In the United States, the picture is the exact reverse: the United States government revenue is 90 per cent from income taxes, and 10 per cent from sales and other indirect taxes. In concentrating on sales taxes, the Soviets seek to *penalize consumption;* by contrast, heavy (and progressive) *taxation of incomes* in the United States—as in some other Western democracies —*hits the productive effort.*

The group with the highest incomes is the same in Russia as in the United States: business managers and executives. Yet, whereas the income tax in the United States goes up to 70 per cent, the top tax rate for Soviet executives is only 13 per cent. As to inheritance taxes: the top rate in the United States is 77 per cent; in the Soviet Union, inheritance taxes were abolished in 1942—another bonus to the affluent elements in Soviet society.

According to official propaganda the problem of social classes has been solved in Soviet society, because from the Marxist viewpoint there can be no class inequality except on the basis of the private ownership of the means of production.

Yet Soviet reality tells a different story. There are at least *three distinguishable classes*. In the first group—numbering a few hundred thousand families, perhaps as many as a million—there are the top government officials, party leaders, military officers, industrial executives, scientists, artists, and writers. The second group is made up of the intermediary ranks of civilian and military officials, collective farm managers, and some of the more affluent skilled workers and technicians in industry; this group forms the middle classes of Soviet society and numbers about four to five million families. The third class is made up of the bulk of the population, the mass of workers and peasants, numbering about fifty million families.

What is remarkable about social stratification in communist countries is that the *income spread between the different classes has been steadily widening*, while it has been continuously narrowed in the democratic nations of the West through taxation and other measures. Moreover, within the bulk of the population, the working class, the *difference between wages of skilled and unskilled workers* has been constantly on the increase in the Soviet Union, whereas in democratic nations this differential has been systematically reduced, largely owing to the pressure of free labor unions. The differential between skilled and unskilled worker is about three times greater in the Soviet Union than in the United States.

The growing inequality between and within classes in communist states is one of the most explosive sources of unrest and revolt. The East German workers who rebelled in 1953 and the Polish and Hungarian workers who rebelled in 1956 objected less to the ideology of communism than to the brutal economic exploitation to which they were exposed, an exploitation that meant austerity for the masses of the people and affluence for a small privileged clique of party bosses and government officials. The reality of communist economics thus taught the workers that the mere transfer of property from private to public ownership did not in itself bring about a new society built on justice and equality.

As Aristotle said over two thousand years ago, the main question is not *who* owns property, but *how* property is used.

How Incomes Vary in the Soviet "Classless" Society

	Monthly Earnings (in Rubles)[1]
Scientist (academician)	800-1,500
Minister (head of government ministry or department)	700
Opera star	500-2,000[2]
Professor (science)	600-1,000
Professor (medicine)	400-600
Docent (assistant professor)	300-500
Plant manager	300-1,000
Engineer	100-300
Physician, head	95-180
Physician, staff	85-100
Teacher, high school	85-100
Teacher, primary school	60-90
Technician	80-200
Worker, skilled	100-250
Worker, semiskilled	60-90
Worker, unskilled	27-50

[1] The official rate of exchange is 1 ruble = $1.11. The actual purchasing power of the ruble is, however, slightly below the dollar.
[2] The top salary at the Bolshoi Theater has been reported as 500 rubles a month. Outside appearances increase the artist's income.

Source: Monthly Labor Review (April 1960).

In our own day, the experience of communist economic change teaches again that the principal issue is not whether the government owns the means of production, but *who owns the government.*

Sources of strength in communism

Among communism's sources of strength, the most important is probably the enormous *widening of the base from which the elite is recruited.* Before World War I, the Russian elite—in government, the army, business, science, and the arts—was drawn from a relatively small social group of upper-class and upper-middle-class background. There was a tremendous gap between the small governing classes of Russia, in intimate contact with Western Europe, and the vast inchoate masses of peasants. The communist revolution, particularly in its first impetus, swept away distinctions of class, sex, or nationality and opened up a new world of opportunity for people who had hitherto been excluded from opportunity of any sort. Industrialization, perhaps the most dynamic key in creating new opportunities in science and government as well as in industry, formed a *new managerial class*, recruited on a very wide basis, for which there was no precedent.

A quick glance at the social background of the top leaders of the Soviet Union today gives us a fair idea of the Soviet leadership as a whole:

Leader	Occupation of Father
Aristov	fisherman
Brezhnev	steel worker
Gromyko	artisan
Kosygin	lathe worker
Mazurov	peasant
Podgorny	foundry worker
Polyansky	peasant
Shelepin	railroad worker
Shelest	peasant
Shvernik	poor worker
Suslov	peasant

These top leaders are typical representatives of the men who run Russia's industry, government, and armed forces. Those Westerners who have dealt with them agree that they are able and confident, full of drive and energy. In the United States, these men would be corporation executives, political and military leaders, and top government officials—the very same jobs they hold in the Soviet Union. Because their ideas and aims seem irreconcilable with Western ideas and objectives, many persons have been blinded to their high technical and executive ability.

The competition for leadership positions in the Soviet Union is more ruthless than in the democratic world, the premium for success greater, and the penalty for failure harsher. The successful manager who overfulfills his production quota is rapidly promoted and his rewards are—in relation to the rest of the population—more ample than in capitalist countries. The incentive system is more fully developed than in the United States; the bonus for the typical Soviet executive amounts to 25-50 per cent of his base salary. By contrast, only about half of American corporations have bonus schemes at all, and where bonuses are paid they typically amount to only 10-20 per cent of base pay.

The penalty for failure is also greater than in capitalist countries. Under Stalin, managerial failure could result in slave labor or even execution; in more recent years, the manager who fails in his production job is more likely to be fired and downgraded to a less responsible job. This harsh emphasis on performance may seem ruthless, but it works—if results are the only things that count.

The less a position in the elite is directly tied up with politics, the more recognition can be given to talent and merit. As long as a leading surgeon, chemist, mathematician, engineer, or industrial executive keeps his mouth shut (politically speaking) and opens it only for the purpose of expressing his loyalty to the regime, he will generally (but not always) be left alone. The more a position in the ruling group is tinged with politics, the more criteria besides merit and talent become relevant and frequently decisive.

Rapid *industrialization* is the second main source of communist strength, in Russia as well as in other communized states. Before World War I, Russia was an overwhelmingly agricultural country; Russian industrial power was very low, ranking behind the United States, Britain, Germany, France, Japan, and Austria-Hungary. After World War II, Russia moved up to second place, preceded only by the United States. Industrialization in all communist states is concentrated on heavy industry, the base of military power.

In absolute figures, industry in Russia and the communist states still lags considerably behind the United States and her allies. But what is alarming is the rapid rate of industrial growth in the communist states, which considerably exceeds that of many Western nations. Even if it be argued that the communist states have now the initial advantage of backward countries undergoing rapid industrialization, and that their present rate of expansion cannot be indefinitely maintained, the Western nations will have to step up their own productivity and rate of industrial growth if the present balance of industrial power, still heavily in favor of the noncommunist states, is not to be lost.

Fast economic growth is not something which automatically comes out of either communism or capitalism but is the result of hard work and know-how. Within the communist group of nations, some have shown faster economic progress than others, and the same is true of the capitalist world. Specifically, the Soviet Union has no superior record of economic growth as compared with *all* capitalist nations. While it is true that the Soviet Union has, in the period of 1950–1965, grown faster economically than the United States, other capitalist nations have done better than the Soviet Union. As the table below shows, the growth record of the Soviet

From *Straight Herblock* (Simon & Schuster, 1964).

It's "split-level living" . . .

Union during 1950–1960 was much more impressive than during 1960–1965, and the superior performance of Japan as compared with Russia in 1960–1965 is particularly striking. However, the eyes of the world are focused on the comparative economic growth of the Soviet Union and the United States rather than of the Soviet Union and Japan. During 1950–1960, the Soviet rate of growth was more than double that of the United States; during 1960–1965, the Soviet growth rate was only slightly above that of the United States. For the whole decade of 1960–1970, the projected annual average Soviet growth rate is 4.5 to 5.5, as compared with an estimated American average annual growth rate of 4.5—on the assumption, that is, that the relative slowdown of the Soviet economy and the unprecedented American boom of 1961–1965 will both continue through the remainder of the decade.

Average Annual Rates of Economic Growth for Seven Major Economies
(Per Cent)

COUNTRY	1950–1960	1960–1965	1960–1970 *(projected)*
Japan	8.8	9.1	7.2
West Germany	7.5	4.8	4.1
Soviet Union	6.8	4.9	4.5-5.5
Italy	5.9	5.2	5.6
France	4.3	4.8	5.0
United States	3.3	4.6	4.5
Great Britain	2.6	3.4	3.3

Source: Joint Economic Committee, Congress of the United States, *Dimensions of Soviet Economic Power* (1963), and *New Directions in the Soviet Economy* (1966).

In gearing economic policy to the requirements of national power, the Soviet Union has made particularly strenuous efforts to close the gap with the United States in such key commodities as iron, steel, coal, petroleum, electricity, and cement. Increased production of these commodities also pays off propagandistically, because most underdeveloped countries look upon steel, for example, as a symbol of industrial progress and power. Part of the slow increase of steel production in the United States is due to the fact that other products such as aluminum and plastics increasingly replace steel in many uses; moreover, in an advanced economy like the American, people increasingly spend on services, amenities, and luxuries rather than on goods that use steel. Similarly, coal has declined in the United States because petroleum and natural gas have increasingly replaced it as a source of fuel or energy. Moreover, absolute production figures of key commodities do not tell the whole story. In the United States, one-fifth of the output of steel goes into automobiles, and sizable amounts of steel are used in residential building, shopping centers, highway construction, consumer durables, and other facets of the good life, whereas in the Soviet Union steel is the foundation of heavy industry expansion and armaments. Similarly, although the Soviet Union produces nearly one-half of the electricity generated in the United States, these absolute production figures conceal the fact that, in terms of residential use, the American home uses eight times as much electricity as does the Soviet home.

Valid as these arguments may be from a strictly economic viewpoint, they make little impact—politically and propagandistically—in the underdeveloped countries. To them, steel is still the number 1 barometer of economic strength and progress, not the amount that people spend on eating out, entertainment, vacations, and other pleasant amenities that are little affected by steel production.

Production of Selected Key Commodities, 1950, 1965

		Soviet Union	United States
Pig iron (million metric tons)	1950	19	60
	1965	66	82
Steel (million metric tons)	1950	27	88
	1965	91	121
Coal (million metric tons)	1950	261	502
	1965	578	475
Petroleum, crude (million metric tons)	1950	38	266
	1965	243	385
Natural gas (billion cubic meters)	1950	6	193
	1965	129	450
Electric power (billion kilowatt hours)	1950	91	389
	1965	507	1,220
Cement (million metric tons)	1950	10	37
	1965	72	65

Source: Joint Economic Committee, and Soviet Central Statistical Administration.

The third major area of Soviet strength is in *education and science.* The Soviet launching of the first sputnik on October 4, 1957 came as a bombshell to those who still had the illusion that Russia was largely a country of illiterate peasants. Yuri A. Gagarin's first manned orbital flight on April 12, 1961 showed that the Soviet lead in space exploration was still very impressive. Triumphs of this kind are the result, not of short-term crash programs, but of long, sustained effort over many years. According to the most authoritative American analysis, the increase in the years 1926–1952 of Soviet professional manpower was as follows: engineers, ten times; teachers, five times; and physicians, four times. (Nicholas DeWitt, *Soviet Professional Manpower,* National Science Foundation, 1955, p. 247.) Since 1952, the Soviet expansion in education has progressed at an even more rapid rate. By 1958, the proportion of the age group 15-19 enrolled in secondary schools and of the age group 20-24 enrolled in institutions of higher learning was highest in the United States but higher in the Soviet Union than in the major Western European countries.

The intense demand for a higher education or advanced professional training in the Soviet Union is also expressed in the constantly rising proportion of students who receive their training through extension or correspondence courses. In the 1940's and 1950's regular day students outnumbered extension and correspondence students by a considerable, but steadily declining, margin. Since 1960, the number of regular full-time students has been consistently well below one-half of the total number of students admitted to institutions of higher learning and professional training, whereas in the United States as in other Western nations the number of regular full-time students generally ranges between 75-90 per cent of all students taking college and university courses.

Looking at Soviet and American higher education in the four decades of 1926–1965, we find the following results: the Soviet Union has trained 2.5 times more engineers than the United States and is continuing to train engineers at an annual rate that is about three times higher than in the United States. The total pool of engineers and physicists is now greater in the Soviet Union than in the United States, and the gap is growing year by year. In agricultural specialties, the Soviet Union has trained over twice as many as the United States, and this ratio is increasing in favor of the Soviet Union. By contrast, the United States has trained three times more graduates in the humanities and social sciences than the Soviet Union, and the American superiority in these areas largely accounts for the continuing over-all lead of the total number of American college students over the total enrollments in Soviet institutions of higher learning and training.

In the field of medicine, the Soviet Union has trained 2.5 more physicians than the United States, and in the last several years the annual number of Soviet medical graduates has been three times higher than in the United States, although the Soviet population is only 15 per cent higher than that of the United States. In 1965, there were 21 physicians per 10,000 population in the Soviet Union but only 15 per 10,000 population in the United States. The shortage of doctors is so severe in the United States that thousands have to be imported—many from poor, underdeveloped countries with comparatively low standards of medical training. In 1965, more than one out of four interns and resident physicians in American hospitals came from abroad, mostly from underdeveloped countries. In New York City, one-half of the hospital staff is foreign. In several states, more than half of the resident physicians in hospitals were educated abroad. Over 90 per cent of medical students from Asia never return home, because their medical skills are so urgently needed in the United States.

The impressive Soviet effort in higher education and specialized professional and technical training is not always matched—not yet, at least—by superior qualitative performance. In medicine, for example, not a single major medical discovery or drug has come out of the Soviet Union since 1917. Within the existing emphasis on engineering and science, priority goes to engineering rather than to basic scientific research. Before 1917, one Nobel Prize went to a Russian scientist (Pavlov, 1904). Since 1917, three and a half Nobel Prizes in science have been awarded to Russians. In basic scientific discovery, Soviet scientists have so far been behind small countries like Austria, Sweden, Switzerland, and Denmark, not to speak of major countries like the United States, Germany, Britain, and France.

The emphasis on engineering can also be seen in the greatest Soviet triumph—space satellites. From the launching of the first sputnik in 1957, the Soviets have maintained superiority in rocket power required to send heavy vehicles into outer space. The United States has launched more space satellites than the Soviet Union, but these vehicles were much lighter than the Soviet ones. While lacking the rocket power of Soviet satellites, American satellites have been gathering much more scientific information in the fields of cosmic radiation, meteorology, and communications. Yet superior engineering in greater rocket power is one of the decisive elements in modern weaponry, particularly intercontinental missiles.

The Soviet commitment to education as a major goal of national policy is expressed in many ways. With a national income that is only about 40 per cent of that of the United States, the Soviets spend proportionately twice as much of their national income on education as is done in the United States. The Soviet professor receives eight times the wage of the average factory worker, whereas the American professor receives only one and one-half to two times the American worker's pay. Tuition, textbooks, and medi-

"How about 'Russian Scientists Say' . . . ?"

cal care are free of charge in Soviet universities and institutions of higher learning, and dormitory quarters—extremely crowded as they may be—cost only a few rubles per month. In addition, 80 per cent of Soviet students receive monthly stipends ranging from 25 to 55 rubles; the latter figure equals the minimum monthly wage of an urban worker. Students in fields such as mining, electronics, and chemical engineering receive the highest stipends, and an additional bonus of 25 per cent is given to those students who maintain a consistently excellent record.

The Soviet system of higher education tries to utilize the maximum of the available brainpower; the main method of recruiting talent is through written and oral examinations. By contrast, one-third of the top quarter of graduating high-school students in the United States does not go on to college—for economic reasons, in most cases.

Soviet leaders fully realize that the race for educational and scientific leadership may decisively contribute to the ultimate outcome of the struggle between East and West. For example, in the effort to harness the hydrogen bomb reaction for the production of electric power, success would mean a vast new source of energy for billions of years. While at the start of the 1960's the United States led in this vital area, by 1966 the Soviet investment of money and manpower was nearly double that of the United States, according to the Atomic Energy Commission. (*The New York Times*, July 10, 1966.) In the field of planetary exploration, the Soviet Union has been spending five to ten times as much as the United States. While continued Soviet advances in exploring Mars and Venus would not necessarily have immediate military results, the political and psychological effects in the race for scientific leadership would greatly enhance Soviet prestige.

Communist Expansion Since 1939

	YEAR	AREA (SQUARE MILES)	POPULATION
USSR Annexed			
1. Part of Rumania	1940	19,400	3,700,000
2. Estonia	1940	18,300	1,200,000
3. Latvia	1940	25,400	2,100,000
4. Lithuania	1940	23,000	3,000,000
5. Part of East Prussia	1945	5,400	1,200,000
6. Eastern Czechoslovakia	1945	4,900	730,000
7. Eastern Poland	1945	69,900	11,800,000
8. Part of Finland	1940	17,600	450,000
9. Tannu Tuva	1944	64,000	65,000
10. Japanese Possessions	1945	17,800	433,000
Communist Regimes Established			
11. Albania	1946	10,700	1,300,000
12. Bulgaria	1946	42,800	7,300,000
13. Czechoslovakia	1948	49,300	14,000,000
14. Eastern Germany (Including Soviet sector of Berlin)	1949	41,500	18,500,000
15. Hungary	1947	36,000	10,000,000
16. Poland	1947	121,100	26,500,000
17. Rumania	1948	91,600	17,000,000
18. Communist China (Not including Tibet)	1949	3,281,000	582,000,000
19. Outer Mongolia	1945	626,000	1,000,000
20. North Korea	1948	48,500	9,000,000
21. North Vietnam	1951	72,000	12,000,000
22. Tibet (Annexed by Red China)	1951	469,000	1,200,000
23. Cuba	1958	44,218	6,000,000

Finally, the most direct and dangerous source of communist strength lies in *military power*. Although the Soviet citizen consumes only one-fifth to one-fourth of the American standard of consumption, and although the whole Soviet national product is but 40 per cent of the American, the Soviet government spends about the same amount on military preparedness as does the United States. The per capita income in Red China is less than one-fortieth that of the United States, but its armed forces are equal in size to those of the United States, and it has consistently devoted large resources to the development of nuclear weapons, even during the near-famine period of the early 1960's. For Red China's rulers, guns come not only before butter but even before rice.

The vast expenditures on building up military strength have paid off in communist imperialist expansion. Since the outbreak of World War II in September, 1939, the Soviet Union has acquired an area larger than all the New England and Middle Atlantic States with a population of over 25 million. In addition to these outright annexations, the Soviet Union established, by armed force, communist governments in Eastern Europe, with a combined population of over 100 million. Red China conquered and annexed Tibet.

Never before in history has imperialistic expansion acquired so much in so short a time.

By contrast, the Western powers have given freedom and independence to over 800 million people in former colonies since World War II.

Sources of weakness in communism

The first source of weakness is the stress on *conformity*. The most distinguishing quality of a leader is his courage to be different, to have new ideas, to be in a minority, even in solitude. Yet as time goes on, the leader in communist regimes is increasingly being replaced by the bureaucrat, the yes-man. The era of the purges in Russia in the middle 1930's was the conflict between the leaders who had made the Revolution and the bureaucrats who administered it. Conformist as prerevolutionary Russia was, it was a paradise of diversity compared with the communist regime. Antigovernment parties of all types, including radical and social parties, functioned openly, and the press reflected all political viewpoints. *Pravda,* which became the official organ of the Communist party after the Revolution, started publication in 1912; it suffered occasional harassments, but it was published.

Lenin, Trotsky, Stalin, and Khrushchev were all products of pre-communist Russia. Malenkov, Stalin's immediate successor, was the first Big Brother in Russia who was a product of communist rule. He proved not to possess the qualities of a leader; in 1955, he was removed as Prime Minister, and in 1957 he was purged by Khrushchev and exiled to Central Asia. Both Brezhnev and Kosygin are also the product of communist rule. Brezhnev was trained in land surveying and metallurgical engineering, but his main profession became, early in his career, professional party work. Kosygin was trained as a textile engineer and spent most of his career in economic and administrative positions, avoiding involvement in ideological or political controversies and conflicts within the Communist party.

Both men lack the despotic ruthlessness of Stalin and the colorful flamboyance of Khrushchev. Brezhnev's and Kosygin's rise to power was marked by efficient bureaucratic performance rather than by impressive personal leadership. Instead of Stalin's limitless autocracy and Khrushchev's personal rule with its unpredictable periodic swings from more authoritarian to more lenient attitudes, the Soviet Union may be entering—if Brezhnev and Kosygin reflect a new long-term trend—an era of totalitarian organization men, of "totalitarians in grey flannel suits."

In some respects, this type of totalitarianism may be more liberal than under Khrushchev (not to speak of Stalin), as in the approach to the farm problem or in giving greater managerial authority to industrial executives. In other respects, this new type of communist totalitarianism may be more conservative and restrictive than under Khrushchev. At the Twenty-Third Communist Party Congress in Moscow in 1966, it became clear that the new regime under Brezhnev and Kosygin did not favor the Khrushchev-type persistent criticism of the "era of the cult of personality"—the official communist euphemism for "Stalinism." This curb on criticizing Stalinism aims at preserving the stature and prestige of the Communist party, which to professional organization men like Brezhnev and Kosygin is more important than ideological controversies over the merits and demerits of Stalinism in the evolution of Soviet communism. However, only time will tell whether a modern industrial society of over 230 million people can be successfully run by a small oligarchy of men whose background is party bureaucracy and industrial management rather than the broader—and tougher—experience of competitive political leadership.

Under Lenin, orthodox conformity was required in social and political thought, but science and the arts were relatively unaffected. Under Stalin, the party line was applied to the physical sciences and the arts as much as to social science. After Stalin's death in 1953, requirements for orthodoxy were relaxed more in the physical sciences than in the arts. When Boris Pasternak received in 1958 the Nobel Prize in literature for his novel *Doctor Zhivago* (which was not allowed to be published in Russia), he was subjected to an organized campaign of vehement attacks and threats. Officially condemned as a traitor by the communist leaders, Pasternak was spared further humiliations by his lonely death in 1960.

Yet, despite the fate of Pasternak, a number of outstanding Soviet writers, particularly Ilya Ehrenburg among the older authors and Yevgeny Yevtushenko among the younger poets, continued to challenge the rigid party orthodoxies. The publication of *One Day in the Life of Ivan Denisovich,* by Alexander Solzhenitsyn, late in 1962 was perhaps the high point of the literary "thaw" permitted by the government. Although this story of life in a Soviet slave labor camp is cast in the form of a novel, the author wrote from personal experience, having spent the years 1945–1953 in such a camp. As the activities of the more liberally minded Soviet authors and artists grew, Khrushchev intervened again, publicly attacked Ehrenburg and Yevtushenko by name, and warned writers and artists to toe the party line.

Under Brezhnev and Kosygin, the trend toward some liberalization in art and literature has been reversed in the direction of more conservative pressure and control. In 1966, two Russian writers, Andrei Sinyavsky and Yuli Daniel, were sentenced to seven years and five years of "strict regime labor camp," for having published "anti-Soviet" works in foreign countries under the pen-names of Abram Tertz and Nikolai Arzhak. Although the trial was closed to foreign reporters, its proceedings became known abroad. The conduct of the trial—and the official attacks against the two writers before the trial—as well as the stiff sentences shocked even communist leaders in some Western countries who publicly warned the Soviet rulers that the trial had done the Soviet Union more harm than the writings of Sinyavsky and Daniel. However, shortly after the trial Brezhnev reiterated in his opening speech at the Twenty-Third Communist Party Congress (March

29, 1966) the hard-line position of the new regime of being "invariably guided by the principles of the partisanship of art, a class approach to the appraisal of everything that is being done in the sphere of culture." Also, under the new regime publications of the type of *One Day in the Life of Ivan Denisovich* have been effectively discouraged. The literary "establishment" under party control has frequently attacked the "negativism" and "nihilism" of some young Soviet writers for emphasizing the shortcomings of Soviet life under Stalin or at present.

In the field of biology the Soviet agronomist Trofim D. Lysenko gained world-wide notoriety. Lysenko attacked all accepted biological knowledge by claiming that acquired characteristics can be inherited. When many biologists in the Soviet Union revolted against this theory, which is contradictory to all known and controllable facts, Lysenko addressed the Lenin Academy of Agricultural Sciences on July 31, 1948, on "The Situation in the Science of Biology." After damning traditional scientific biology, Lysenko made this statement: "The question is asked in one of the notes handed to me what is the attitude of the Central Committee of the Communist Party to my report. I answer: The Central Committee of the Party examined my report and approved it."

Thus, a question of utmost scientific importance was settled by the fiat of the Central Committee of the Communist Party rather than by the experimental method of the decadent capitalist scientists. Vavilov, the leading Russian geneticist and the outstanding opponent of Lysenko, was arrested in 1941 and exiled to Siberia where he eventually died. After Stalin's death, Khrushchev continued to support Lysenko, in spite of severe criticisms of Lysenko by fellow scientists. After Khrushchev disappeared from the scene in 1964, Lysenko's influence declined, because the new Soviet rulers refused to give him Communist party support.

The fate of psychoanalysis under communism is another case in point. Until 1930, psychoanalysis was tolerated in the Soviet Union, having attracted considerable attention in Russia long before the Revolution. After 1930, psychoanalysis gradually fell into disfavor, and in 1936 the Communist party officially decided that psychoanalysis was incompatible with Marxism-Leninism-Stalinism. After having been branded by the Nazis as false because of its Jewish origin, psychoanalysis was condemned by communists as a web of false bourgeois concepts and was finally assailed as an "ideological instrument of American imperialism"!

In the field of pure and applied philosophy, the communists

have done much housecleaning too. Their opposition to more conservative thinkers was to be expected, but eventually they took on progressive thinkers also. John Dewey, for example, has been roundly condemned for his pragmatic philosophy, which patient communist research has revealed to be yet another cleverly disguised instrument of American imperialism.

Another method of literary assassination is through enforced ignorance. After having talked to hundreds of Russians, a young American writer found that not one of them had ever heard of John Stuart Mill. After spending a year at Moscow University, the same writer summed up his impressions as follows: "You find fourth-year psychology students, for instance, who can quote Pavlov but have never read Freud; fifth-year economics students who have never examined a single criticism of the labor theory of value canonized by Marx; teachers of contemporary Western literature who know nothing about Nabokov, and an entire History of the Soviet Period Department which has not read, and has little hope of reading, Trotsky." (George Feifer, *The New York Times Magazine,* November 22, 1964, p. 50.)

Stalin felt as much at home with music as with the other arts. In January, 1948, the Central Committee of the Communist Party of the Soviet Union decreed that all music must henceforth be popular, simple, and tuneful; at the same time the committee condemned the "formalism" of the best known composers in Russia, such as Shostakovich and Prokofiev. The attack was also directed against instrumental music in general and chamber music in particular, which, the composers were told, "the people did not care for," and the production of more vocal music was urged instead. In some instances, the communists not only have attacked modern art as "formalistic," "remote from the people," and "bourgeois"—the usual epithets—but have imitated the Nazis faithfully enough to charge some works of art with being "cosmopolitan."

After Stalin, official Soviet hostility to modern art and music continued under Khrushchev as well as under Brezhnev and Kosygin. After visiting the first Soviet exhibition of abstract paintings in Moscow in 1962, Khrushchev summarized his artistic judgment by saying that they could have been painted by a "donkey's tail." After this public statement by Russia's most authoritative art critic, other Soviet leaders quickly fell in line by demanding that even wallpapers and textiles had to get rid of abstract designs which were nothing but expressions of "bourgeois decadence," "vulgarity," and "abstractionism."

After Khrushchev, the systematic attack on abstract art continued with unabated—and even intensified—force. In 1966, for example, Oskar Rabin, perhaps the best known of contemporary young Russian painters, was attacked for having permitted an exhibition of his expressionist and symbolist paintings in London. For years, Rabin earned his living as a railroad laborer but devoted his spare time to painting. His "underground" paintings appealed to foreign residents in Moscow who recognized his talent and bought his pictures. This support enabled him to devote all his time to painting. Because of his unorthodox style, he was denied membership in the Artists Union, thus being barred from officially permitted showings of his works in the Soviet Union. After committing the crime of allowing the exhibit of some of his paintings in London, Rabin was attacked by Soviet spokesmen as a painter of "paranoiac visions," as a "miserable wretch who has gone astray in his ideas and in his art." The official cultural journal in the Soviet Union, *Soviet Culture,* urged Rabin and other "underground artists" to discontinue any connection with Western art dealers: "Do you think that these profiteers value you as artists? They spit on you. You are useful to them only as political commodities to help bourgeois propaganda. This is your only value to the West." By contrast with the official Soviet damnation of Rabin as a "paranoiac" and "miserable wretch," Western students of Russian life and civilization find Rabin in the great artistic tradition of his country: "He evokes the same profound melancholy and human nostalgia that we find in the great Russian writers." (Jacques Catteau, "Oskar Rabin, Painter," *Survey,* October 1965, p. 84, with reproductions of some of Rabin's paintings.)

Why this persistent Soviet hostility to modern trends in art, music, and literature?

Fifty years ago, abstract music and painting and expressionism in literature started out as small movements; while the following has grown, it is still a minority everywhere. Simple folk tunes in music, smiling factory workers and collective farmers in paintings—these types of art are not only more suitable for communist propaganda, but they also express the level of taste of a Stalin, Khrushchev, or Brezhnev. It does not matter too much whether a British Prime Minister or an American President likes modern art or not, but it matters a great deal how the First Secretary of the Soviet Communist Party feels about it.

Second, there is the element of individual revolt in modern art and music, including jazz. Modern art is a rebellion against centuries-old conventions and forms and is therefore suspect. Moreover, modern art expresses free-flowing individuality and imagination, thus lessening the importance of the group, the people. The Soviet leadership thus looks with suspicion at this individualistic streak in modern art and literature, just as Dostoevsky was long consigned to relative obscurity, for he stresses individual tragedy, guilt, and responsibility rather than class war as the ultimate source of the human condition.

Finally, there is in modern art a deliberate split between the minority of the artistic vanguard and the mass of the people. While this is true everywhere, it is more serious in communist countries that uphold the official dogma of the identity of party leaders and the people. According to this dogma, there is always perfect identity of outlook and feeling between the intellectual leadership and the masses of the people. Modern art, on the other hand, provides an illustration of an intellectual and artistic minority being ahead—or at least separate from—the people. This separation of artistic minority and people runs counter to the Soviet-communist dogma of identity between the "toilers of the mind" and the mass of peasants and workers. This disparity could be resolved either by foisting modern art on the people or by silencing the artists. The second solution is politically much easier, and it also has the advantage of reflecting the esthetic reactions of the Soviet political rulers.

In literature, the communists have no use for the classical theme "boy meets girl." Instead, officially approved communist art (called "socialist realism") revolves around a new theme: "Boy and girl meet machine, production rises, and all three live happily ever after." Under the Brezhnev regime, Khrushchev has often been attacked for talking too much about material affluence under communism and thereby neglecting the ideal of the "new man" communism is trying to create. Soviet writers have therefore been admonished to avoid a "confined outlook on life" and a "concern with petty events" and to foster, instead, "revolutionary-creative energy." At the Twenty-Third Communist Party Congress in 1966, numerous statements by Brezhnev and other party leaders clearly indicated that writers would be henceforth expected to toe the party line more rigidly than under Khrushchev. While this heavy hand of bureaucracy in literature does not necessarily suggest a complete return to the Stalinist approach to recalcitrant writers, the general tendency has been to go backward rather than forward.

Much will depend on how the "angry young men" among contemporary Soviet writers will react to this conservative trend under Brezhnev.

One of the most hopeful aspects about communist indoctrination and thought-control is that they have proved much less effective than they were believed to be. The remarkable thing about the Hungarian Revolution of 1956 was the predominant role of young people in the fight for freedom. Most of the fighters were in their teens or early twenties; all were products of communist monopoly in education and mass communication.

In Russia too, fifty years of communist indoctrination have not proved as successful as the Soviet leaders and the outside world thought. After Khrushchev's anti-Stalin speech before the Twentieth Congress of the Communist Party of the Soviet Union on February 25, 1956, there was a breath of fresh air, for a time at least, and young people began to show strange feelings and interests. University students pinned foreign broadcast texts to bulletin boards, raised unorthodox questions in party-sponsored meetings, and otherwise made a nuisance of themselves. Yet in spite of frequent harassments by police and university authorities, spontaneous student groups have spread from Moscow and Leningrad to many other Soviet universities. In these groups, an American visitor to the Soviet academic scene reports: "There is 'free' philosophy, not 'official' philosophy. They discuss books by Russell, Sartre, Camus: they listen to discussions on existentialism and totalitarianism, in which 'totalitarian society' is used to denote ambiguously the Soviet order." (Lewis S. Feuer, *The New York Times Magazine*, August 18, 1963, p. 80.)

In recent years, some especially rebellious—and courageous—students and young poets have even put out underground magazines, mostly devoted to poetry and social criticism. Written in mimeographed form and circulating in a few dozen or a few hundred copies, these illegal literary magazines are published, often only in a few issues, until the secret police discovers the identity of the editors and throws them into jail. The same treatment may also be given to students who do not commit the more serious crime of illegal publication but merely talk too much in front of fellow "students" who in reality work for the police. While such rebellious students still are no more than a very small minority among Soviet students, their influence may grow if there is no return to the harsh methods of Stalinist repression. Whenever totalitarian rulers grant "a little freedom" to their subjects, they inevitably discover that it cannot remain static and either grows or has to be repressed.

Despite Soviet anti-foreign, and particularly anti-American, hate propaganda over five decades, Soviet youth shows an insatiable hunger for foreign styles, fashions, and music, particularly if they are American. Jazz, forbidden for many years as the music of decadent American capitalism and characterized as "wild orgies of cavemen," became the rage of Soviet youth as soon as the ban was slightly lifted in 1956. Louis Armstrong, Stan Kenton, Duke Ellington, and Erroll Garner are among the jazz idols of the Soviet hit parade. The pathetic craving of Soviet youngsters for Western "culture" is most dramatically evidenced by their enthusiasm for Elvis Presley, the secret weapon of the United States in the struggle with austere communism.

In 1962, the Soviet authorities—following again the theory of "a little freedom"—opened two "youth cafés" in which young people could listen to jazz over coffee or soft drinks. Yet two establishments for a city of six million quickly proved insufficient, and within a year jazz could be heard in many places in Moscow and in some other major cities. Seeing that jazz was too powerful to be stopped, the government decided to exercise some control over it by accepting and working with it. In the spring of 1965, the Soviet Composers Union, which controls and runs Soviet music, and the Young Communist League (*Komsomol*), which controls Soviet youth in the age group of 14-26, held auditions of jazz groups in order to determine which groups would be allowed to play and what type of jazz could be played. A few months later, the award-winning combos gave the first officially sponsored jazz concert at the 1965 Moscow Jazz Festival.

Although finally tolerated, jazz must still tread softly and not "go wild" by official party standards of musical taste. At the annual congress of the Young Communist League in 1966, for example, attacks were made again on "pathological dances" and "hysterical music," thus warning Soviet youth not to go too far in its addiction to foreign, particularly American, dances and melodies. For a time, the twist was attacked as evidence of decadent capitalism, but attempts to substitute authentic Soviet dances bearing such names as "Slag Heap" and "Enthusiasts' Dance" failed to stir the deeper emotions of Soviet youth. Eastern Europe is an important source of supplementing tame Soviet jazz. Visiting Polish and Yugoslav bands cater to those who look for "progressive" jazz and even bolder new horizons in modern music still frowned on by official Soviet tastemakers.

The craving of Soviet youth for foreign ways of feeling and acting is partly due to their pent-up curiosity after having been cut off from the ouside world for so long. Partly, and perhaps more importantly, it is due to something deeper—a sense of dullness and frustration produced by Soviet conditions of living. Over and over, Soviet youth express their feeling to foreign visitors in these words: "It is so boring here. Life is so dull." On a trip through the Soviet Union from the Baltic to the Pacific Far East, an American correspondent asked a young Soviet professor what kind of man the Soviet system was trying to create. The young professor replied: "Yes—I can tell you. They want all mankind to be bored bores." (*U.S. News & World Report*, January 20, 1964.)

If the lack of freedom will not eventually make Soviet youth rebellious, the dullness and austerity of Soviet life perhaps will.

One form of such rebellion is the attempt to leave the Soviet Union without permission. It is extremely difficult for Soviet citizens to go abroad even for a short visit. Whereas only a few hundred Soviet citizens are permitted each year to visit the United States as tourists, generally traveling in groups and accompanied by representatives of the secret police, around 10,000 to 15,000 American tourists annually visit the Soviet Union. When it comes to permanent emigration, Soviet citizens generally do not even bother to apply, as the desire to emigrate is considered evidence of hostility to the government. Thus, some more adventurous souls try to leave the country illegally. According to the Soviet criminal code, high treason—punishable by death—includes "fleeing abroad or refusing to return from abroad." Under Stalin, the death penalty was often used, but under both Khrushchev and Brezhnev the penalty has generally been reduced to imprisonment for 5-10 years. What worries Soviet authorities is that many of these would-be escapers from the Soviet Union are young people from good families whose parents are party members. Another form of rebellion is in the economic field, such as black marketeering, theft of state property, and other serious economic offenses. In 1961, the death penalty was introduced for such crimes, and during the following three and one-half years about 300-400 persons were executed for these offenses. (*Survey*, October 1965, p. 70.)

The *main weakness of communism*, however, is the *discrepancy between ideal and reality*. Its leaders proclaim lofty ideals for the renewal of mankind and yet use inhuman means, age-old instruments of oppressive despotism. One of the deepest insights of the liberal way of life is that *means and ends cannot be too sharply separated* from each other and that the nature of the means employed in realizing an end will determine the character of the end itself. Communism acts in total disregard of this axiom and purports to build a new fellowship of love and fraternity with the knout and the slave labor camp or "correctional camp," as the milder form of forced labor is now called.

One of the most powerful original messages of communism was its protest against social inequality and privilege based on class and caste. Yet in communist Russia a class system is being created that exceeds by far the class system Marx sought to supersede. In addition, communism has created the caste of political commissars, men who do not feel themselves accountable to man or God, men for whom the control of the Communist party apparatus, the army, and police is the final source of power.

Finally, the gap between promise and performance can be clearly seen with regard to the *freedom of nations.* The communist promise is international brotherhood and equality of all nations. In the Soviet Union itself, a fervent cult of the Great Russians has been built up in recent years; outside of the Soviet Union, the Russians have carried on a foreign policy that is openly and cynically imperialistic.

Revolts against Soviet communism

In 1948, Yugoslavia was more communized than any of the Soviet satellites in Eastern Europe. Tito's crime in 1948 was not abandoning communism in favor of capitalism, but the much worse offense of trying to regain national independence for the peoples of Yugoslavia from Moscow. The Soviet Union mobilized all its resources of propaganda and subversion to overthrow Tito and his brand of national communism. At the time, few people thought Tito could defy Moscow successfully. Yet the unlikely happened, and Yugoslavia is still independent. Since 1955, the Soviet Union has come to realize that an independent Yugoslavia is here to stay and has been compelled by the force of circumstances to come to a *modus vivendi* with the Tito regime. Yet Titoism is, by communist admission, a disease rampant throughout the communist world. No communist state or party is free from it. Titoism, or "national communism," reflects a people's natural desire to be free from foreign domination, an issue over which many empires have come to grief in the past.

Political and economic controls were relaxed in Yugoslavia following the break with Moscow. The peasants were given the choice of returning to individual farming, and the overwhelming majority chose without much hesitation to abandon the collectives. As a result, the production of food greatly increased, and Yugoslavia's economic development pushed forward at a rapid pace. Also, American military and economic aid—amounting to nearly $3 billion in the years 1945–1966—greatly helped Yugoslavia to maintain its independence and improve its economy.

Foreign books and newspapers are obtainable in Yugoslavia, although in limited quantities only, and there is a considerable exchange of students and teachers with Western Europe and the United States. Foreign movies are shown, and Western plays are performed on the Yugoslav stage. Restrictions on travel abroad or even emigration to a foreign country have been much relaxed—more so than in any other communist state. In 1965, about 700,000 Yugoslavs traveled abroad, and in 1966 about 250,000 were in temporary employment abroad, mostly in West Germany, France, and Switzerland. The prime ambition of many of these temporary workers abroad is to save enough so that they can return to Yugoslavia with a car of their own.

Yet the communist leadership in Yugoslavia reminds the people from time to time that there are limits to freedom in a communist state. The fate of Milovan Djilas is a case in point. Djilas was a lifelong friend and one of Tito's closest aides both during and after World War II. But in the early 1950's, Djilas began to express democratic ideas. He urged a free press and free public discussion, and he even dared to suggest that Yugoslavia be permitted to have more than one party. This was too much for the communist rulers. Djilas was tried in 1955 and sentenced to three years in prison. In 1957, a book by Djilas entitled *The New Class* was smuggled out of Yugoslavia and published in New York. In his book, Djilas exposed communism as nothing more than an instrument of the communist ruling class (the "new class") for the exploitation and domination of the Yugoslav people. A new trial followed in which he received another seven years of imprisonment. Released from prison in 1961 for reasons of health, Djilas went to work on another book, *Conversations with Stalin,* describing the talks he had had with Stalin in 1944–1948. The book was published in 1962 in New

York; Djilas was tried again, and this time he received nine years of prison. A communist from early boyhood, Djilas spent three years in prison under the anticommunist regime of Yugoslavia before World War II. Under communism, he has found out how much more efficient communist repression is than that of the preceding system he helped to destroy.

The silencing of Djilas did not permanently extirpate what he stood for. A young assistant professor of philosophy, Mihajlo Mihajlov, published in 1965 *Moscow Summer*, a highly critical report on his impressions during a trip to the Soviet Union. Mihajlov was arrested, tried, and sentenced to nine months of imprisonment; he was released from prison a few months later. In 1966, Mihajlov announced—both in Yugoslavia and in foreign papers—that he planned to publish "an independent democratic magazine." He was arrested again, tried, and sentenced to one year of imprisonment for having "disseminated false information about Yugoslavia." Like Djilas, Mihajlov is a socialist, but an uncompromising democrat, opposed to all forms of totalitarianism. Also, he expressed deep religious sympathies, which are not popular in official communist circles. Whereas in capitalist democracies young assistant professors are often confronted with the academic imperative "Publish or Perish," in communist regimes they have to face the political imperative "Don't Publish or Perish."

After Tito's rebellious break with Moscow in 1948, the next major explosion took place on June 16 and 17, 1953, in East Germany. Food conditions had steadily deteriorated under Soviet exploitation and East German communist mismanagement, and there was less food than during World War II. Even bread and potatoes, the staple diet of communist economic planning, were scarce.

The spark which fired the smouldering resentment of the people was a government announcement on May 28, 1953, that workers' wages would be cut further unless they produced at least 10 per cent more than in the past. On June 16, building workers on Stalin Avenue in East Berlin started a spontaneous strike and marched toward government headquarters. The strike spread quickly throughout East Germany on that day and the next, and in many communities the workers were in command of the situation, occupying police offices, liberating political prisoners, and setting government and Communist party buildings on fire. Many members of the police either took a wait-and-see attitude or even went over to the rebels. Before long, the rebels demanded, in addition to more tolerable living conditions, free elections, free labor unions, and the end of Soviet domination.

Hesitating at first to intervene directly, the Soviet forces quickly realized that the communist regime would soon be overthrown completely, and thousands of Soviet tanks moved into the major strongholds of rebellion, suppressing it in a few days. Several hundred Germans died in the uprising, hundreds were wounded, and about 50,000 were imprisoned.

The East Germans continued to show their distaste for communist rule in the one way still left open: mass flights into West Germany through the escape hatch of free West Berlin. In the years 1950–1961, about four million East Germans fled to West Germany, or nearly one-fifth of the entire population of East Germany. What made this mass exodus particularly painful to the communist government was the fact that the refugees included disproportionately large numbers of young people, skilled workers, and professional people. The Soviet government realized that, should the masss flight of East Germans into West Germany continue for another decade or two, East Germany would soon become a country without people, and all that might be left would be the Soviet occupying army and its loyal puppet government of Walter Ulbricht. As a result, the East German government sealed off the borders between East and West Berlin on August 13, 1961, by hastily erecting a barbed-wire and concrete barrier. More perhaps than any other action of communist policy, the Berlin Wall has come to express, before the whole world, the nature of communism as a vast prison.

Exactly three years after the uprising in East Germany the Poles revolted. On June 28, 1956, thousands of workers of the Stalin Steel Works in Poznan went on strike early in the morning and moved toward the center of the city, chanting "bread, bread, bread," singing Polish national songs, carrying the old Polish national flags, and refusing to disperse despite the tank formations quickly brought into the city by the communist authorities. Before long, the striking workers occupied the Communist party headquarters and the radio station and set the city prison on fire after freeing the prisoners. In the ensuing battle with army and police, a battle that lasted for several days, about 200 Poles lost their lives, thousands were wounded, and many more thousands arrested.

Militarily, the rebellion was successfully repressed, but politically it unleashed a chain of events which is still in the making. In October, 1956, Wladyslaw Gomulka was elected First Secretary of the Polish Communist Party. This announcement came as a bombshell, because Gomulka was known as the leader of Titoism or "national communism" in Poland and had spent several years in prison for that crime.

For a while, the Russians considered full-scale occupation of the country and the re-establishment of Stalinism by force. But the Poles stood their ground, and Poland had won, for the time being, its struggle for some degree of national independence, although its government continued to be communist dominated.

One of the most popular moves of the new government under Gomulka was to permit the peasants to dissolve collective farms and go back to private farming. As a result, food production rose, leading to improved living conditions of the urban population as well. In industry too, the harsh controls over workers were relaxed, and industrial production moved steadily forward from its previous low. Private enterprise in business and trade has been permitted on a moderate scale, such as in the case of bakers, tailors, plumbers, repairmen, and skilled craftsmen in the building and tourist trades. In addition to these internal measures aiming at the improvement of its economy, Poland has also benefited from American economic aid, amounting to close to $1 billion in the years 1945–1966.

In 1957, the Polish government released Cardinal Wyszynski, the symbol of Catholic resistance to communism, from prison and permitted religious instruction in public schools. Poland became the only country behind the Iron Curtain to have a Catholic university (in Lublin) as well as a network of Catholic schools from kindergarten to secondary school. This new attitude of greater tolerance was also extended to literature and the arts. Modern tendencies in painting and music are eagerly discussed and practiced, and American jazz is played as enthusiastically as anywhere in Europe. Also, Western books and newspapers are obtainable in Poland. Arriving in Warsaw from Moscow, one is amazed to see large quantities of French, English, and German books in display windows of Polish bookstores—a sight one cannot even dream of as yet in the Soviet Union. Numerous Polish teachers, writers, and students have visited Western countries, including the United States, and American scholars and students have visited Poland. They all find deep eagerness among the Polish people to maintain close contacts with the Western world. The Poles have always considered themselves the last outpost of Western civilization on the European Continent, the cultural boundary between Europe and

Asia, and they are still looking desperately to the West for encouragement and inspiration.

In foreign policy, the Polish government since 1956 has treaded softly, because "Poland's neighbors are not Australian shepherds," as Poles are being reminded by their leaders. Poland is a member of the Warsaw Pact, the Moscow-sponsored military counterpart to NATO, including Russia, Bulgaria, Czechoslovakia, East Germany, Hungary, and Rumania. Even many noncommunist and anticommunist Poles realize that their government can no more openly and directly offend Russia than can Finland, which also, though democratic and independent, must refrain from any foreign policy that could be construed as anti-Soviet by the Kremlin.

For the time being, totalitarianism of the Stalinist type is dead in Poland, but as yet it is uncertain how much liberty the individual citizen will be permitted under the Gomulka regime or a regime led by any other "national communist." For a few years after the changes in 1956, freedom of religion, speech, and the press was relatively high. From 1960 on, the government has gradually nibbled away at these liberties, without daring to abolish them in a single stroke. Censorship of newspapers has been tightened, and some of the more liberal magazines have been banned. The communist government and party leaders have made it plain that they will not allow any liberalization which will endanger their own positions of power and the existence of the communist dictatorship.

This hardening of government policy has also been clearly seen in the growing harassment of the Catholic church. In 1961, the government prohibited religious instruction in public schools. Injecting a note of offensive insult to the fervently Catholic Polish population, Gomulka appointed as Minister of Education a man who had previously served as the head of the Polish Association of Atheists. Since 1960, the government closed and confiscated some Catholic schools and harassed others through discriminatory and harsh tax measures. Increasingly, the authorities have openly attacked church leaders on the ground that they teach loyalty to their church rather than to the government. In his Palm Sunday sermon of April 11, 1965, Cardinal Wyszynski answered the communist government as follows: "It is monstrous that we Catholics must reject God because there is a group of people, with power and public funds, wishing it. Where is reason? Where is democracy? In the name of law must we reject God? Is it a monstrosity to demand this from the nation. We must not keep silent."

The events in Poland in 1956 immediately raised hope and passion in Hungary. On October 23, 1956, university students, quickly joined by thousands of industrial workers, held a mass meeting in Parliament Square. Expressing their sympathy for the Polish fight for freedom and independence, they put forward a series of demands, including among others: the evacuation of Russian troops from Hungary; free elections; free labor unions and the right to strike; revision of workers' wages and a complete reorganization of the economy; the immediate release of political prisoners and the return of Hungarians deported to the Soviet Union; removal of the statue of Stalin; and, finally, reorganization of the compulsory system of farm collectives.

The political police turned a peaceful meeting into bloody rebellion by firing on the students and workers. The fighting quickly spread throughout the whole country. The workers declared a general strike, and the freedom fighters were soon joined by the regular Hungarian army and police. On the communist side, the Hungarian political police were joined by powerful Russian tank forces. Yet the incredible happened. The freedom fighters won their struggle, and on October 29, 1956 Hungary was free. Political authority was exercised by the representatives of popular organizations, and almost at once dozens of democratic newspapers began to be published. Communists were nowhere to be seen, and statues of Stalin were publicly burned. Also, political prisoners were set free. The best known among them was Cardinal Mindszenty, who had been imprisoned since 1948.

However, this period of Hungarian freedom and independence lasted for only five days. On November 3 close to 200,000 Soviet troops and 5,000 tanks moved into Hungary to suppress Hungarian freedom. After a week of heavy fighting, the revolution was put down. Prime Minister Nagy was kidnapped by the Russians and later executed. Over 35,000 Hungarians were killed in the fighting, and many more wounded. Many thousands were deported to Siberia, and over 200,000 managed to escape to Austria. The physical destruction of the towns was worse than that suffered by Hungary in World War II, when she was a major battleground for many months.

Despite their military defeat by Soviet tanks, the Hungarians learned several lessons. First, the spectacle of rebelling workers trampling and burning the red flag as the symbol of oppression destroyed the myth, once and for all, that Soviet communism represents the cause of the workers. Throughout the whole Hungarian

Revolution, the Hungarian Workers' Council, and local workers' councils across the nation, were the center of anti-Soviet and anti-communist activity.

Second, the Hungarian Revolution proved that the communist regimes in Eastern Europe, installed by Soviet armed force in the first place, in the last resort still depend on that force for their survival. Without the massive deployment of Soviet troops and tanks, the Hungarian Revolution would have decisively triumphed, as there was very little resistance on the part of the few native communists. In 1966, approximately 75,000 Soviet troops were still stationed in Hungary.

Third, the Hungarian Revolution revealed the inefficacy of communist indoctrination. The revolution was touched off by university students—the products of communist education and indoctrination.

Pavlov, the great Russian physiologist of the nineteenth century, discovered in his experiments with dogs the phenomenon of conditioned reflexes through continued repetition of the same stimuli. The communists have tried to apply Pavlovian techniques to humans, in order to transform man into a conditioned reflex machine, behaving automatically and unthinkingly in accordance with a predetermined pattern inculcated in him by his masters.

The evidence of the Hungarian Revolution, particularly as supplied by the resistance of youngsters in their teens and early twenties, suggests that—despite Pavlov and communist indoctrination—there is still a difference between man and dog.

Finally, the Hungarian Revolution gave the death-blow to the theory, obsessively clung to by the free world, that revolution in a totalitarian police state is impossible. According to this theory, revolution was possible in the eighteenth or nineteenth century because the government did not then possess the powerful weapons of suppression available to it in this century. The Hungarian Revolution has proved that the mind of man is still king, as it has always been, and that totalitarian governments of the twentieth century cannot rely exclusively on terror any more than could despotism in the past.

During the first years after the crushing of the Hungarian Revolution, many people inside and outside Hungary thought that the heroic effort of the nation had been in vain. Communist dictatorship was harsher than before the Revolution, and for a while it seemed more Stalinist than the Soviet Union itself. In the end this reasoning—an implied defense of inert submission to communist totalitarianism—proved wrong. The very fact of the Revolution encouraged tendencies toward more national independence in other communist states. From 1960 on, Albania has been able to defy the Soviet Union by siding with Red China in its conflict with Russia. Rumania, always held up as a perfect example of a docile satellite, has increasingly asserted her independence since the early 1960's.

Under the Soviet plan for Eastern Europe, Rumania was to concentrate on producing foodstuffs and raw materials rather than on building an industry of her own. She openly defied Russia and has been pushing rapid industrialization, regardless of whether it fits Soviet plans or not. In the process of building up her industry, Rumania has also sharply increased her trade with Western countries, while her trade with the Soviet Union has fallen drastically. In the years 1955–1964, the share of noncommunist countries in Rumania's foreign trade rose from 20 per cent to 33 per cent, whereas the share of the Soviet Union dropped from 69 per cent to 41 per cent in the same period. In the cultural field, Rumania abolished in 1963 the compulsory teaching of Russian in grade and high schools and closed the official Soviet Russian Language Institute and Russian bookstore in Bucharest. A French cultural office was opened in Bucharest, and Rumanians were again able to read at least some Western authors previously forbidden.

In the field of foreign policy, Rumania has condemned Red China with less ardor and enthusiasm than any of the communist states of Eastern Europe, and the Rumanian communists have appealed to both Russia and Red China to end their quarrel, thus trying to maintain Rumanian independence and increased influence in the Sino-Soviet rift. In 1966, Rumania even dared to propose the ending of all military blocs, both East and West. While this proposal had little practical effect, it ran counter to the official Soviet concept that the foreign policy of the communist Warsaw Pact states is completely peaceful, whereas NATO is nothing but an expression of American imperialism. Though Rumania soon declared she had no intention of leaving the Warsaw Pact, she had managed to convey an impression of independence vis-à-vis the Soviet Union.

In Hungary herself, the harsh government installed by the Soviet army after the repression of the Revolution in 1956 gradually realized that Soviet tanks were not enough if the country was to regain some measure of political stability. By 1963, this movement of relaxing the most oppressive controls gathered considerable momentum; thousands of political prisoners were released under a general amnesty, and the government eased its stringent controls in industry and farming. Writers and artists were given greater freedom of expression, and noncommunists were appointed to important positions. Whereas the previous slogan had been "He who is not for us is against us," the new official slogan became "He who is not against us is with us." In 1965, Janos Kadar, the head of the Hungarian Communist party, publicly expressed his concern about the continuing lack of popular acceptance of communism, in spite of the more lenient methods used in the preceding few years. In urging intensified party efforts, he asked: "What would be the good of having a few hundred thousand very radical communists if the rest of the people turned against the ideas of communism?" (*The Economist*, August 28, 1965.) Relaxation of travel restrictions was another measure in the policy of appeasing the people. In 1965, about 100,000 Hungarians were permitted to travel to Western countries. Such permits were generally given to people whose failure to return would not be an economic loss to the nation or to those who left behind hostages (such as wives and children) in order to ensure their return. All in all, in her internal policy Hungary has come close to Poland and Yugoslavia, but in her foreign policy she continues to follow, as Poland does, the line laid down by the Kremlin.

The reverberations of the Hungarian Revolution were not confined to Europe, however. In 1959, the Tibetan people revolted against Red China, which had conquered Tibet by armed force in 1950. Red China had to fight heavy battles for several weeks before the rebellion was put down. Thousands were killed, and over 40,000 Tibetans, including the Dalai Lama, their "god-king," fled into neighboring countries, mostly into India.

The Hungarian Revolution provided a conclusive answer to the variety of Soviet reactions to deviations of satellites from the Moscow line. Why did the Soviet Union tolerate the changes in Yugoslavia and Poland toward "national communism" of a more liberal variety, while it suppressed by military force the uprisings in East Germany, Poznan, and Hungary?

The answer to these questions may be found in this consideration: in both Yugoslavia and Poland, the changes were brought about *from the top*. They were palace revolutions within the top leadership of the Yugoslav and Polish Communist Parties, whereas the movements in East Germany, Poznan, and Hungary stemmed *from below*. The Soviet people themselves are used to palace revolutions within the communist leadership; by allowing Titoism and Gomulkaism, the Soviet leaders demonstrate to the Soviet people that changes in a communist state can come only from the top. Had the Soviet Union given in to the popular pressure and uprisings in East Germany, Poznan, and Hungary, such examples might have set a dangerous and provocative precedent for possible changes in the Soviet Union itself. By tolerating Tito and Gomulka and saving them from true popular democracy, the Soviet leaders think of their own necks.

The Sino-Soviet conflict

The most explosive conflict within world communism is as yet to come: Red China against the Soviet Union. Basically, it is a struggle over power, but like every power struggle it has other elements as well.

First, there is the issue of nationalism, or Chinese against Russians. For over three hundred years, Russia has expanded her empire in Asia, frequently at the expense of China. Russia has, therefore, traditionally feared the prospect of a strong and united China ruled by an effective central government, the kind of government that communist totalitarianism has established in Red China since 1949. From the traditional Chinese viewpoint, the Russians are meddlesome troublemakers, imperialist expansionists, and—by the standards of the ancient Chinese civilization—a horde of crude barbarians. In the eyes of the Chinese, Russians are not (as they appear to some Westerners) semi-Asiatic or semi-Oriental, but full-fledged Europeans and, as such, barbarians by definition.

Even under Stalin, Titoism showed that the force of nationalism was stronger than the myth of "international proletarian solidarity and fraternity." If the nationalism of little Yugoslavia could prevail against Stalin, the nationalism of a great power like China, the Chinese feel, is even more destined to prevail against a mere Khrushchev or Brezhnev. Marx or no Marx, over 800 million Chinese will not forever accept the idea that the 230 million motley peoples of the Soviet Union are the leaders of the communist world. The Chinese are quite familiar with the Confucian saying, "When two men ride on a horse, only one can sit in front." The Chinese are determined that they, not the Russians, will sit in front.

Closely connected with the traditional force of nationalism is the issue of population and resources. Over 800 million Chinese inhabit a densely populated area, with an annual increase of population running to about 12 million people. By contrast, the 230 million inhabitants of the Soviet Union live in a much vaster territory, and the annual increase of population is only about 3 million. On the Russian side of the common border, the land is empty and

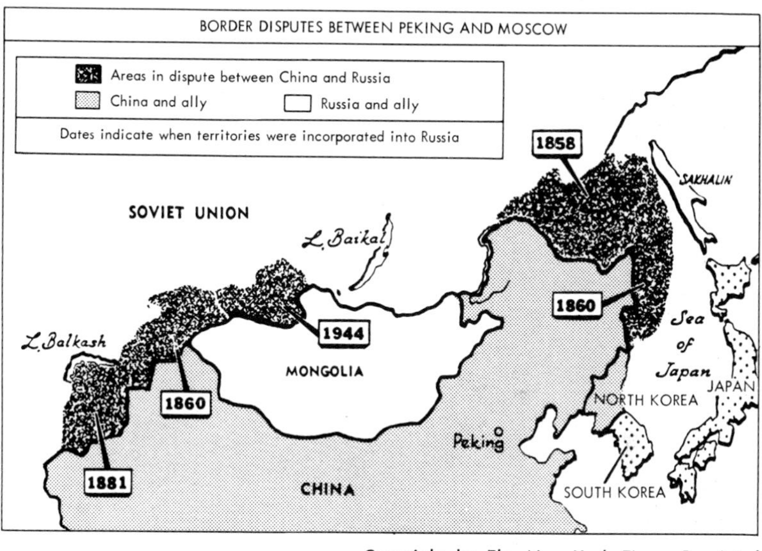

Copyright by *The New York Times.* Reprinted by permission.

the population very sparse. On the Chinese side, the land is overcrowded. This growing gap between the Soviet ratio of people and resources on the one hand and the Chinese ratio on the other may someday lead to Chinese expansion at the expense of Soviet territory.

In particular, the Chinese have publicly proclaimed in recent years that they do not recognize the imperialist treaties and conquests at the expense of China in the past. This is of particular concern to Russia, since she took more territory from China than any other imperialist power. The major areas in dispute include vast Far Eastern stretches of land, from the mouth of the Amur River down the Pacific coast of Siberia and reaching west as far as Lake Baikal. Today, this area of untold natural riches is inhabited by 9 million Soviet citizens. The Chinese feel that, with more intensive cultivation of the soil, at least 100 million Chinese could live there—albeit on a lower Chinese standard of living. Next,

Red China has also shown desires for the "liberation" of formerly Chinese territories in Soviet Central Asia, covering an area of about 0.5 million square miles and 10 million people. This is rich land with a great potential in food and fibers. Finally, there is Outer Mongolia, with over half a million square miles and only one million population. A Chinese province from 1686 to 1911, it became a Russian protectorate in 1912–1919 and again a Chinese province in 1919–1921. In 1921, Outer Mongolia became an independent state in form, but in fact it was closely linked with Moscow. Red China has tried to gain a foothold in Outer Mongolia, playing on racial affinity and historical ties, but Russian influence has so far remained uppermost. One of the main reasons for Russia's success is the fact that she has been giving considerable economic aid to Outer Mongolia—about $200 million and more annually, one of the highest per capita aid expenditures of any country anywhere. In 1966, the Soviet Union and Outer Mongolia concluded a military security treaty, giving the Soviet Union the right to station troops in her ally's territory, thus bringing Soviet armed forces right up to the Chinese border.

While the Soviet leaders have repudiated many of the internal policies of the tsars, they are not willing to give up the fruits of tsarist conquest, be it in favor of the Chinese or of anybody else. So far, the Red Chinese have publicly stated that they do not wish to settle the issue of these disputed areas by force, but by peaceful negotiation at "the appropriate time," that is, when China is strong enough to bargain effectively with the Soviet Union. Chinese maps now indicate the area of the country before and after the foreign imperialist grabs of Chinese territory. By coincidence, Russia always appears in these maps as the foremost imperialist, helping herself to more Chinese territory than any other imperialist state of the past. Since such maps are published in the officially prescribed school books in Red China, a whole generation is growing up eager to regain the lost territories.

Far from dismissing these territorial ambitions of the Red Chinese as idle speculation, the Soviet government has taken them seriously. In 1963, the Soviet government began a drive to double the population of the disputed areas in the east within a decade and supplemented this campaign with detailed economic plans designed to attract, and provide for, a rapidly growing population. Even if this project of doubling the population of the Soviet Far East were to succeed, the Chinese population is multiplying so much faster than the Soviet that it is doubtful whether the Soviets can ever match the Chinese population pressure by transferring its own people in sufficiently large numbers to match the Chinese density of population in even an approximate manner. In the meantime, the Red Chinese have embarked on an intensified settlement program at two crucial frontiers with the Soviet Union: Northern Manchuria and Sinkiang. The Soviet authorities are aware of this Chinese pressure on their borders, and Soviet border guards in the Far East and Central Asia are on constant alert against "enemy violators." Border clashes have occurred on numerous occasions, and each side blames the other for the intense military activities on the border. Speaking on June 1, 1966, in the Soviet Far East near the Chinese border, Soviet President Podgorny said that the Soviet armed forces in the Far East "are valiantly guarding this vibrant region, created by the hands of our forefathers and covered with the sweat and blood of our people." Shortly afterward, the Red Chinese government charged the Soviet government with "making military deployment along the Chinese border in coordination with United States imperialist encirclement of China."

Soviet fears of a resurgent China have also been seen in the economic field. During the first years of the communist regime in China, from about 1950 to 1957, Soviet aid and advice were significant in the total economic planning of Red China. After 1957, tensions gradually developed, and the Soviets took measures against Red China where they could be most painful: in the economic sphere. In 1959, the first repatriations of Soviet advisers, experts, and other technicians took place; by the middle of 1960, these repatriations were about finished. Interestingly, Soviet aid to Red China—even in the early years of closest cooperation—never included the atomic field, a precautionary measure for which the Soviet leaders later could claim much credit in their country. However, the Soviet Union did not only cut off all technical aid after 1960. In some instances, the departing Soviet technicians even took with them the plans of the projects they were engaged on, as was the case in the huge Sammen Narrows Dam on the Yellow River.

Moreover, the Red Chinese have also suffered a considerable decline of trade with the Soviet Union and the Eastern European communist states. Russia and communist Eastern Europe exported to China 12 per cent of their total exports in 1958 but only 4 per cent in 1965; conversely, China exported to Russia and communist Eastern Europe 66 per cent of her total exports in 1958 but only 30 per cent in 1965. Since Chinese imports from Russia and Eastern

Europe included arms, machinery, and industrial raw materials, the sharp drop in trade has hit Red China very hard. Also, China will not soon forget that even during the three catastrophic years (1959–1961) of the Chinese economy the Soviets insisted on Chinese repayment of earlier loans in foods and consumer goods, in both of which China was desperately short. Paradoxically, while in theory Red China tries to appear more virulently anti-Western than the Russians, she has greatly increased her trade with noncommunist countries since 1958. Between 1958 and 1965, China's exports to Japan quadrupled, her trade with Western Europe almost doubled, and her trade with other noncommunist nations also doubled.

Diplomatically, too, the Soviet Union and Red China have different interests, for reasons of geography if for no other. For the Soviet Union, the problem of Germany and the more specific issue of Berlin are the key problems in Europe—in both of which Red China has shown very little interest. By contrast, Red China's number one issue in Asia is the conquest of Taiwan—a matter which is of little concern to Russia. In the struggle between India and Red China, the Soviet Union has not even pretended to be a neutral. From the beginning of the Chinese aggressions against India in 1959, the Soviet Union at first refused to side with the aggressor and later openly aided India with jet fighters, transport planes, helicopters, and other equipment. She also helped India to build her own factory producing Soviet-type jet fighters.

The case of India illustrates the two divergent approaches of Red China and Russia to the goal—shared by all communists everywhere—of spreading communism throughout the world, particularly the underdeveloped world. The Soviet approach has been that the first objective is to get a foothold in an underdeveloped country through economic aid, propaganda, and subversion, with the immediate objective of neutralizing and minimizing Western (particularly American) influence as rapidly as possible. If subsequent events develop along hoped-for lines, then the Soviet approach fully envisages Soviet support for local civil wars and minor international wars fought with conventional weapons.

By contrast, the Red Chinese approach to the problem of communizing the underdeveloped countries is different. In the first place, the Chinese argue that Soviet economic aid should go only to communist states (like China herself) or those well on the road to becoming communized but not to "capitalist regimes" like India or Egypt. As to the spreading of communism in underdeveloped

Reprinted from Bill Mauldin, *I've Decided I Want My Seat Back* (New York: Harper & Row, Publishers, 1965). Reprinted by permission.

"I'm an awakening giant myself. Who'll we have for breakfast?"

countries, the Chinese urge Soviet support for more direct—that is, armed—action. Chinese communist leaders often quote Mao's famous statement that "political power grows out of the barrel of a gun." In looking at the world at large, the Chinese communist leadership seeks to apply the lessons of its own conquest of power. In China, the communist revolutionaries established strongholds in the countryside and then proceeded to encircle and conquer the beleaguered cities. In present-day Chinese communist thinking, North America and Western Europe are "the cities of the world," and the "contemporary world revolution also presents a picture of the encirclement of cities by the rural areas." (*Peking Review*, September 3, 1965, p. 24.) This means that "the cities of the world" (North America and Western Europe) must be conquered by the "rural areas of the world," or Asia, Africa, and Latin America, in the same way in which the cities of China were conquered by the rural areas during the communist civil war in China. The Red

"Damned Communists!"

Chinese leaders frankly admit that Red China must be the "base area for the world revolution."

The Soviet Union hopes to communize the world through leadership in economics and science, propaganda, subversion, and minor wars short of all-out nuclear war. The Chinese position is that such a nuclear world war is not inevitable, because the West is unlikely to strike back with nuclear weapons if pushed harder than the Soviets are willing to do. However, the Red Chinese reason, should the risk of nuclear war materialize, such risk must be accepted, because nuclear war would see, not the end of mankind, but of capitalism, on the ruins of which communism would triumph everywhere. For the Chinese, a loss of 200 million people in a nuclear conflict would still leave enough Chinese to carry on. For the Soviet Union, a similar loss of 200 million people would mean the destruction of the whole country, and Soviet leaders are therefore less comfortable about the prospect of nuclear warfare.

Thus, Sino-Soviet differences are not primarily based on different interpretations of communist dogma. In a general way, the Soviet approach toward the communization of the world expresses the attitude of a country that has acquired much self-confidence and that feels that time is on its side. By contrast, Red China has accomplished relatively little, as measured by the standards of other great powers (like the United States or the Soviet Union), either in the field of economic development or scientific leadership. She is therefore in a hurry and willing to take greater risks in direct action. Moreover, in the case of India, for example, the national interests of China and Russia would be different and very likely opposed, even if Lenin had never laid down any guidelines for communizing the world. Both Russia and China have one major interest with respect to India: to see to it that India does not become subservient to China (as viewed by Russia) or to Russia (as viewed by China). By aiding India in her self-defense against Chinese imperialism, Russia today is doing no more than trying to preserve the balance of power in Asia, just as in Europe Britain has for centuries sided with the states that were threatened by an expansionist power on the European continent.

The competition between China and Russia is taking place on all continents, both within communist states as well as within communist parties in noncommunist states. In Europe, Albania, the poorest of the communist states, has come under the influence of Red China. In Asia, Africa, and Latin America Red China portrays herself as the true leader of the poor, have-not nations, whereas Russia is pictured as being too busy with keeping what she has, and not dedicated enough to world revolution. In Asia, Red China leads over the Soviet Union in North Vietnam, whereas Soviet influence is paramount in the communist regime of Outer Mongolia. Among the Asian communist movements, Soviet influence is dominant in Ceylon, Japan and India, although in all three cases there are strong pro-Peking factions.

Many Asian Communist parties deliberately adopt an attitude of nonalignment in the Sino-Soviet conflict in order to obtain greater freedom of action by playing one side against the other. Some of the Asian, African, and Latin American parties are truly neutral between Moscow and Peking; others are nonaligned but favoring to some degree one side or the other. In some cases, the local Communist parties have been rent by internal dissension over the Sino-Soviet issue to such an extent that factions and splinter groups have developed, threatening the unity of the movement as a whole.

From the beginning of 1963 on, the Chinese communists have persistently played on one major theme in their conflict with Russia, a theme that has particular relevance in the underdeveloped countries: color. A mockery of anything even remotely related to Marx or Lenin, the theme of race and color may well become the most powerful weapon in the hands of the Chinese against the Russians. Fully aware that the majority of the world's people are nonwhite and that in most underdeveloped countries the colored vastly outnumber the whites, Red China is trying to create the image of Russia as but another white imperialist power, seeking to impose its will on the poor, nonwhite masses in Asia, Africa, and Latin America. Thus, when the Soviet Union signed the partial nuclear test ban agreement with the United States and Great Britain in 1963, Red China refused to join, because she was eager to get ahead with her own atomic weapons program. Yet very soon she publicly attacked the agreement as another example of the Russians joining with the white imperialist "haves" against the "toiling masses" of the nonwhites throughout the world. In the last few years, a favorite propaganda theme of Red China against the Soviet government ("Soviet revisionist leading clique," in Chinese communist semantics) has been the charge that Russia "is pursuing a policy of Soviet-U.S. collaboration for world domination." (*Peking Review*, September 2, 1966.)

In spite of all the tensions and conflicts between Red China and the Soviet Union, the nations of the free world should not forget that the Sino-Soviet conflict is not over the issue of whether to bury the noncommunist nations, but *how* to bury them. Freedom will survive only if the policies of the free nations are flexible enough to cope with both the Chinese and Soviet methods of communist expansion.

The issue of communism

The communists assert that the issue which divides the world is the clash between individual, capitalist enterprise and public, collective ownership of the means of production and distribution in industry and agriculture.

This communist analysis of the world situation is concurred with, oddly enough, in capitalist countries by some extreme conservatives, men who claim to be the most uncompromising foes of communism. Such men constantly acknowledge the validity of the Communist party line by asserting that the preservation of free enterprise is the supreme goal of the free world and that the main threat of communism lies in its opposition to private enterprise.

Yet to accept this communist-conservative interpretation of the present world struggle is to fall into an erroneous analysis of the facts and an even more disastrous formulation of policy. The partial socialization of basic industries in Britain and in the Scandinavian countries has proved that varying forms of industrial ownership and organization do not in themselves constitute a source of conflict. The staunchest allies of the United States are Britain and Norway in Europe, Australia and New Zealand in the Pacific, and Israel in the Near East—nations with the strongest socialist movements in the world. The Anglo-American alliance after World War II, culminating in the North Atlantic Treaty Organization, is the closest association of the United States and Britain ever formed in time of peace, and on the British side it was initiated and carried through by the socialist Labor government.

Socialists in Britain, as in other countries, understand that their disagreement with certain aspects of American capitalism, or even with capitalism in general, is a minor issue compared with their disagreements with totalitarian communist imperialism.

What makes communism an issue of peace or war is not its opposition to capitalism, but its determination to impose its philosophy by force of arms. *The proper division of the world, therefore, is not between communism and capitalism, but between nations that seek to spread their system by infiltration, subversion, and civil war, and nations that honestly and sincerely wish to maintain peace.*

The internal economic system—be it capitalism, socialism, a mixed economy, or communism—is of no necessary relevance to the main issue of world peace and the right of nations to be free.

Similar to the error of confusing communism with anticapitalism is the equally common error of confusing it with *antidemocracy.* However understandable the emotional and intellectual revulsion of free men from communist totalitarianism, they must not lose sight of the fact that communist antidemocracy is no more the main issue than communist anticapitalism. Numerous antidemocratic regimes throughout the world are gladly accepted by the free nations as allies in the struggle against communism, just as they were welcomed earlier in the struggle against fascism. Many Latin American states are governed by antidemocratic (or, at least non-democratic) regimes. Turkey has had for over forty years various forms of dictatorship; if the main division of the world were between democracy and dicatorship, Turkey (as many another nation) would be a weak candidate for the democratic side, yet she is helping to resist imperialist aggression.

From a practical viewpoint, the identification of communism with antidemocracy and anticapitalism plays right into the hands of the communists, since both capitalism and democracy (as understood, for example, in the United States) are not typical, but rather exceptional, in the world at large. If Western policy were to limit admission to the alliance of the free nations to a select group of a few countries happily matching the economic and political institutions of Britain or the United States, the resulting group of states would be hopelessly inadequate in meeting the threat of communism.

From the viewpoint of international ethics and common sense, the main interest one country has in another is the latter's willingness to preserve the peace. Only when autocracy is accompanied by aggressive imperialistic designs does it become a danger to the world. And then what is dangerous in it is its aggressiveness, not its autocracy. The two should not be confused.

If the free nations draw the line sharply between themselves and the communist orbit, the issue can be presented in the age-old terms of human liberty versus serfdom and slavery. Thus expressed, the issue will be clear wherever men and women prize liberty, and communist propaganda will fail in its attempt to picture the world struggle as one between Wall Street and the peoples of the world. If the free world would thus commit itself to the fight for human liberty against communist aggression as the main issue of the present crisis, there is little doubt of the ultimate outcome of the struggle.

FOR FURTHER READING

Abramov, Fyodor, *The New Life: A Day on a Collective Farm.* New York: Grove Press, Inc. (Black Cat Books), 1963.

Barghoorn, Frederic C., *Soviet Foreign Propaganda.* Princeton: Princeton University Press, 1964.

Bergson, Abram, *The Economics of Soviet Planning.* New Haven: Yale University Press, 1964.

Berlin, Isaiah, *Karl Marx.* New York: Oxford University Press, Inc., 1948.

Campbell, Robert W., *Soviet Economic Power,* 2nd ed. Boston: Houghton Mifflin Company, 1966.

Cantril, Hadley, *The Politics of Despair.* New York: Collier Books, 1961.

Chinh, Truong, *Primer for Revolt: The Communist Takeover in Vietnam.* New York: Frederick A. Praeger, Inc., 1963.

Cohen, Arthur A., *The Communism of Mao Tse-tung.* Chicago: University of Chicago Press, 1965.

Djilas, Milovan, *The New Class.* New York: Frederick A. Praeger Inc. (Praeger Paperbacks), 1959.

Draper, Theodore, *Castroism: Theory and Practice.* New York: Frederick A. Praeger, Inc., 1965.

Ebenstein, William, *Great Political Thinkers,* 3rd ed., chap. 23. New York: Holt, Rinehart & Winston, Inc., 1960.

———, *Modern Political Thought,* 2nd ed., chap. 9. New York: Holt, Rinehart & Winston, Inc., 1960.

———, *Political Thought in Perspective,* chaps. 24, 25. New York: McGraw-Hill Book Company (McGraw-Hill Paperbacks), 1963.

Eckstein, Alexander, *China's Economic Growth and Foreign Trade: Implications for U.S. Policy.* New York: McGraw-Hill Book Company, 1966.

Fischer, Louis, *The Life of Lenin.* New York: Harper & Row, Publishers (Harper Colophon Books), 1966.

Granick, David, *The Red Executive.* Garden City, N.Y.: Doubleday & Company, Inc. (Anchor Books), 1961.

Halperin, Morton H., *China and the Bomb.* New York: Frederick A. Praeger, Inc., 1965.

Hodgkinson, Harry, *Double Talk: The Language of Communism.* London: George Allen & Unwin, 1955.

Hook, Sidney (ed.), *World Communism: Key Documentary Material.* Princeton: D. Van Nostrand Co., Inc. (Anvil Books), 1962.

Horelick, Arnold L. and Myron Rush, *Strategic Power and Soviet Foreign Policy.* Chicago: University of Chicago Press, 1966.

Horowitz, Irving Louis, *Three Worlds of Development: The Theory and Practice of International Stratification.* New York: Oxford University Press, Inc., 1966.

Inkeles, Alex and Kent Geiger (eds.), *Soviet Society: A Book of Readings.* Boston: Houghton Mifflin Company, 1961.

Joint Economic Committee, Congress of the United States, *New Directions in the Soviet Economy.* Washington, D.C.: Government Printing Office, 1966.

Koestler, Arthur, *Darkness at Noon.* New York: Mentor Books, 1948.

Korol, Alexander G., *Soviet Research and Development: Its Organization, Personnel, and Funds.* Cambridge, Mass.: M. I. T. Press, 1965.

Lowenthal, Richard, *World Communism: The Disintegration of a Secular Faith*. New York: Oxford University Press, Inc. (Galaxy Books), 1966.

Masaryk, T. G., *The Spirit of Russia*, 2nd ed. New York: The Macmillan Company, 1955.

Mihajlov, Mihajlo, *Moscow Summer*. New York: Farrar, Straus & Giroux, Inc., 1965.

Miller, Margaret, *Rise of the Russian Consumer*. London: The Institute of Economic Affairs, 1965.

Nove, Alec, *The Soviet Economy*, rev. ed. New York: Frederick A. Praeger, Inc., 1966.

Pasternak, Boris, *Doctor Zhivago*. New York: Mentor Books, 1959.

Rubinstein, Alvin Z., *Communist Political Systems*. Englewood Cliffs, N.J.: Prentice-Hall, Inc., 1966.

Scalapino, Robert A. (ed.), *The Communist Revolution in Asia: Tactics, Goals, and Achievements*. Englewood Cliffs, N.J.: Prentice-Hall, Inc., 1965.

Shulman, Marshall D., *Beyond the Cold War*. New Haven: Yale University Press, 1965.

Solzhenitsyn, Alexander, *One Day in the Life of Ivan Denisovich*. New York: Bantam Books, 1963.

Thayer, Charles W., *Guerrilla*. New York: New American Library (Signet Books), 1965.

Wetter, Gustav A., *Soviet Ideology Today*. New York: Frederick A. Praeger, Inc., 1966.

Wolfe, Bertram D., *Marxism: 100 Years in the Life of a Doctrine*. New York: The Dial Press, Inc., 1965.

Yevtushenko, Yevgeny, *A Precocious Autobiography*. New York: E. P. Dutton & Co., Inc., 1963.

Zawodny, J. K., *Death in the Forest: The Story of the Katyn Forest Massacre*. Notre Dame: Notre Dame University Press, 1962.

Totalitarian Fascism

Social background of fascism

Communism was the first major twentieth-century totalitarian revolt against the Western, liberal way of life; *fascism* was the second. Stripped to its essentials, fascism is the totalitarian organization of government and society by a single-party dictatorship, intensely nationalist, racialist, militarist, and imperialist. In Europe, Italy (1922) was the first to go fascist, followed by Germany (1933). In Asia, Japan became fascist in the 1930's, gradually evolving totalitarian institutions out of its own native heritage. In the Western Hemisphere, a semi-constitutional government of a landed oligarchy was destroyed in Argentina in 1943 in a revolt of dissatisfied officers, and a fascist dictatorship was subsequently built up under the leadership of Colonel (later General) Perón, lasting until its overthrow in 1955.

Clearly, then, whereas communism is the form of totalitarianism typically linked with poor and underdeveloped nations (Russia in Europe, China in Asia), fascism is the form of totalitarianism that typically grows in wealthier and technologically more advanced nations (Germany in Europe, Japan in Asia). In the Americas, Guatemala, one of the poorest and most backward nations, for years encouraged the growth of communism until the pro-communist regime of President Arbenz was overthrown in June, 1954; Cuba under Fidel Castro is a more recent example of communism in the Americas. Fascism, on the other hand, saw its most intense development in Argentina, the wealthiest of the twenty Latin American republics.

Whereas communism is very largely the product of predemocratic and preindustrial societies, fascism is *postdemocratic* and *postindustrial:* fascism is impossible in countries with no democratic experience at all. In such societies, dictatorship may be based on the army, the bureaucracy, or the personal prestige of the dictator, but it will lack the element of mass enthusiasm and *mass support* (not necessarily majority support) characteristic of fascism. Moreover, although no fascist system can arise in a country without some democratic experience (as in Germany or Japan), there is not much likelihood of fascist success in countries that have experienced democracy over a long period, such as Switzerland, Scandinavia, Holland, England, or the United States.

Paradoxically, experience has proved that, in general, the more violent and terroristic fascist movements are, the more popular support they tend to have. Thus fascism in Germany was both the most brutal and the most popular political movement; in Italy fascism was less popular and less brutal. Such fascist dictatorships based on mass support are not to be confused with traditional dictatorships such as existed in Europe in several countries during the 1930's, particularly in the Balkans and Eastern Europe. The present authoritarian dictatorships in Spain and Portugal, too, are essentially traditional, relatively moderate, and rest on the established forces of the bureaucracy and army.

In Latin America, there also are numerous dictatorships, but they are not fascist (with the exception of Argentina from 1943 to 1955) because they typically rest on the personal magic of one man, usually a general. Relying as he must on the good will of his army, the Latin American dictator has no need for, and rarely has, the mass support that characterizes fascism. Popular political movements hardly enter the picture.

The second condition essential to the growth of fascism is a considerable degree of industrial development. There are at least two principal points of contact between fascism and relatively advanced industrialization. First, fascist terror and propaganda require a good deal of technological organization and know-how. Second, as a system of *permanent mobilization for war,* fascism cannot hope to succeed without considerable industrial skills and resources.

It may be argued that the connection between fascism and modern industry goes even deeper. Every industrial society brings about social and economic tensions. Such tensions can be dealt with in one of two ways: the liberal way or the totalitarian way. The liberal society recognizes the variety of economic interests and their necessary conflict (such as between labor and management, agriculture and industry, skilled and unskilled workers) and seeks to reconcile such conflicts by the experimental method of peaceful, gradual adjustment. The totalitarian fascist state either denies that there are divergent social interests (abhorring as it does the notion of variety, especially in the form of departures from state-imposed uniformity) or, if it half-heartedly concedes the existence of divergent social interests, it resolves such differences by force.

The difference between communism and fascism on this point may be briefly (and with some oversimplification) formulated in this way: communism is the totalitarian way of *industrializing a backward society;* fascism is the totalitarian method of *solving conflicts within an industrially more advanced society.*

In its social background, fascism has particularly appealed to two groups: first, a numerically small group of *industrialists* and *landowners* who are willing to finance fascist movements in the hope of thereby getting rid of free labor unions. Industrialists are not, as a class, any more fascist-minded than other social groups; in countries with strong liberal and democratic traditions, for example, industrialists are no better and no worse than other people as far as their faith in the democratic process is concerned. But where democracy is weak, as in Germany, Italy, or Japan, it takes only a few wealthy industrialists and landowners to supply fascist movements with ample funds.

Where the pressure of public opinion is strongly democratic and liberal, individual industrialists who are inclined toward fascism will find that supporting fascist groups is bad business; but where democratic traditions are weak, leaders of big business like Thyssen and Krupp in Germany, or the Mitsui trust in Japan, found it possible to side openly with the cause of fascism.

The second main source of fascist support—and numerically by far the most important—comes from the lower middle classes, mostly in the salaried group. Many persons in this class dread the prospect of joining (or rejoining) the proletariat and look to fascism for a salvation of their status and prestige. The salaried employee feels jealous of big business, into whose higher echelons he would like to rise, and fearful of labor, into whose proletarian world he would hate to descend. Fascism very cleverly utilizes these jealousies and fears of the salariat by propagandizing simultaneously against big business and big labor. Although such propaganda is neither logically nor politically consistent, its very inconsistency both reflects and appeals to the confusion of the salaried class, uncertain as that class is where to turn politically.

In the United States, anxiety over preserving one's threatened status has been one of the main psychological forces exploited by the Radical Right (John Birch Society, Minute Men) and by fascist groups. This status anxiety has been centered, above all, on the rising power of organized labor, which is perceived as a threat to the existing status quo. In addition, American fascist and semi-fascist propaganda has focused on white fears of the rising status of Negroes. As in other countries, racial hostility is stronger in psychologically more insecure lower middle-class groups than in the better educated and more affluent middle and upper classes.

Paradoxically, organized labor frequently contributes to this uncertainty and demoralization of the salariat without meaning to do so. For psychological reasons, white-collar workers are generally unwilling to organize into unions. As a result, the *incomes of workers,* particularly those organized in unions, *have tended to improve much faster than the incomes of salaried employees.* As the gap between the economic status of workers and that of salaried persons widens, the latter become more and more resentful of losing what they consider their rightful place in society and may turn to fascism, which promises to keep unions and other upstart organizations under control. The leaders of organized labor may point out that the weak economic position of salaried persons is their own fault and that such persons are in error in refusing to organize and bring pressure upon their employers; such arguing points, however, though they may be logically valid, are psychologically ineffective. In times of prosperity the divergence between labor and the salaried class may not be too upsetting politically, but in times of crisis and depression the smallest class antagonisms may turn into political dynamite.

Another important social group that has shown itself particularly vulnerable to fascist propaganda is the military. Even in a strong and well-established democracy, professional military people tend to overestimate the virtues of discipline and unity; where democracy is weak, this professional bias of the military becomes a political menace. Thus, in the early stages of Nazism in Germany, the military class of the nation either openly supported Hitler or at best maintained an attitude of benevolent neutrality. The top military leaders of Germany knew that a high proportion of Nazi bosses were criminals and unscrupulous psychopaths, yet they supported the Nazi movement as a step toward the militarization of the German people. In Italy too, fascism in its early stages received considerable support from army circles, and in Japan fascism developed with the active and enthusiastic support of the army, which had every reason to be the main pillar of a regime committed to imperialist expansion. In Argentina, semi-constitutional government was overthrown in 1943 in a revolt of the "younger officers," under Perón, who set up his own brand of fascism, named *peronismo* after him.

Yet it should be pointed out that the military often also play a leading part in getting rid of fascist and other kinds of dictatorial government. Perón himself learned this lesson in 1955, and the same thing has happened to several other Latin American dictators since the end of World War II. Once fascism is established, people often look to the army as one of the last remaining bulwarks of decency and legality. Therefore, fascism (as is also true of communism) indulges in periodic purges of the armed forces, because fascist leaders realize that the army is one of the few institutions left that enjoy genuine popular respect.

Although fascism is not a direct or necessary result of economic depression, as Marxist-communist theory suggests, there is a relation between the two. In times of depression, fear and frustration undermine faith in the democratic process, and where the faith in rational methods weakens, fascism is the potential gainer. The small businessman blames big business for his troubles; big business puts the blame on the unreasonableness of the labor unions; labor feels that the only way out is to soak the rich; the farmers feel that they are not getting enough for farm products and that they are made to pay too high prices for manufactured goods; city people envy the security of the farmers ("always something to eat and a roof over your head"); and—worst of all—there is the large mass of unemployed people.

What democratic nations have failed to understand sufficiently is that the worst feature of unemployment is not economic suffering (which can be mitigated by adequate relief), but the feeling of being useless, unwanted, outside of the respectable ranks of society. It is among these spiritually homeless that fascism makes serious inroads during a depression: by putting an unemployed person into a uniform, a fascist movement makes him feel that he "belongs," and by telling him that he is a member of a superior race or nation, such a movement restores some of his self-respect.

The Black Muslims—more akin to fascism than to communism—have sought to exploit the feeling of "not belonging" among American Negroes. The rate of unemployment is, in prosperity and depression, twice as high among Negroes as it is among whites, and many Negroes therefore feel excluded from existing society both racially and economically. In their propaganda the Black Muslims have tried to make the Negro feel that he belongs to a superior race and that he must dissociate himself from the corrupt and unjust white world, by force if necessary. In their appeal to racialism and change by force, in their pride in African culture, and in their promise of building independent Negro political communities on American soil, the Black Muslims thus aim at restoring Negro self-respect.

The sense of not belonging is, in a way, characteristic of life in modern industrial society in general. Industrialization and urbanization have debunked and frequently destroyed traditional values, without always providing adequate substitute values in their place. The disorientation and confusion resulting from these effects of industrialization provide the social and psychological background of fascism and its attempt to restore the old, preindustrial way of life in a modern nation.

It can thus be seen that the Marxist interpretation of fascism in terms of class (identifying fascism with capitalism in decay) is not borne out by the facts. *Fascism cuts across all social groups;* wealthy industrialists and landowners support it for one reason, the lower middle classes for another, psychopaths and criminals for another still. Finally, there are the many nationalists and chauvinists in every country who prove themselves vulnerable to promises of conquest and empire. In terms of explicit programs, fascist movements must make the most contradictory promises to satisfy all their adherents; such contradictions are one main weakness of fascism. Yet in terms of implicit psychological background, fascism looks within all social groups for the great common denominators, *frustration, resentment,* and *insecurity.* These psychological attitudes can easily be turned into hatred and aggression, against both internal and external "enemies."

Because these social and psychological attitudes are not the monopoly of any one social class, fascism manages to appeal to large masses of people in some countries. When Adolf Hitler joined the Nazi party in 1919, he was Member No. 7. Yet within fourteen years Nazism became the greatest mass movement in German history, including in its ranks members of all groups of German society, from hobos to members of the imperial family and the royal houses of the German states. By 1932, the Nazi vote had mounted to 14 million, and in March, 1933, 17 million Germans (almost half the total vote) voted for Nazism; several more millions voted for nationalist and militarist parties that were Nazi in all but name. It is obvious that 17 million voters cannot consist exclusively of wealthy bankers and industrialists and that only a party with a national, rather than class, appeal can obtain such high votes. In no other country has fascism ever been as widely popular as in Germany, but there has been no fascist regime anywhere without some popular support.

Psychological roots of totalitarianism

In countries like Germany and Japan, the clue to the understanding of fascist tendencies lies in broad social forces and traditions. In those countries, the authoritarian tradition has been predominant and democracy is still a very frail plant. As a result, a German or Japanese with fascist tendencies is no outcast and may be considered perfectly well adjusted to his society. Even when his society explicitly condemns fascism, as it is likely to do each time it loses a war, much in the implicit habits and customs of German and Japanese life tends toward the authoritarian way of life, and from authoritarianism to fascism there is only a step. In democratic societies such as Britain or the United States, on the other hand, the appeal of fascism can be more fruitfully judged from the angle of individual psychology. Empirical studies in the United States have shown that 10 per cent of Americans are strongly authoritarian and about 20 per cent partly authoritarian. (T. W. Adorno and others, *The Authoritarian Personality,* 1950.)

The traditional analysis of political dictatorship has been centered on the motivations of dictatorial leaders, driven by lust for power and sadistic cravings for domination. The followers and subjects of a dictatorship are viewed exclusively as "victims" who just happen to fall into the misfortune of oppressive rule. Every insurance company knows that some persons are more accident-prone than others, and every policeman knows that some persons are more likely to attract criminals than others.

Similarly, it is not too farfetched to suggest that some people and some nations are more "dictatorship-prone" than others. Plato's psychological insight led him to suggest in his *Republic* that constitutions grow not "from stone to stone," but "from those characters of the men in the cities which preponderate and draw the rest of the city after them." The very existence of an authoritarian mass movement like fascism depends on the *desire* of many persons *to submit and obey.*

Rational democrats may not understand why anyone should prefer to obey rather than take the responsibility of making decisions for himself; they take it for granted that men *should* make their own decisions rather than have their actions dictated by others. But this democratic stereotype overlooks the *comforts of irresponsibility* to many persons. Children love the feeling of being sheltered and secure behind the benevolent power and authority of their parents. The mark of the mature adult is his willingness and capacity to stand on his own feet, to take responsibility and be independent of others. Yet relatively few persons ever attain this sort of maturity; the process of growing up, as every adolescent knows, is painful, and many rebel against a cold world where they must struggle for themselves without the omnipotence and omniscience of parental love and security. In all human beings there is a *latent tendency toward dependence* based on the parent-child relationship, although some people manage to achieve a more self-reliant adulthood than others. The totalitarian system, whether communist or fascist, appeals to people who, for whatever personal reasons, look for the father-child relationship, for security through dependence.

What are some of the empirically ascertainable traits that characterize the authoritarian personality, particularly the personality attracted to the fascist type of authoritarianism? First, a tendency to conform compulsively to orthodox ideals and practices; emotional rigidity and limited imagination; excessive concern with problems of status and strength; strong loyalty to one's own group ("in-group") coupled with vehement dislike of outsiders ("out-group"); and stress on discipline and obedience rather than freedom and spontaneity in human relations (education, sex, family, religion, industry, government). The "herd-minded" (or "ethnocentric") element in the fascist personality is perhaps the single most important one, although no one element in itself conclusively defines a personality as authoritarian.

The key role of the *family* in the formation of basic attitudes seems to be brought out by all clinical and theoretical studies; but the family is not, after all, an isolated and independent agent. Rather it reflects the predominant social goals and values and constitutes to the child the cultural and psychological representative of society at large.

No person is ever completely authoritarian or completely democratic, just as no human being is ever an utter devil or a perfect angel. In each case it is a question of quantity and degree, although differences of quantity eventually become differences of quality. Although there has been no major fascist mass movements in the United States so far, it is a matter of record that some Americans looked upon German and Italian fascism in the 1930's as the "wave of the future" (as it was called in a book of that title) and that others sympathized with Argentine fascism in the 1940's and 1950's.

Dependence and submission in a totalitarian society—fascist or communist—give a person the security for which he hungers but deny him self-expression and self-assertion, the needs for which are as deeply embedded in human nature as the desire for security. Thus denied, these drives turn into repressed hostility and aggression, for the expression of which fascism provides two channels, one for the ruling class, one for the ruled. Within the apparatus of the dictatorial party and government, there is the pattern of the cyclist: crouching before the superior above, pressing down on the subordinate below. Only the leader need not crouch before anyone—he only presses down. Below the top leader—"Big Brother," as Orwell called him in *1984*, the classic fictional portrait of totalitarianism—although each member of the party and government hierarchy must kowtow to someone above him, in return he may tread on those below him.

Persons outside the ruling class, however, have no one to command; they can only obey. How can they express their hostility and aggressiveness? Since the vast majority of the people in a totalitarian state form the group of those who can only take, but not issue, commands, this is a serious problem for every dictatorship. Although officially the dictator claims that he is universally beloved, he knows that there is much repressed hatred and hostility directed (or capable of being directed) toward him and his regime.

The answer of totalitarian dictatorships is to *direct this latent hostility of the people against real or imaginary enemies.* For the communist, the enemy may be the bourgeois, Trotskyites, Titoites, or Wall Street. Hitler first chose the Jews as the target of German aggression; once given a direction for their savagery, the Germans were not satisfied until they had sent six million Jews from central and Eastern Europe to the gas chambers. Later new enemies took the place of the Jews: Britain, the United States, Churchill, Roosevelt, Bolshevism, the churches. Finally, when they felt that the end was close, Hitler and his cohorts unleashed their vengeance on the Germans themselves; if they had to go down, the German people had to be destroyed with them. In a more recent fascist regime, peronist Argentina, American imperialism and international finance were the chief targets of fascist hate propaganda.

To men who cannot be masters of their own lives, fascism promises mastery over other peoples; and if fascism cannot deliver the triumphs it promises, the hatred of the people may turn against their leaders, as it did against Mussolini, who was tried before a partisan committee in northern Italy in April, 1945, excuted, and then publicly hung from a lamp-post in Milan. Having taught his people violence and hatred, he reaped himself what he had sown.

The psychological interpretation of totalitarianism—fascist or communist—is of particular value where the prevailing cultural pattern is not authoritarian, where it takes some personal quirk to break with the democratic pattern of the environment. Thus, in societies like Britain or the United States, the psychological analysis of people who have embraced communism or fascism is of great value because there emerges from such an analysis a definite pattern of personality factors that is typical in many American fascists or communists.

Yet it would be futile to explain the historical strength of fascism in Germany or Japan, or of communism in China or Italy, by means of personal psychology. It may be argued that an American or Englishman who embraces communism or fascism is not well adjusted, comes from a broken home, or has had an unhappy childhood, but the same can hardly be said of 17 million Germans who voted for Hitler in 1933 or of the many millions of Frenchmen and Italians who have persistently voted communist since the end of World War II. Where totalitarianism assumes the proportions of a mass movement, the main avenue of analysis must be that of the great social, economic, and cultural forces and traditions of a nation.

Whereas the cure for an American fascist or communist may be found on the psychoanalyst's couch, the cure for five million Frenchmen who vote communist is more take-home pay every Saturday and a more decent life all round. Similarly, the origins of fascist totalitarianism in Germany, Japan, and Argentina lie deeper in the collective lives of those nations than can be revealed from a study of individual personalities. There was plenty that was wrong in Hitler's personality as viewed through non-German eyes, but to the 17 million Germans who identified themselves with him in the election of March 1933, he must have been an admirably adjusted personality.

Elements of fascist doctrine and policy

Although fascism, like communism, is a movement that exists everywhere, it has no such authoritative statement of principles as communism has; moreover, there is no one country, at present, directing a fascist world conspiracy. During the Nazi regime (1933–1945), Germany was the most powerful of the fascist states then in existence, and world fascism was very largely directed, financed, and inspired by German brains and money. Since the defeat of the fascist Axis (Germany, Japan, Italy) in World War II, however, there has been no really major fascist state; Argentina never possessed anything like the world-wide influence that Nazi Germany had until 1945.

The absence of a universally recognized authoritative statement of fascist principles is not total. Hitler has left in *Mein Kampf* (1925–1927) a trustworthy guide to his thought, and Mussolini's *The Doctrine of Fascism* (1932), a moderate statement of fascist principles, expresses the Italian brand of fascism. The latter has served as a model for most other fascist movements in the world because it is more universal in outlook; Nazism, a specifically German brand of fascism, has proved for that reason less suitable for export.

Although there is no *Fascist Manifesto* with undisputed authority among fascists, it is not too difficult to state the principal elements of the fascist outlook:

(1) Distrust of reason
(2) Denial of basic human equality
(3) Code of behavior based on lies and violence
(4) Government by elite
(5) Totalitarianism
(6) Racialism and imperialism
(7) Opposition to international law and order

(1) The *distrust of reason* is perhaps the most significant trait of fascism. The rational tradition of the West stems from Greece and is one of the three basic components (the other two being

Jewish monotheism and Christian love) that have given the West its characteristic culture and outlook. Fascism rejects this Greek root of Western civilization and is frankly *antirationalist,* distrusting reason in human affairs and stressing the irrational, sentimental, uncontrollable elements of man. Psychologically, fascism is *fanatical* rather than reflective, *dogmatic* rather than open-minded; as a result each fascist regime has its taboo issues such as race, empire, the leader, and it is the nature of a taboo issue that it must be accepted on faith and cannot be critically discussed. During the fascist regime in Italy (1922–1945), Mussolini's picture was shown in every classroom in the country over the caption "Mussolini is always right."

The communist states have the taboo issue of Marxism-Leninism, a set of final truths that must not be questioned. In addition, there are the more passing taboo subjects as defined by the top party leaders in Russia, Red China, or Yugoslavia.

As a matter of basic principle, *democracy recognizes no taboo issue:* there is no subject that cannot be questioned or challenged, not even the validity of democracy itself. In practice, of course, democracies do not always live up to that ideal. Thus, it was argued by some in the 1950's that in the United States the question of the validity of democracy was on its way to becoming a taboo issue, especially since the Supreme Court's 1951 decision upholding the constitutionality of the Smith Act of 1940 (under which the advocacy of the duty, desirability, necessity, or propriety of revolution is a criminal offense).

The individual, too, may have taboo issues, dark corners in his heart or mind that must not be pulled out and subjected to rational examination. The mentally healthy individual has few or (ideally) no taboo issues because he is able to face reality as it is and does not insist on living in a dream world in defiance of reality. Psychologically, the existence of taboo issues in the individual or in a group, party, or nation is due to a sense of insecurity or guilt, or both.

Under conditions of stress and strain, the individual as well as the collective group may take refuge in the temporary shelter of the taboo, postponing the facing of reality but unable to shut it out forever. Since totalitarian regimes permanently operate in a state of high tension and crisis, the taboo is part and parcel of their normal environment. Democracies succumb to the temptation of the taboo, and its false security, only in periods of exceptional strain; it is significant that the Supreme Court's decision on the Smith Act took place in 1951, at the height of the Korean war. In the 1960's, a more tolerant and reflective mood prevailed, and the Supreme Court has greatly liberalized its views of the 1950's on the constitutionality of revolutionary propaganda and organizations.

(2) The *denial of basic human equality* is a common denominator of fascist (as well as communist) movements and states. True enough, democratic societies do not always live up to the ideal of human equality, but they are subject to attacks of conscience if they fail, and they at least accept equality as the long-term goal of public policy. By contrast, fascist societies not only accept the *fact* of human inequality but go further and affirm inequality as an *ideal.*

The concept of human equality goes back to the three roots of Western civilization. The Jewish idea of one God led to the idea of one mankind, since all men as children of God are brothers among themselves. The Christian notion of the inalienability and indestructibility of the human soul led to the ideal of basic *moral* equality of all men. Finally, the Greek-Stoic concept of reason led to the oneness of mankind on the basis of reason as the most truly human bond that all men have in common.

Fascism rejects this Jewish-Christian-Stoic concept of equality as soft and nonsensical and opposes to it the concept of inequality, which can most simply be spelled out in the contrast of superiority and inferiority. Thus, in the fascist code, men are superior to women, soldiers to civilians, party members to nonparty members, one's own nation to others, the strong to the weak, and (perhaps most important in the fascist outlook) the victors in war to the vanquished. The chief criteria of equality in the Western tradition are man's mind and soul, whereas the fascist affirmation of inequality is based ultimately on *strength.*

(3) The fascist—like the communist—code of behavior stresses *violence and lies* in all human relations, within and between nations. From the democratic viewpoint, politics is the mechanism through which social conflicts of interest are peacefully adjusted. By contrast, the fascist view is that politics is characterized by the *friend-enemy* relation. Politics begins and ends, in this fascist way of thinking, with the possibility of an enemy—and his *total annihilation.* The democratic antithesis to the friend is the *opponent,* and in democratic nations the opponent of today is considered the potential government of tomorrow. (The opposition in the British Parliament is officially called "Her Majesty's Loyal Opposition,"

and the leader of the Opposition receives a special salary to do his job well.) The fascist knows only enemies, not opponents, and since enemies represent evil incarnate, total annihilation is the only solution. This doctrine applies to domestic as well as to foreign enemies; thus, the Nazis first set up concentration camps and gas chambers for German citizens and later used the same facilities on non-Germans.

Contrary to common opinion, *concentration camps* and *slave labor camps* are not incidental phenomena in totalitarian systems like fascism and communism but are of their very core. It is in the concentration and slave labor camps that totalitarian regimes seek to destroy the legal and moral person in man and to deprive him of the last residue of individuality. The technique of brainwashing used by fascists and communists deliberately seeks to break a man's mind to the point where he will publicly confess to crimes he did not commit and perhaps could not have committed. After a period of brainwashing, the victim no longer has a mind of his own; he merely plays back, like a record, what is expected of him.

By institutionalizing organized mass murder in concentration and slave labor camps, totalitarian regimes demonstrate to the entire population what is in store for anyone in disfavor with the men in power, and at the same time they provide the shock troops of the regime with a peacetime outlet for savagery and fanaticism. Immediate death is often considered too humane a penalty by such regimes; moreover, the slow death of concentration or slave labor camps has a greater demonstration value than the clean, old-fashioned method of the execution squad or the gallows.

(4) *Government by elite* is a principle that fascists everywhere frankly oppose to the "democratic fallacy" that people are capable of governing themselves. The concept that only a small minority of the population, qualified by birth, education, or social standing, is capable of understanding what is best for the whole community, and of putting it into practice, is not an invention of twentieth-century fascism. Plato, one of the founders of Western political philosophy, strongly believed that only one class, the "philosopher-kings," are fit to rule society. The contrary belief, that the people as a whole are capable of self-rule, is of relatively recent origin and has successfully worked only in limited areas of the globe.

Although the fascist idea of government by a self-appointed elite (a fascist government usually shoots its way into power) is undemocratic, such a government does not always lack popular approval. Strange as it may seem to the democrat, who expects everybody to behave as he does, people throughout history have frequently approved of autocratic governments. Approval alone, however, is no evidence of democracy. What makes a government democratic is that it always depends on popular consent given in free elections. In fascist regimes, even when the government enjoys popular approval, it is carried on independently of popular consent, without free elections, a free press, or a freely functioning opposition.

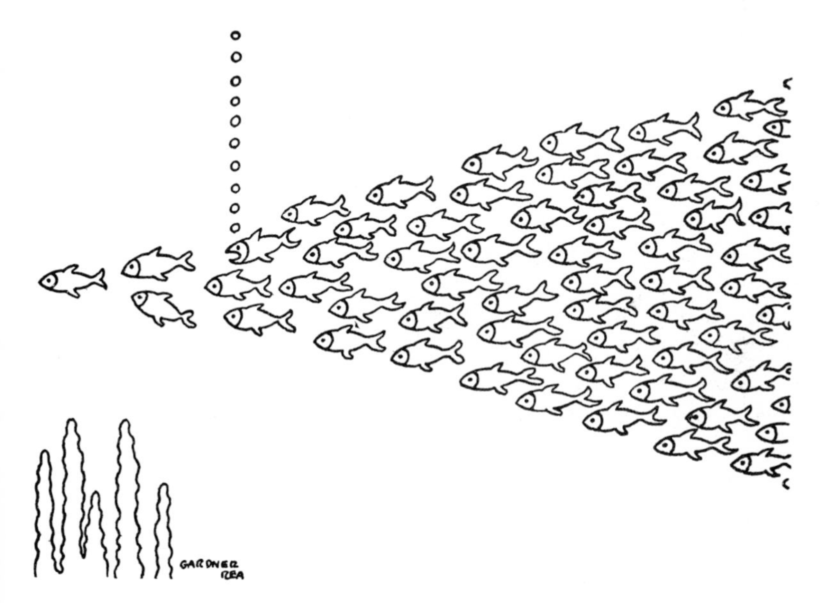

Drawing by Gardner Rea; © 1957 The New Yorker Magazine, Inc.

"God knows what we'd do if anything should ever happen to him!"

The fascist *leadership principle* expresses the extreme form of the elite concept. It fully reflects the irrational nature of fascist politics; the leader is considered infallible, endowed with mystical gifts and insights. In a conflict between popular opinion and the fascist leader, the will of the latter prevails; the leader represents the public interest, the way all people would think if they knew what was best for the whole community (what Rousseau called the "General Will"), whereas the people express only individual whims and desires not necessarily in harmony with the public good (Rousseau's "Will of All").

The emphasis on leadership is contrary to the fascist enforcement of orthodoxy and conformity. Hitler, Mussolini, and Perón grew up in nonfascist societies with considerable free competition. So far it has been impossible to appraise the leadership qualities of a generation born and bred under fascism. The German, Italian, and Argentine brands of fascism did not last long enough (1933–45 in Germany; 1922–45 in Italy, and 1943–55 in Argentina) to supply conclusive evidence on the matter.

(5) *Totalitarianism* in all human relations characterizes fascism as a way of life rather than as a mere system of government. There are many dictatorships, particularly in Latin America, in which the authoritarian principle is applied only in government. If the people do not make any trouble politically and do not interfere with the rule of the dictator and his henchmen, they can lead their own lives pretty freely. Education, religion, business, and agriculture are not touched very much by the political dictatorship. By contrast, fascism is totalitarian; it employs authority and violence in *all* kinds of social relations, whether political or not.

With regard to women, the largest discriminated-against minority of the world, fascism is antifeminist. Women should stay in their place, said the Nazis, and their concern should be the famous three K's—*Kinder, Küche, Kirche.* Since women are unable to bear arms they are automatically second-class citizens according to the fascist view and are excluded from leadership positions in government or party. They have the right to vote, but since this right in fascist countries means only the right to be enthusiastic about the leader and his party, it is not much of a practical asset. Within the family the father is the leader, and both his wife and his children get a strong taste of domestic authoritarian government, which has more effect on their everyday lives than the operations of the remote political government in the capital. In the extreme case of modern fascism, Nazi Germany, the contempt for women was finally demonstrated in the official ridicule of the institution of marriage as a false Jewish-Christian prejudice, and German women were encouraged to produce children for the fatherland outside of wedlock.

Fascist countries also make a point of refusing to employ women extensively in schools. From the fascist viewpoint, schools are to teach discipline and obedience, specifically to prepare the boys for military service and the girls for related domestic activities. In a program of such importance, fascist educators feel women teachers have no place.

Thus it can be seen that fascist totalitarianism, unlike the old-fashioned dictatorships of Latin America, is *totalitarian in its objective:* to control all phases of human life, political or not, from the cradle to the grave. It begins the control even before the cradle, by pushing definite population policies, and has been known to reach into the grave, so to speak, to decide whether a dead person should have a burial at all and, if so, in what form.

But fascism is also *totalitarian in its means.* It will use any form of coercion, from verbal threats to mass murder, in obtaining its ends. By contrast, the classical authoritarian dictatorship was, and is, more restrained in its means and resorts to murder only on a limited scale. Thus, whenever a Latin American dictator is ousted he is usually permitted by his opponents to assemble his family and peacefully depart to a foreign country.

(6) *Racialism and imperialism* express the two basic fascist principles of inequality and violence as applied to the society of nations. Within the nation, fascist doctrine holds, the elite is superior to the rest and may impose its will upon them by force. Similarly, between nations the *elite nation* is superior to others and is entitled to rule them. German fascism went furthest in its racialist and imperialist policies. A straight line led from the theories of the superiority of the German-Nordic "race" to the mass murder of millions of people. The German objective of world domination included the elimination of some nations through genocide and the enslavement of the rest. After the expected defeat of Britain and Russia, the United States was to be next on the list. The Japanese race theories found their practical imperialist expression in the concept of "co-prosperity," under which Japan would prosper by exploiting Asia and the Pacific.

Italian fascism was for a long time (from 1922 to 1938) remarkably free from exaggerated race theories; early Italian propaganda in this general field concentrated on the idea of reviving the old Roman empire. In 1938, however, Mussolini discovered that the Italians were a pure and superior race, and he became more closely tied to Hitler Germany.

In Argentina, the Perón government strongly emphasized the mission and destiny of Argentina and accompanied this doctrine of Argentine superiority with a deliberate policy of imperialism. Peronist imperialism, probably out of respect for the tremendous power of the United States in the Western Hemisphere, which makes any fascist territorial ventures highly dangerous, limited itself to economic, political, and ideological expansion; but Argentina built up a vast armament industry, and her neighbors could not help wondering against whom this Argentine war potential was to be used. Only the overthrow of the Perón dictatorship in 1955 removed these fears of Argentine imperialism.

Racialism and imperialism are not an exclusive monopoly of fascism. Although communist theory rejects both, Russian communism is strongly imperialistic. After World War II a Great Russian cult was built up differing only in degree from the Great Russian superiority concept as it was officially held in pre-Bolshevik Russia. More recently, Red China has made use of the propaganda argument of race and color in her struggle with Russia for supremacy in the communist world and for leading the underde-

Baldy in The Atlanta Constitution.

". . . Sure we've complied, here's our Negro!"

veloped countries—mostly inhabited by nonwhites—toward communist revolution.

In the democracies too, there is a tradition of racialism; in the United States, for example, racial discrimination has seriously corroded the vitality of democratic ideals. Called (by the Swedish social scientist Gunnar Myrdal) "the American dilemma," the race issue in the United States may ultimately decide the fate of the democratic way of life at home and abroad.

The communists have concentrated much of their propaganda in Asia and Africa on British imperialism and American racialism; both points have proved effective in many of the underdeveloped countries, and if the communists have frequently failed to make converts out of such propaganda, they have at least succeeded in paralyzing Anglo-American influence by fostering a position of neutralism.

(7) *Opposition to international law and order* is the logical outcome of the fascist belief in inequality, violence, racialism, imperialism, and war. Whereas nonfascists (with the exception of out-and-out nonresisting pacifists) accept war as a tragic fact, which should be abolished, fascists raise war to the level of an ideal, because, as Mussolini put it, "war alone brings up to their highest tension all human energies and puts the stamp of nobility upon the peoples who have the courage to meet it."

Any type of international organization assumes some form of government by consent, which is directly contradictory to the fascist principle of *government by force*. Also, equality of states before the law of nations is a basic principle of international order. The fascist concept of the elite leads, as we have seen, to the leadership of one nation over the society of nations as it does to the leadership of one man within the nation's government. Fascist states, therefore, shy away from international organizations in which they are expected to abide by majority decisions and in which government is carried on by methods of discussion rather than by force.

The fascist regimes of Italy and Germany had no use for the League of Nations; Germany withdrew in 1933 and Italy in 1937. In the United Nations, peronist Argentina consistently played a lone wolf role. In the Organization of American States, she did all she could to prevent effective cooperation between the United States and the Latin American republics—a policy that was later faithfully copied by Cuba under Castro.

In sum, it can be seen that the fascist theory and practice of international politics are not so different from those of communism. Both accept force and war as the vehicles of resolving differences.

For the communist, the concept of *class* plays the dominant role in the struggle, whereas fascism sees in *race* and *nation* the key concepts in the dynamics of change.

In practice, both communism and fascism lead to the same thing in international relations, although their theoretical starting-points differ. When Germany and Russia finally clashed in 1941, the reason was not ideological but practical; they could not agree on the division of the spoils. Since Russia was not satisfied with German proposals for dividing up the world, Germany attacked Russia as an obstacle on its path to world dominion.

Fascist economics: the corporate state

The corporate state applies fascist principles of organization and control to the economy. The fascist economy is subdivided in state-controlled associations of capital and labor, and each association has a monopoly in its trade or occupation. *The one-party state is the ultimate arbiter of conflicts between capital and labor.*

The philosophy of the corporate state rests on two assumptions. First, man (except for the small ruling elite) should not be politically articulate as a citizen but only as a worker, entrepreneur, farmer, doctor, or lawyer; general political problems are assumed to be too complicated for the mass of the people, who are only expected to understand issues that bear directly on their vocational or professional work. Second, members of the small ruling elite are supposed to understand broad problems that affect the whole society, and they alone are therefore qualified to govern the community. This conception is Platonic in origin, and in modern times antidemocratic thinkers like Burke and Hegel have supported it against the claims of the democratic theory.

The democratic conception rejects this corporate approach to economic and political organization for several reasons. In the first place, it is not always easy to separate economic from political aspects. Tariffs seems to be a purely economic issue, yet they directly affect political and diplomatic relations with other states.

Immigration seems at first sight to be an economic problem, yet delicate psychological and diplomatic issues are involved in it. Economic aid to other nations, as the United States has learned in the last twenty years, has profound military and political aspects as well as economic effects.

Second, the democratic theory holds that only the man who wears the shoe knows where it pinches—the mystic knowledge and insight of the ruling elite are no substitute for the experience of the ruled—or, as Aristotle put it, the guest is a better judge of the meal than the cook. Fascists insist that the cook not only ought to be the final judge of his product but also should impose his judgment on the guests, by force if necessary.

Finally, the democratic theory rejects the fascist assumption that members of one particular class are superior in judgment to the rest of the people and are therefore the nation's natural rulers. Formal education can supply knowledge only, not judgment. Judgment is not something that can be learned in fascist schools for leaders; it is the result of character, intelligence, experience, and personal philosophy. Formal training and education in leadership, party doctrine, public administration, history, and politics do not necessarily add up to true leadership. Jesus did not obtain a Ph.D. in religion, Socrates did not not attend a school of education, Lincoln did not major in political science, and Churchill never went to college at all.

The kind of wisdom and moral courage that make up the essence of leadership may be greatly aided by formal education, but the two should not be confused. The democratic theory thus rejects the assumption of fascist doctrine that only a small elite has insight into the public good. From the democratic viewpoint, only God has a perfect understanding of Truth with a capital *T*, but every man is capable, at least partially, of seeing truth with a small *t*.

What the one-party state with the secret police and concentration camps is to the political side of fascist regimes, corporatism is to fascism's social and economic aspects. Just as in the political sphere fascism replaces the pivotal concept of individual liberty with unlimited state authority, so in the economic sphere it rejects the conception of a free welfare economy—be it capitalist, socialist, or middle-of-the-road. The objective of the corporate state is the *power of the state* rather than the welfare of the individual. More specifically, the ultimate objective of the corporate organization of the economy is the preparation of a *permanent war economy,* because aggressive imperialism is the ultimate aim of fascist foreign policy.

The Italian fascist regime, installed in 1922, set up a corporate state that was to show to the Italians and the world that fascism was not mere reaction, directed against liberal capitalism and socialism, but a new creative principle of social and economic organization. The economy was divided into syndicates of workers, employers, and the professions. Only one syndicate was recognized in each branch of business or industry, and although membership in a syndicate was not obligatory, the payment of dues was. The officials of the syndicates were either fascist politicians or persons of reliable loyalty to the fascist regime. In effect, these associations of workers and employers were nothing but instruments of state policy, with no will or life of their own. Since each syndicate had a monopoly of organization in its field, state control was made that much easier.

To make this method of control more nearly complete, the fascist government established *corporations* which were administrative agencies in a given industry designed to unite and control the associations of *workers and employers* in that industry. According to law, the syndicates were autonomous; in fact, however, they were run by the state. The corporation, supreme instrument of fascist economic organization, made no pretense of autonomy, being as it was nothing but an administrative agency of the state and in no way different from the prisons and the other tools of fascist government by force and propaganda.

Despite the same name, the fascist corporation is, of course, not to be confused with the business corporation in the United States. They have nothing whatever in common. The fascist corporation is a government agency, whereas the American business corporation is a company of limited liability, owned by private citizens, and engaged in business.

In the final analysis, the much advertised corporate state was no new principle of social and economic organization, but merely a sign of the fact that in the totalitarian system of fascism economic relations, like all other aspects of society, could not be left to the free interplay of the competitive liberal society. In his speech of November 14, 1933, Mussolini stated that the essential bases of the corporate state were a *single party,* a *totalitarian government,* and an atmosphere of *strong ideal tension.* The Fascist Party provided the first two essentials of the corporate state, and the strong ideal tension was brought about by the ceaseless propaganda of expansionist imperialism.

The first real test for the corporate state in Italy, the best-developed historical example so far, came with that country's entry into World War II in June 1940. Fascist Italy revealed itself to be wholly unequal to the task of fighting a major war, not only from the military and political viewpoint, but also from the standpoint of economic efficiency. For twenty years the corporate state had sacrificed the welfare and happiness of a poor people to the dream of a powerful empire and the megalomania of a would-be conqueror of continents. Yet when the first real test of battle came, Italian fascism failed on the economic front even more than on the military front. The economic legacy of the corporate state was not wealth and empire, but the loss of the colonies, poverty, and destitution.

After the execution of Mussolini in the spring of 1945, the Italian people destroyed whatever vestiges were left of the corporate state and embarked upon a new chapter of economic rehabilitation, based on a mixture of economic liberalism and political democracy. In the last analysis, much of the economic ruination of Italy wrought by fascist corporatism was ultimately paid for by the American taxpayer, as the United States poured billions of dollars into Italy after World War II to help her stand on her own feet again. Since 1950, the Italian economy has been one of the fastest growing economies in the world and has provided standards of living undreamed of during the fascist era.

In the Western Hemisphere, Colonel Perón, speaking for the fascist regime in Argentina just after the successful *coup* of June, 1943, declared his admiration for the fundamental conceptions of the corporate state at the very moment when Italian fascism, the model and inspiration of Argentine fascism, had reduced Italy to ashes and ruins. To Argentina as to other nations, the corporate state under Perón brought inflation and meatless days—meatless days in a country that formerly had been the largest exporter of meat in the world. Above all, corporatism in Argentina (called *justicialismo*) meant the end of free labor unions and their replacement by government-sponsored puppets. The employing class, too, was put under the control of the government. Finally, the peronist regime followed the corporate systems of other fascist states by dedicating the economy to the hasty development of heavy industry and the manufacture of armaments. Thus, *justicialismo*, which set out to defend justice against both capitalism and socialism, ended up as the servant of an imperialistic dictator and his political machine, until both were overthrown in 1955.

Peronism: the case of Argentina

The defeat of the Axis in World War II has by no means removed the threat of fascism forever. In terms of military security, to be sure, the chief danger now confronting the free nations is the danger of communist aggression; there has been no major threat of fascist aggression after the defeat of the great fascist powers, Germany and Japan. As an attitude of mind, however, and as a reflection of social and political authoritarianism, fascism has shown that it can survive temporary defeats; only a few years after fascist regimes led Germany and Italy to disaster and humiliation, neo-fascist organizations in both countries brazenly resumed operations.

The case of Argentina is more complex, and it proves that the Western Hemisphere is not immune from the virus of fascism. In 1943, a group of discontented younger officers overthrew the existing democratic regime, which was far from being perfect but which nevertheless was democratic. The officers were under the leadership of Colonel Juan Perón, who in several years in Italy as a military attaché had become a fervent admirer of Mussolini and of fascist ideas. As soon as the peronist clique took over, Argentine foreign policy became openly hostile to the democratic nations in World War II and friendly to the fascist powers. On March 27, 1945, when the war was practically over, Argentina, in order to be admitted to the San Francisco Conference under the terms of the Yalta agreement, declared war on Japan, as well as on Germany "in view of the character of the latter as an ally of Japan." Thus the pro-fascist and pro-Nazi sentiment of the peronist regime was manifested in the wording as well as the timing of its declaration of war.

Perón at first stayed in the background but then took over the ministries of war and labor. The war ministry gave him control over the armed forces, with which he could supplement the deep affection in which the people allegedly held him. Control over labor removed, as in other fascist states, any threat of organized mass action. The radio was completely subordinated to the government, and the opposition was deprived of access to it. In the newspaper field, Perón leveled his sights at *La Prensa,* one of the five or six great newspapers in the world, having an old and revered tradition of independence. First the peronist government tried to cajole and harass *La Prensa* into submission by administrative subterfuges rather than by open action. When all pressures and threats failed, Perón seized *La Prensa* early in 1951 and converted it to the pro-government, fascist line. *La Prensa's* owner, Dr. Ezequiel Paz, obliged to flee to the United States to save himself from prison, was the most famous Argentine refugee; but he was just one of the many who sought asylum in the other American republics and in France and England.

In most of its policies, the peronist regime followed the techniques and aims of Hitler and Mussolini. Yet in one respect—and a very important one—Perón showed intelligence considerably superior to that of his models and masters. Without exception, all the other fascist dictators—like all communist dictatorships—abolished political parties other than the ruling party; and since there could be no regular elections without opposition candidates, fascist elections became plebiscites in which the voters were presented with a major issue and asked to vote yes or no. The votes in fascist elections were usually announced to be somewhere in the neighborhood of 99.6 per cent in favor of the dictator.

It is at this point that Perón improved on Hitler and Mussolini. Perón apparently had too much of a sense of humor to announce to the world that 99.6 per cent of his people insisted on his leadership. He was satisfied with considerably less. In the presidential elections of 1946 Perón was elected by a majority of only 55 per cent, a figure that gave the election the appearance of having been fought under conditions of free campaigning. Nothing was further from the facts, for early in 1944 all political parties had been abolished. This measure hurt the opposition parties more than the government, and it was only shortly before the elections, in late February of 1946, that political parties were reconstituted. Much of the election campaign was conducted in a state of siege, a favorite measure in Latin American dictatorships, under which the government can legally suspend all rights of individual civil liberty. The opposition parties and their leaders were subjected to physical terror from a mob that operated under government protection. In many cases, the police itself used violence against antiperonists, and there were numerous murders in the campaign.

In 1949, Perón had the Argentine Constitution of 1853 changed because under it immediate re-election of the President was illegal.

A modest man, Perón claimed he did not wish to run for the presidency again, but as a patriotic Argentine he finally gave in to the mounting pressure from all sides and allowed himself to be drafted. The election of November, 1951, gave Perón a victory of over 60 per cent, still way below the 99.6 per cent victories of the other fascist dictators.

In the 1951 election, terror against opposition parties was practiced even more openly than in 1946. Hundreds of candidates were jailed during the campaign for no worse crime than daring to run against the existing regime, and conditions were so chaotic that two presidential candidates were out of the race even before the campaign was over. The socialists withdrew from the campaign altogether when it became apparent that the whole thing was a farce. Their candidate for the presidency had been imprisoned, as were hundreds of leaders of other parties, six weeks before the election. In typically fascist fashion, the government declared that it had discovered a subversive plot, and a state of siege was once again proclaimed, so that ruthless terror could be legally employed. In the congressional elections of April 25, 1954, the peronist slate obtained two-thirds of the popular vote. Every radio station was compelled to broadcast Perón's speeches, and the opposition was unable to get any radio time for its candidates. This monopoly of the government was supplemented by many other forms of discrimination, and occasional terror, against the opposition. It was remarkable in the election of 1954, as in 1946 and 1951, that so many Argentines still dared to vote against the peronist regime.

Late in 1954 Perón started his campaign against the Roman Catholic Church; this was the beginning of his undoing. After persisting in that campaign for several months, he was excommunicated by the Vatican on June 16, 1955. On that same day, the Argentine air force and parts of the army staged an armed uprising, but it failed. Three months later, provincial units rebelled again, and this time Perón's fate was sealed when the entire navy went over to the rebels. Only four days after the outbreak of the revolution, on September 19, 1955, Perón quietly slipped away in a Paraguayan gunboat, fleeing eventually to Spain. Since there was virtually no resistance to the revolutionary forces, Perón had to escape in a hurry.

What he left behind came as a shock to the Argentine public. Many were aware that agriculture and industry were in a mess, that public finances were in chaos, that graft was widespread, that Perón's nearest relatives were among the leading grafters, and that honesty and integrity had just about disappeared from public life. But few people knew much about Perón the man, as distinct from Perón the dictator.

In his several homes were found stacks of Argentine currency, totaling millions of dollars; boxes of gold money and valuables made of gold and silver; fabulous jewels of his late wife, Eva Perón, and foreign bank books. It was estimated that his bank deposits in foreign banks must be worth many millions of dollars. Since Perón had always posed as an anticapitalist and friend of the poor, the extent of his private wealth and grafting came as a shock to many of his followers.

The transition from peronism to constitutional government was not easy. Although direct experience with fascism—as with communism—has an immunizing effect, Argentine democracy missed the opportunity provided by the downfall of the peronist dictatorship. Mentally still living in the nineteenth century, the opponents of peronism, particularly in the professional and upper classes, thought that constitutional government could endure without social and economic reforms on a broad scale. The new regime thus failed to win over the labor unions, which had previously been wooed by the peronist regime. As a result, only a few years after Perón's ouster, the peronists were able to become the largest single party, deriving their strength mainly from working class and lower middle-class voters.

In 1962, the peronists won about one-third of the popular vote, thus constituting a serious threat to democratic government. President Frondizi, who had shown little ability in coping with the renewed pressure of peronism, was removed from office by the military. In the presidential elections of 1963, a moderate, Arturo U. Illia, was elected, while peronism suffered a sharp decline. Yet this decline proved very short-lived. In the congressional elections of 1965, the peronists emerged again as the strongest single party, winning almost 30 per cent of the popular vote. The administration of President Illia showed itself unable to solve the political problems of peronism, the social problems of poverty, and the economic problems of inflation.

In 1966, constitutional government was abolished by a military *coup*, whose victorious leaders proclaimed their intention of staying in power as long as would be necessary for the "rehabilitation" of Argentina. Constitutional government following the ouster of peronist fascism thus lasted for only eleven years. The present military dictatorship is of the more traditional Latin American authoritarian type rather than fascism, but—like peronism—it would not have come into power if the Argentine democratic forces had shown themselves more alert to the causes, rather than the symptoms, of fascist or authoritarian dictatorship.

The military dictatorship installed in Argentina in 1966 was no novelty in Latin America or in Argentina itself. Authoritarian political dictatorships have come and gone in Latin America, but the peronist regime was the first example in the Western Hemisphere of a full-fledged fascist state, totalitarian in objectives and means. The peronist era of 1943 to 1955 proved a poor schooling for constitutional government. The future will tell whether the military regime set up in 1966 will throw Argentina back into the older patterns of authoritarianism with some respect for the rule of law or whether it will move in the direction of fascist dictatorship.

Is fascism still a threat?

Is fascism still a threat in the leading democratic nations? The tendency now is to say, emphatically, no. On balance, this may be the right answer, but to say that fascism is unlikely to take over the government of the United States, for example, is not to say it may not be a serious menace. To the extent that an *anti-intellectual tendency* exists in this or any other democracy, it undermines the faith in rational processes; whereas such a tendency need not lead straight to fascism, it prepares the mentality without which there can be no effective fascist movement. Racialism, to the extent that it still exists, is another source that feeds the fascist potential in the United States, as in other democracies. Democracy as known before no longer exists in South Africa, for example: racialism and democracy just do not mix. While South Africa still has a multi-party system and a mild (and harassed) opposition press, it has steadily moved in the direction of the fascist police-state. It practices such methods as imprisonment without trial, confinement of "dangerous" persons to specific localities, forced residence of millions of Negroes in assigned reservations, and censorship of books, movies, and radio according to racialist concepts. The racialism that started out in South Africa to be directed solely against the Negroes later turned against the Indians and finally took in the whole English-speaking part, nearly one-half, of the white popu-

Reprinted by permission from *Saturday Review.*

"Yes, son, this is what happens to a country when the eggheads take over."

lation. Conversely, to the extent that there has been progress in race relations in the United States—and the progress in the last twenty years has been very substantial—the chances of fascism in the United States have decreased.

The *cold war* with world communism has been another contributing factor in the revival of fascism. Because fascism and democracy are both opposed to communism, some democrats have wrongly concluded that democracy and fascism are natural allies in the struggle against communism, overlooking this important distinction: the quarrel between communism and fascism results from the inability of burglars to agree over the division of the loot, whereas the quarrel between communism and democracy is that between the burglar and the law. The same quarrel exists between fascism and democracy.

Possibly the most dangerous softening up of democratic resistance to fascism is the destruction of democratic habits and institutions, not by outside attacks, but within the citadel of democracy itself. If there is any fascist threat to democracy today—and there is—it no longer comes from Berlin, Rome, and Toyko. It derives its parasitic strength from the inertia and apathy of the citizens of a democracy, because without such civic diseases there can be no support for demagogues and fearmongers who seek to aggrandize themselves at the expense of the whole body politic.

It should be kept in mind that the practical alternative is not between 100 per cent virtue and 100 per cent sin, but always between mixtures with varying proportions of ingredients. The danger in a democracy like the United States is not outright fascism on the German, Italian, or Argentine patterns, but the insidious and unnoticed corroding of democratic habits and institutions by prefascist and profascist attitudes. Huey Long, who as governor of Louisiana in the early 1930's set up the nearest thing to a fascist dictatorship in the United States, once jokingly said that if fascism ever came to the United States, it would be under the slogan of 100 per cent Americanism.

Long was right. The open, self-confessed fascist will not get a sympathetic hearing in the United States because the verbal symbols of fascism are identified too profoundly with evil in the American mind; the fascist fellow traveler, the crypto-fascist, the proto-fascist, the prefascist, and the profascist are more dangerous than the plain unhyphenated fascist. By publicly declaring himself to be what he is, the fascist cannot work under the mantle of respectability. A politician with fascist leanings who denies that he is a fascist and who emphasizes his patriotism can do much more harm than the admitted fascist who is not permitted to work within the institutional framework of public life. The danger of not recognizing this prefascist attitude is that, should it become full-fledged fascism (as it well might in an economic depression or in some other disaster of the sort that periodically shakes men's faith in democracy), recognition of it as a threat may come too late for those whose earlier judgment was too lenient.

FOR FURTHER READING

Adorno, T. W. and others, *The Authoritarian Personality.* New York: Harper & Row, Publishers, 1950.

Arendt, Hannah, *The Origins of Totalitarianism,* 2nd ed. New York: Meridian Books, Inc., 1958.

Baumont, Maurice and others, *The Third Reich.* New York: Frederick A. Praeger, Inc., 1955.

Bettelheim, Bruno, *The Informed Heart: The Human Condition in Modern Mass Society.* New York: Free Press, 1960.

Blanksten, George I., *Perón's Argentina.* Chicago: University of Chicago Press, 1953.

Bullock, Alan, *Hitler: A Study in Tyranny.* New York: Bantam Books, 1955.

Chabod, Federico, *A History of Italian Fascism.* London: Weidenfeld & Nicolson, 1963.

Cohen, Elie A., *Human Behavior in the Concentration Camp.* New York: W. W. Norton & Company, Inc., 1953.

Ebenstein, William, *Fascist Italy.* New York: American Book Company, 1939.

———, *The German Record.* New York: Holt, Rinehart & Winston, Inc., 1945.

———, *The Nazi State.* New York: Holt, Rinehart & Winston, Inc., 1943.

Fromm, Erich, *Escape from Freedom.* New York: Holt, Rinehart & Winston, Inc., 1941.

Germino, Dante L., *The Italian Fascist Party in Power.* Minneapolis: University of Minnesota Press, 1959.

Gilbert, G. M., *The Psychology of Dictatorship.* New York: The Ronald Press Company, 1950.

Halperin, S. William, *Mussolini and Italian Fascism.* Princeton: D. Van Nostrand Co., Inc. (Anvil Books), 1964.

Hoess, Rudolf, *Commandant of Auschwitz.* New York: Popular Library, 1961.

Kirkpatrick, Ivone, *Mussolini: A Study in Power.* New York: Hawthorn Books, Inc., 1964.

Nathan, Peter, *The Psychology of Fascism.* London: Faber & Faber, Ltd., 1943.

Neumann, Sigmund, *Permanent Revolution,* 2nd ed. New York: Frederick A. Praeger, Inc., 1965.

Orwell, George, *1984.* New York: New American Library (Signet Books), 1950.

Payne, Stanley G., *Falange: A History of Spanish Fascism.* Stanford: Stanford University Press, 1961.

Schapiro, J. Salwyn, *Liberalism and the Challenge of Fascism.* New York: McGraw-Hill Book Company, 1949.

Schweitzer, Arthur, *Big Business in the Third Reich.* Bloomington: Indiana University Press, 1964.

Shirer, William L., *The Rise and Fall of the Third Reich.* New York: Crest Books, 1962.

Viereck, Peter R. E., *Metapolitics: The Roots of the Nazi Mind.* New York: Capricorn Books, 1961.

Warren, Robert Penn, *All the King's Men.* New York: Random House, Inc. (Modern Library), 1953.

Weber, Eugen, *Varieties of Fascism.* Princeton: D. Van Nostrand Co., Inc. (Anvil Books), 1964.

The Democratic Way of Life

Democratic Capitalism

Two conceptions of democracy

In 1948, George Bernard Shaw proposed that, in order to eradicate misunderstanding and confusion about the meaning of democracy, the leading scholars and thinkers of the world be convened and the issue be settled once and for all. Unfortunately, the root of the trouble lies deeper. Disagreements about the concept of democracy are not semantic, but reflect differences of a more fundamental nature.

When a representative of the United States, Britain, or France talks about democracy, he frequently means the very opposite of what a Russian or Chinese communist has in mind when he uses the same term. Thus at the end of World War II, when the United States, Britain, France, and the Soviet Union occupied Germany, one of their chief objectives was the democratization of Germany. At first all four powers wholeheartedly agreed on the objective, but it soon became evident that the Russian concept was entirely different from the Anglo-American-French understanding of democracy.

The Western powers took the view that bringing democracy to Germany meant free elections; a free press; freedom of political association; freedom of religion, thought, and speech; equality before the law; the right to oppose the government; the right to choose one's job; the right to form free trade unions; the right to move freely within one's country, go abroad temporarily, or emigrate permanently; and—in a general way—the right of every person to develop his mental and moral faculties to the fullest possible extent.

Above all, *freedom from fear* is basic in the Western concept of democracy. No society can be called free unless its citizens feel safe from unwarranted intrusion into their affairs by governmental authorities.

This aspect of democracy has been most aptly described in this way: in a free country, a knock at the door early in the morning means the milkman is there; in a totalitarian country, the same knock might mean the secret police are there, come to snatch a man from his home and family and to jail, exile, or execute him without trial or due process of law.

The communist conception of democratizing Germany was entirely different from the Western. In the first place, when the communist speaks of democracy, he has in mind, not government *of* the people, nor government *by* the people, but, as a leading Soviet philosopher puts it, "whether this or that policy is carried out in the interests of the people, in the interests of its overwhelming majority, or in the interests of its minority." (G. F. Aleksandrov, *The Pattern of Soviet Democracy*, 1948.)

Which doctrine reveals whether government is carried out *in the interests of the people?* Marxist-Leninist doctrine. Who interprets the doctrine correctly? The Communist party. Who in the Communist party determines the party line? The Politbureau, a group of a dozen men or so. Who in the Politbureau determines its general policy? The top communist leader who controls the party, army, and police. If the leader loses control over any one of these key elements of power—as happened to Khrushchev in 1964—he is removed and becomes an "un-person."

Communists call the essentials of democracy—freedom of speech, press, and association, equality before the law, and all the other fundamental democratic rights and liberties—*formal* democracy, as compared with the *real* democracy of communism, in which the means of production are owned by the state. In this communist conception, the traditional democratic freedoms assume a new meaning.

Freedom of the press? By all means, provided the newspapers function "in conformity with the interests of the toilers." (Article 125 of the Constitution of the Soviet Union.) Freedom of speech? Completely and unqualifiedly, provided the speaker's words support the communist cause.

Two criteria determine, in communist thinking, whether a government deserves to be called democratic: first, the nature of the economic system it operates and, second, the kind of foreign policy it pursues.

The case of Germany illustrates the importance of the economic system. In the elections of West Germany in 1953, only 2.2 per cent of the vote was for the Communist Party. After being outlawed in West Germany in 1956, the party remained legal in West Berlin. In the West Berlin city elections of 1958, the communists obtained 1.9 per cent of the vote, and in the elections of 1963 only 1.3 per cent. Yet from the communist viewpoint, West Germany is a dictatorship because the *interests* of its population are not determined by the one party that knows what is best for the Germans, the Communist Party. In particular, as long as capitalism exists in Germany there can be no democracy there, the communists say, because capitalism is by definition a dictatorship of the wealthy over the poor, even though a majority of the latter may vote in its favor. From the communist viewpoint, West Germany today could be called a democracy only if the Communist Party supported by 2.2 per cent of the popular vote, ruled Germany, because only the Communist Party could rule in the interests of the German people.

By contrast, in the Soviet view East Germany is a true democracy, because it has abolished capitalism and operates a state-owned and state-run economy. The fact that a communist one-party dictatorship rules East Germany in total dependence on Soviet military force, the fact that this artificial regime has to keep its population imprisoned behind frontiers of barbed wire and concrete walls to prevent mass flights into West Germany, the fact that political prisons and "correctional" labor camps have been set up—all this is irrelevant to the communist proof of democracy.

The second criterion which, in communist political thinking, determines whether a government is democratic is foreign policy. In the view of Chinese communists, for example, Albania is a true democracy, because it sides completely with Red China on foreign policy (and particularly so in the Chinese campaign against the Soviet leadership). For this very reason, Albania is—in Soviet eyes —not a democracy, but a "deviationist, power-mad oligarchy." Should the Albanian communist government tomorrow switch sides and line up with Moscow against Peking, it would become a shining example of democracy in the Soviet judgment, although Albania might continue its internal system of extreme totalitarianism, more Stalinist than that of any other European communist state.

Democracy as a way of life

From the above illustration, the principal characteristics of the Western concept of democracy as a way of life clearly emerge:

(1) Rational empiricism
(2) Emphasis on the individual
(3) Instrumental nature of the state
(4) Voluntarism
(5) The law behind the law
(6) Emphasis on means
(7) Discussion and consent in human relations
(8) Basic equality of all human beings

(1) *Rational empiricism* is perhaps the most important single element in the free way of life. It is based on confidence in reason and in the applicability of reason not only to physical nature but also to human relations. Dogmatists—such as communists or fascists—*know* what the truth is; for communists the concept of class is the ultimate in truth, whereas to fascists race and nation are the last repositories of truth. Since the dogmatist is so sure that he knows, he need not inquire further; his aim is to strengthen what he knows already, and he brands whoever questions his knowledge guilty of intellectual subversion. The psychological and historical relation between dogmatism in philosophy and authoritarianism in politics is clear: absolute certainty of knowledge leads to fanatic enthusiasm in sentiment, which in turn leads to intolerant repression in government.

In contrast, empiricism, first fully developed by John Locke (1632–1704), is based on the idea that *all our knowledge derives from experience.* In this conception, truth (with a small *t*) is tentative, changing, and subject to constant checking and verification.

Since the history of both physical science and social thought is full of truths that turned out to be wholly or partly untrue, the rational empiricist refuses to believe, as the dogmatist believes, that mankind ever has arrived, or ever will arrive, at final answers. One of the most paradoxical puzzles of the progressive enlargement of knowledge is that, as our understanding and knowledge of a particular problem or field increase, the awareness of our ignorance increases at an even faster rate. Many a problem solved—

in the physical as in the social sciences—creates more new problems than existed before the solution.

It takes a lot of knowledge and inquiry to know what one does not know. The man who was first aware of his ignorance was probably, in the evolution of human thought, the first scientist; for, aware of *what* he did *not* know, he set about finding an answer. Without Newton's "solution" of the problem of gravity, there would have been no new world of physical phenomena unlocked by Einstein. Without the "solution" of the problem of government by the democratic method in the modern world, there would have been no Tocqueville discovering in his *Democracy in America* (1835) the new world of political problems created by the democratic solution.

The rational empiricist therefore views truth, in the study of nature as much as of man, as an endless process and considers the knowledge or truth of today no more than a *probability,* to be changed if new facts are brought to light. Bertrand Russell writes in his *Philosophy and Politics* that the genuine liberal says not "This is true," but "I am inclined to think that under present circumstances this opinion is probably the best."

Science and democracy also share the emphasis on procedure, on *how,* not what, answers will emerge as the result of the quest for true knowledge. The main justification of freedom of expression in both science and democracy is broader than the mere satisfaction of individual persons' desires for self-expression and self-fulfilment, defensible as that criterion alone may be. In science, the whole scientific community depends on, and feels entitled to, the free gathering and communication of all possible data and ideas. Similarly the political community of democracy depends for its very existence on the unhindered expression of the widest range of facts and opinions before a decision is made.

Ideally, a legislative body in a democracy acts like a judge who renders his decision after he has listened to all sides presenting arguments that may be material or immaterial, important or unimportant. In fact, the oldest legislative body—the British Parliament—began, and functioned during the first few centuries of its existence, as a High Court: and even now the upper house of Parliament, the House of Lords, serves as Britain's supreme court. To this day, all democratic legislatures follow the British parliamentary procedure originally developed in a framework of judicial proceedings.

What most distinguishes a democratic from a totalitarian legislature is therefore not the final product, what laws are made in either institution, but what procedures are followed. Above all, democratic procedure requires, as do the judicial and scientific procedures, that *all sides of an issue be heard.* From this basic procedural requirement stem the essential democratic liberties of speech, publication, assembly, and association. By contrast, totalitarian "parliamentary" procedure allows only one side, the "party line," to be presented. The truth is already there, before any debate or discussion—*if* there is any debate or discussion, for cheering and applause often take their place.

It is probably no coincidence that rational empiricism and democracy have developed more or less simultaneously in England, France, and the United States. In England, for example, John Locke, the founder of empiricism, is still the most persuasive exponent of political liberalism. In the United States, empiricism has been the dominant school of thought, culminating in John Dewey (1859–1952), whose application of rational empiricism to philosphy and politics has been a lasting contribution to the American liberal heritage.

(2) The *emphasis on the individual* sharply separates liberal democracy from both fascist and communist totalitarianism. In the eyes of the liberal democrat, no social or political institution, be it a local boy-scout group, a party precinct, or the state, has a purpose of its own other than to serve and aid the individual in living a fuller life.

In the totalitarian doctrine, the state is the master, the individual the servant. Hegel, the intellectual ancestor of both fascism and communism, says in his *Philosophy of Law* (1821) that the individual finds his liberty in obeying the state and the fullest realization of his liberty in dying for the state. Only when the individual dies for the state does he lose the last trace of any personal whimsicality and uniqueness and become completely a part of the state.

By contrast, Locke sees the indestructible essence of man in resisting, rather than in blindly obeying, the state. The liberal principles of life, liberty, and the pursuit of happiness are thus the exact opposite of the authoritarian concept of citizenship as duty, discipline, and death for the state.

Thomas Jefferson, one of the greatest liberal individualists of all time, remarked in a letter to Colonel William Stephen Smith, dated November 13, 1787, that "the tree of liberty must be refreshed from time to time with the blood of patriots and tyrants." The Declaration of Independence, too, states that life, liberty, and the pursuit of happiness are among the unalienable rights of man and that "whenever any form of government becomes destructive of these ends, it is the right of the people to alter or to abolish it, and to institute new government, laying its foundations on such principles, and organizing its powers in such form as to them shall seem most likely to effect their safety and happiness."

The historical roots of individualism are three: first, the Jewish concept of one God leads to the idea that all men, as children of God, are brothers to each other. Second, the Christian doctrine of the indestructibility of the human soul maintains that whatever social, economic, and political inequalities may exist, all men possess a spiritual equality and uniqueness that no earthly power can override. Third, in the Stoic view, the one principle of action that governs all things is *to be at one with oneself,* to know oneself, and to act in conformity with one's rational principles and purposes. The true self of man, according to the Stoics, is not his flesh or bones, but the faculty that uses them, his *reason,* the part of man that more than anything else characterizes him as human.

At no time, of course, has this individualism been fully accepted, and the counterforces of totalitarianism always threaten it. At the present time, in particular, the threat of all-destructive atom and hydrogen bomb war leads to a strengthening of anti-individualist attitudes, stressing the idea of "let's close ranks" rather than "let each man decide what is right or wrong and act accordingly."

(3) The *instrumental theory of the state* views the state as a mechanism, to be used for ends higher than itself. Both Plato and Aristotle, the founders of Western political theory, conceived of the state as an organic entity, with a life and purposes of its own, superior to the purposes of the individual. Plato and Aristotle thought of the state as the *highest moral good,* the source of moral values and spiritual enrichment for the individual.

From the Jewish-Christian viewpoint of religion, the instrumentalist theory of the state maintains that the highest values in man's life relate to God and that no earthly law can claim to supersede God's. The function of the state is to maintain peace and order, so that men can pursue their activities devoted to higher ends. From the rational-humanist viewpoint, the instrumentalist theory of the state affirms that the ability of the individual to use his reason in discovering what is right and wrong is the ultimate test of political authority and that the state therefore cannot turn evil into good or wrong into right solely because it possesses the means of physical coercion.

The liberal doctrine stresses society far more than the state; in the classical liberal doctrine—and to a considerable extent today—*society is considered basically self-sufficient,* and *the state is to step in only when the voluntary efforts of society fail.*

The instrumentalist theory of the state thus relegates the state to a supplementary position. As long as individuals can get along without the state, the liberal bias is against the state, even if the state could do the same thing a little better.

In the totalitarian state, the assumption is always in favor of the state, because it is credited with omniscience and omnipotence. Thus the totalitarian state organizes and controls not only the sensitive areas of the economy, education, and religion, but even chess players and Sunday afternoon hikers, because the state does not wish to leave any activity to the free discretion of its citizens.

(4) By contrast, the democratic theory sees in the principle of *voluntarism* the very lifeblood of a free society. Fellowship can most deeply be experienced in small, voluntary groups. Such groups were first formed in seventeenth-century England on a religious basis, and to this day the English-speaking world abounds with thousands and thousands of religious sects that are small in size and entirely voluntary in nature.

Later, the principle of voluntary association was applied in the field of politics (parties), education (private schools), and economics (labor unions and employers' associations). In charity, the Red Cross and local community chests testify to the fact that there is still a strong sentiment for retaining voluntary activity. Even in England, which has national health and social security programs covering every person from the cradle to the grave, there has been a reassertion of the importance of voluntary organization in social welfare, supplementing the governmental programs.

(5) The concept of *the law behind the law* flows directly from the *federal* view of state and society in classical liberalism. Society is conceived as an aggregate of diverse voluntary associations, and the state itself is looked upon as an essentially voluntary body because its authority is derived from the consent of the governed. Whenever authority is organized on a federal basis, there has to be a higher law defining the relationships of the parts among each other and of each part to the whole.

Classical liberalism, therefore, has always adhered to the idea that the relations between state and society, between government and individual, are ultimately defined by a law higher than that of the state. In fact, classical liberal thought in Britain and the United States assumes that the *law is not the product of the state, but precedes it.* The right to life, liberty, property, and the pursuit of happiness is not a gift of the state to the individual, but precedes the state. The function of the state in relation to man's basic rights is to protect and define such rights, not to create them.

In the United States, in particular, the concept of the law behind the law has never been challenged as the foundation of American political thought and experience. The Declaration of Independence specifically recognizes it, and the Constitution has also recognized that no legislative body can make laws without due process or laws that otherwise violate basic principles of reason. The very existence of the United States is, of course, due to the insistence that above the law then ruling, the law of imperial Britain, there was a higher law to which the revolutionary colonists pledged allegiance.

Opponents of democratic government have charged that this concept of a higher law, making government dependent upon the consent of the governed, opens the door to rebellion and anarchy. In his *Two Treatises of Government* (1690), John Locke answers this charge with three counterarguments. First, Locke concedes that the democratic theory of government admits of the possibility of rebellion, but he denies that it does so more than any other theory. When the people are made miserable, they will rebel under any form of government; let the governors be "sacred and divine, descended or authorized from heaven, give them out for whom or what you please, the same will happen." Second, Locke says, men do not rebel "upon every little mismanagement in public affairs," or "for light and transient causes," as the Declaration of Independence puts it. Third, and here Locke moves from the defensive to the offensive, government by consent coupled with the right of the people to rebel is "the best fence against rebellion."

Locke could only guess in 1690 whether his arguments would be proved by experience, because democracy was then still a thing of the future. Yet experience has proved him perspicacious. The British and American systems of government, based on the Lockean-Jeffersonian admission of the people's right to rebel against oppression, have proved themselves the stablest and most successful political systems the world has ever seen, and the same may be said of countries (smaller in size but equally great in the glory of freedom) like Holland, Switzerland, and the Scandinavian nations. By contrast, where the higher law has been rejected in the name of law and order, the political results have been blood purges, conspiracies, plot and counterplots, and violent swings from one extreme to another—the political record, specifically, of communist and fascist dictatorships.

(6) The *emphasis on means* in democratic life is based on the realization that ends lead no existence apart from means but are continually shaped by them. The totalitarian makes a clear-cut distinction between means and ends. In his dogmatic way of thinking he is absolutely certain of what the ends are, and possessing this certainty, he pays little attention to the nature of the means. Thus, the communists believe in universal brotherhood and cooperation as their officially professed end, yet they fail to realize that the means employed in bringing about communism—secret police, "correctional" labor camps, thought control, denunciations, repression of dissent—increase hatred and misery rather than diminish it.

One of the main difficulties in separating means from ends is the fact that *in most practical situations a means is simultaneously an end.* Thus, education is for some an end in itself; for others, it is but a means to an end—to a degree, for example. Yet, a degree may again be only a means to the end of a happier, fuller life, or a better job. Again, a better job is not necessarily an end in itself; it is likely to be a means to some higher end, such as expressing a sense of craftsmanship or serving society.

The central position of means in free societies is well entrenched in their living experience. Magna Carta, habeas corpus, and jury trial, to mention but a few roots of liberty in the English-speaking world, are originally all procedural devices, means; and the history of liberty may aptly be described as a history of procedure. In representative assemblies too, it is not the legislative product that distinguishes a democratic body from a nondemocratic one, but the difference of procedure. In the one case, procedure aims at the fullest and fairest guarantee of the right of the minority to be heard; in the other, procedure aims at silencing minorities and bringing about the loudest possible volume of cheers for the dictator.

At present, the danger in democratic societies lies in the possible waning of this awareness that differences over means are the heart of the difference between democracy and totalitarianism. In fighting a totalitarian system like fascism or communism there is a natural tendency to imitate their means, and because the tendency is natural, special efforts must be made to guard against it. In defending democracy, some persons are willing to use means that are bound to destroy the very thing they seek to defend.

(7) *Discussion and consent* are the means by which a democratic society typically settles divergent viewpoints and interests. It is the democratic view that, since no one possesses absolute truth, both sides to an argument may make a contribution to the best possible answer and that the only way to get that answer is to marshal all the available evidence.

The independent voter in a democracy typifies the person who is not willing to commit himself unconditionally to one party, either because he knows too little or (less often) too much about politics, or simply because—whatever his level of political information—he does not expect much from government in any case. In a totalitarian state there are no independent voters, only followers or enemies of the prevailing manner of thought. The importance of the independent voter can be clearly seen in many elections. In 1952 the Republican party selected General Eisenhower over Senator Taft as its presidential candidate, mainly for his wider appeal to independent voters. In contrast, Goldwater's defeat in the presidential election of 1964 was attributed by many to his relatively weak appeal to independent voters.

In the theory of the democratic society, governments derive "their just powers from the consent of the governed" (Declaration of Independence), because the state has no reason for existence other than to serve the people. If the state becomes oppressive and unmindful of the rights of the people, then the democratic theory, as was pointed out earlier, upholds not only the right but the duty to revolt against such government.

This right to rebel can be claimed only where the methods of discussion and consent are blocked by tyrannical despotism; where the channels of discussion are open, as in a democratic state and society, no democrat would claim the right of rebellion against the state.

The communist who today claims the right to revolution as a general democratic privilege utterly distorts this concept for his own purposes. From the democratic viewpoint, *the democrat has the moral right, and duty, to rebel against the totalitarian system, but the totalitarian possesses no such right against the democratic system.*

(8) The *basic equality of all human beings* is a point of democratic doctrine and policy that is frequently misunderstood. No

democrat has ever said that all men are identical but only that in basic respects they are equal. The very uniqueness of each and every person creates a kind of equality that is important in the democratic outlook. From the religious viewpoint of the Jewish-Christian tradition, all men are equal before God; God's challenge to every human being is the same, although men's response to it varies enormously. From the rationalist-humanistic viewpoint, all men share, over and above differences of race, sex, religion, nationality, and class, one common trait: the ability to reason. In this sense, all men are citizens of the world rather than of a particular, distinctive group, and their basic equality derives from what they have in common rather than from what separates them.

The Declaration of Independence makes it perfectly plain that all men are created equal, in the sense that they have certain unalienable rights, such as life, liberty, and the pursuit of happiness. The equality that men receive at birth, according to democratic theory, is thus not in the nature of an outright gift or grant but a loan, as it were, an *opportunity*, a *challenge*. The Jeffersonian phrase "pursuit of happiness" admirably expresses the thought that man does not have the right to happiness, in the sense that the state or his family or friends owe him happiness, but only in the sense that he has the right to *pursue* happiness, unhindered by unreasonable obstacles.

However, equality does not mean, as Plato charged it meant, "dispensing a kind of equality to equals and unequals alike." The contrary is true, of the ideal democracy at least. In practice it is not easy to ascertain when equals are still equal and when they become unequal. Thus, to take an illustration: the most common interpretation of democratic equality is "equality of opportunity." A grave difficulty arises immediately. If all men were endowed with the same talents and abilities, and were born into the same homes, and received the same schooling, giving all an equal opportunity would be a fair solution. Yet people differ in native talent and even more in background and education.

Legislative action cannot equalize the I.Q. of the population, and there will always be differences of ability, drive, and motivation, but laws can make equality of opportunity more real by trying to equalize conditions before the race starts: increased inheritance taxes lessen the impact of inherited wealth, progressive income taxes favor the lower-income groups, and free education (from nursery school to university) benefits the indigent more than the affluent. In other words, equality of opportunity, if it allows ability alone to operate, quickly establishes and perpetuates inequality. *Need, too,* must be considered; it adds to the principle of efficiency that of happiness.

Conditions of political democracy

Of all the aspects of democracy, the political has top priority. Although political democracy is not identical with democracy as a way of life, the instinct of those who tend to identify the two is not unsound. Experience has shown that political democracy, if practiced over any length of time, leads to the extension of the democratic principle to social, economic, and international problems. So far, there is less evidence that social or economic democracy leads to political democracy. Precisely because political democracy merely defines "the rules of the game," it is more far-reaching than social or economic democracy, which is concerned with one particular substantive area of problems.

The first characteristic of democratic government is the maintenance of a political climate in which *political liberty* can thrive. In every society, those who uphold the orthodox views may freely express them. *Political liberty begins at the point where unorthodox opinions may be freely presented, without legal, social, or economic penalties.*

The political liberty of a society can best be measured by the *margin of unorthodoxy* that is *tolerated* in that society. This yardstick enables us to go beyond the crude classification of dictatorship and democracy, which is valid only on a general level. Examining first the totalitarian states by this criterion, we find the least margin of unorthodoxy in Red China today, in the Soviet Union under Stalin, and in Nazi Germany under Hitler; a much wider margin in the Soviet Union under Khrushchev and Brezhnev or in Yugoslavia under "national communism," and the relatively largest unorthodoxy in some traditional Asian, African, and Latin American dictatorships. By comparison with the ideological dictatorships of either the fascist or communist type, the nonideological military dictatorships, such as were set up in Algeria (1965), Ghana (1966), Indonesia (1966), or Nigeria (1966) tolerate a considerable degree of unorthodoxy so long as the authority of the military rulers is not challenged.

Measuring the margin of unorthodoxy in democratic societies,

Reprinted by permission from *Saturday Review.*

"In my opinion, a yes-man is so much dead wood in an organization. Right, Weatherfield?"

we find Britain, France, Scandinavia, Holland, Australia, and New Zealand on the top of the list, while the United States trails somewhat behind. Needless to say, the positions are never fixed, and the range of unorthodoxy constantly changes; by general agreement there is more uniformity and conformity of thought in the United States today than thirty years ago, and there may be less again ten years hence.

The *common agreement on fundamentals* is a second condition indispensable to the successful working of political democracy. The most important agreement, and the one no written constitution can by itself guarantee, is the common desire to operate a democratic system. Where there is no written constitution, as in Great Britain, there is no protection of political minorities or individual nonconformists other than the decency and restraint of the majority. Legally, the British Parliament could outlaw the opposition and introduce a totalitarian state overnight. But the government is not doing that because it is a party to an unwritten agreement to abide by democratic principles.

By the same token, written constitutions are not necessarily a protection. Fascism developed in Italy, Germany, Japan, and Argentina despite written constitutions, and the existence of a democratic constitution in Czechoslovakia after World War II did not restrain the communists from distorting and destroying it.

Even in the United States, the written Constitution is, in itself, no last line of defense of political democracy. There have been times when either the Congress, the executive, or the judiciary—or all three—have shown little respect for political liberties; and there have been other times when the spirit as well as the letter of the Constitution have been faithfully respected. Throughout these ups and downs of American democracy, the Constitution remained the same; the variable was the greater or lesser determination of the people to defend liberty at all cost.

The lesson of all this historical experience is simple: *the strength of a democracy is never greater than the will of the people to uphold it.*

Where agreement on fundamentals is lacking, political democracy suffers from stresses and strains that may well become fatal. An irreconcilable division on fundamentals between major parties may lead to civil war or dictatorship. Such a situation existed in the United States in 1860 when there was no agreement on the basic issue of slavery. In 1930, the German political system was a democracy as far as the paper constitution was concerned; but two-thirds of the electorate wanted to set up totalitarian dictatorships of either the communist or fascist type, and the fascists finally won out in 1933. Obviously, no constitution, however perfect on paper, can save a democracy if the antidemocrats outvote the democrats two to one. A democratic constitution *assumes,* but *cannot* in itself *create,* the will to maintain democratic institutions.

The Fourth Republic of France (1945–1958) provides another example. During its existence, the forces favoring or tolerating republican government based on an omnipotent parliament mustered just a little over one-half of the electorate. On the extreme Left, the communists, dedicated to the principle of totalitarian dictatorship, were supported by one-fourth of the electorate. On the extreme Right, supported by about one-fifth of the electorate, there were groups that either sought to set up a new republican regime based on a strong executive or that aimed at doing away with democracy altogether.

Such disagreement on fundamentals could not work, and it did not work. The Fourth Republic ended in 1958, and the new Fifth Republic was centered on the personality of Charles de Gaulle. A new equilibrium of forces has emerged; the communists, with about 20 per cent of the popular vote, remain the only force opposed to any form of democratic government. Eighty per cent of the popular vote (Socialists, Catholic Democrats, Radicals, Gaullists, and Independents) are united on the formula that French republicanism can be saved only by a strong executive as proposed by de Gaulle. Time will tell whether the Fifth Republic reflects a new French agreement on fundamentals or whether it is but another makeshift solution covering up the absence of such basic agreement.

Is agreement on economic policy a necessary condition of political democracy? A generation ago, this question was answered more often in the affirmative than today. Conservatives frequently expressed apprehension lest the new socialist principle of public ownership undermine the whole fabric of institutions. In contrast, socialists frequently expressed the fear that conservatives would be unwilling to adhere loyally to democratic principles if socialist parties were given a chance to change the economic organization of society by constitutional means and that the propertied classes would put property above constitutional democracy.

Experience has shown that both sides have been wrong. In theory, the disagreement on basic economic policy between conservatives and socialists looked bigger than it has worked out in practice. The conservatives have abandoned much of their old economic laissez-faire position, and the socialists, having considerably modified their economic philosophy, are now satisfied with a program consisting of welfare state legislation and the socialization of only a few basic industries.

The very nature of the democratic process makes the choice of zero versus 100 per cent virtually impossible. Since elections are generally decided by the floating independent vote, which by definition is middle-of-the-road, no extreme program has a chance of being accepted.

Government by more than one party expresses the democratic principle, borrowed from the law, that "the other side must also be heard" (*audiatur et altera pars*). The dogmatic, totalitarian viewpoint holds that there is only one Truth, and from that position to the one-party state there is a direct line. The democratic viewpoint holds that different men perceive different aspects of truth, mainly in the light of their lives and experiences and that there will be at least two sides to any major question.

The communists say that the two-party system is a product of capitalism; that the opposing interests of capitalists and workers must be represented in opposing parties; and that, since capitalism has been abolished in the Soviet Union, there is no need for an opposition party to the Communist party.

This line of argument has serious flaws. In the first place, it wrongly assumes that property is the only line of political party. In Europe, party loyalties are frequently based on religious or ideological loyalties; in the United States the regional factor is often important. Also, the communist argument exaggerates the impact of property on party. Only about 60 per cent of the British working class vote Labor, and in the United States the correlation between income and vote is equally indecisive. If income were the only decisive factor, political prediction would be much easier than professional pollsters have found it to be.

Moreover, if inequalities of income are important politically, the need for a multi-party system is more urgent in the Soviet Union than in the capitalist countries, because the inequality between managers and workers, and between skilled and unskilled workers, is much greater in the Soviet Union than in capitalist countries. There is little doubt that if freedom of association were suddenly introduced in the Soviet Union, parties would be formed for the purpose of asserting the claims of peasants, the unskilled workers, and the various nationalities such as the Ukrainians and White Russians.

Even if capitalism could be abolished in the most democratic manner, there would still be need for more than one party. Assuming a classless society in which all productive property is owned publicly and in which incomes too are relatively equal, there would still be questions of vital concern to the community, questions admitting more than one answer. For example, every state, whether democratic, fascist, communist, socialist, or capitalist, has to decide each year what portion of its national product is to be consumed and what portion is to be saved and invested. Another typical question that every community has to face is how much to spend on social welfare and which groups should be favored—the claims of the old compete with those of the young, education may compete with health. The answer to such questions cannot be found in the form of economic organization.

After all, even when there was no capitalism in the modern sense, there was a multitude of parties. When the suffrage was limited to the propertied classes, as it was in most countries until about one hundred years ago, the existing parties were divided not on the basis of rich and poor, but along other lines—town versus country, secularism versus clericalism, states' rights versus centralism, free trade versus protection, republicanism versus monarchism, slavery versus freedom, to name but a few.

Psychological roots of democracy

Man has lived for about a quarter million years on this planet, yet he has had some knowledge of democratic ideas and practice for only about twenty-five hundred years. Even today, democracy as a way of life exists only in a relatively small portion of the world. Democracy, then, can scarcely be called "natural." On the contrary, the democratic way of life is the most difficult of all; it does not emerge spontaneously and by accident but is the result of deliberate thought, seeking to correct what is natural, all too natural, in human behavior.

Just as the behavior of the child is more natural than that of the adult, the behavior of the authoritarian is more natural than that of the democratic personality. The process of growth and development from childhood to maturity is natural only in the biological and physiological sense, not in the social and cultural sense. Socially and culturally, the transformation of the child into the mature adult demands much forethought, planning, and hard work.

Politically, the authoritarian personality is fundamentally the grownup who has never become mature, the ostensible adult who still accepts the dependency and security characteristic of childhood. By contrast, the democratic personality is the emotionally and intellectually mature adult, the person able to stand on his own feet and shape his life for himself. The mature adult does not need security provided by an external authority; he possesses security within himself. The price of this emotional and intellectual independence is high, since to attain it a person must face responsibilities and make decisions by himself, without being able to blame anyone afterwards if his decisions are wrong.

There is no growing up without making mistakes, and the overprotected child *can* make no mistakes—his father will see to that! Similarly, in a dictatorship, the system prevents the individual from experimenting and acting on his own, so that (in theory, at least) he always does the right thing. By contrast, the process of growing up, of moving away from supervision to personal responsibility, implies the possibility of choosing the wrong thing, of making mistakes; in this sense, *democracy may be defined as the right to make mistakes.*

Implied in this concept is not the desirability of erring for the sake of erring, but the recognition that freedom implies choice between alternatives and that no one can grow to maturity, no one can be truly democratic, without learning to make choices and without occasionally making the wrong choice.

The 200 per cent American defenders of democracy who want to make it a crime for anyone ever to think or act wrongly are trying to have a democracy with authoritarian personalities, people who only think and do what authority has allowed them to think or do.

The attitude of the democratic personality toward the leader is markedly different from that of the authoritarian personality. The latter regards the leader of the nation with a mixture of loyalty and reverence resembling the emotions he first felt toward his parents, particularly his father. The traditional reference to a chief of the state as the "father of the country" is the linguistic expression of a profound psychological tie; the adult in such a society has really never outgrown the father-child relationship.

By contrast, *the democratic personality puts more emphasis on the group than on the leader*. This feeling goes back to that of the rebellious child, who joins with his brothers in a league of equals to destroy the authority of their father. "Liberty, equality, fraternity," the three ideals of the French revolution, express the attitude of the democratic personality against authority.

For this reason, democracies frequently act with deep suspicion whenever a great leader appears. Churchill was opposed in England before World War II because he was "too clever," not average enough, and therefore potentially dangerous. Clemenceau was removed from French public life after World War I because he was too much of a leader. Many American voters who cast their ballot

Reprinted by permission from *Saturday Review.*

"I'll say this about the Horde; it gives you a great feeling of belonging."

against Franklin D. Roosevelt were motivated by the unconscious fear that he was not Mr. Average American. Lincoln attracted the same kind of hatred, although much of it was rationalized in political and ideological arguments.

It is for this reason, too, that impersonal factors like constitutions, charters, and congresses play such an important part in democratic states; leaders come and go, but the institutions continue unimpaired. In contrast, the authoritarian personality thinks in terms of allegiance to a particular person. In Spain and Latin America, for example, political loyalty revolves around the phenomenon of *personalismo;* the political attachment and allegiance are to one particular person rather than to a party, program or constitution. Even democratic parties in such countries usually are split into various factions, each led by one man, to whom his group owes allegiance. But this is even more true, of course, of antidemocratic movements: thus we speak of Hitlerism, Peronism, Stalinism, but not of Churchillism, Eisenhowerism, or Johnsonism.

The formation of the democratic personality is first determined in the *family*. It was Sigmund Freud who emphasized that the first five years are probably the most decisive years of life as far as basic attitudes are concerned. In the early years of life, the home is school, church, and government all rolled into one. In some societies, parents are accorded absolute power over their children; in such societies the family resembles a miniature absolutist state, in which the fiat of the absolute ruler, the father, is the law.

In contrast, democratic family relations give the child the first experience of democracy. In the United States, the family unit resembles, in most cases, a small parliament in which every member feels free to have his say when family decisions are in the making. Children do not expect to be told what to do, what line of work to pick, or whom to marry. Far from being the absolute ruler of an authoritarian family, the American father has often learned to be satisfied if he has a chance to be heard. His hope is not of being obeyed *because* he is the father, but rather (if we can take the cartoonist's word for it, at least) of getting a fair hearing *although* he is the father.

One of Germany's leading child psychologists, Kurt Lewin, came to the United States in 1934 and stayed here until his death in 1945. In 1936 he wrote a paper on "Some Social-Psychological Differences between the United States and Germany" (reprinted in his *Resolving Social Conflicts*, 1948), in which he makes the following observations:

"To one who comes from Germany, the degree of freedom and independence of children and adolescents in the United States is very impressive. Especially the lack of servility of the young child toward adults or of the student toward his professor is striking. The adults, too, treat the child on a much more equal footing, whereas in Germany it seems to be the natural right of the adult to rule and the duty of the child to obey. The natural relation of adult and child in the United States is not considered that of a superior (*Herr*) to a subordinate (*Untergebener*) but that of two individuals with the same right in principle. The parents seem to treat the children with more respect."

The *school* is, next to the home, perhaps the most important single source of a child's basic psychological patterns. What children formally learn in school is much less important than what they pick up unconsciously from the way in which the school operates. Authoritarian societies consider the school as little more than a phase of premilitary training, in which the function of the teacher is to inculcate habits of order and discipline.

In a democratic school system, the main function of the teacher is to help the child develop his own personality and to help him learn *how* to think rather than what to think. The permissive attitude of the democratic school is premised on the assumption that people will generally choose the right way if given the proper help and guidance, and that trust will beget trust.

Also, most democratic societies do not hesitate to run the schools on a coeducational basis and to employ women on a large scale. By contrast, authoritarian schools often separate boys from girls to make sure that the boys grow into tough men rather than soft sissies; also, men are generally preferred as teachers, mainly because only men can play the necessary role of father-substitute.

The democratic nature of the school is also determined by the relation of teacher and parent and that of teacher and political authority. In student government, the students are given the opportunity to learn formal self-government and to make their rules of self-government without interference from the outside. In many colleges, much of the discipline, from exams ("honor system") to staying-out hours, is regulated and enforced by the students themselves. This type of experience teaches a student more about democracy than a reading assignment about the theory and ideals of democracy.

Moreover, the existence of private schools in democracies is a further expression of freedom in education. In totalitarian societies, the state generally abolishes all private schools since there is only one pattern that is right and the state knows what it is and has the means to enforce it. In democratic societies, many important educational innovations have been given their first trial in small experimental schools; if successful, such advances then spread to the public school system.

The attitude toward women in society sharply differentiates the democratic from the authoritarian personality. The authoritarian generally desires to keep women in their place; his scale of values is oriented strongly toward masculine traits and preferences. Many legal codes officially recognize the superior position of the man by declaring him to be the head of the family and by subordinating his wife to him in matters of property and other basic issues.

Feminism is not only the creed of rebellious women who wish to assert their equality, but also the feeling of democratically inclined men who resent the treatment of women as inferiors just as they resent the treatment of any other human being as an inferior on the basis of race, for example, or religion, or nationality. As in other cases of intolerance and inequality, the democratic personality is keenly aware of the fact that *unfair and arrogant treatment is harmful not only to the person so treated, but also to the person who metes it out.* This aspect of racial segregation was recognized by the Supreme Court when it declared racial segregation in pub-

Drawing by Peter Arno; © 1949 The New Yorker Magazine, Inc.

"I hate *everybody*, regardless of race, creed, or place of national origin."

lic schools unconstitutional in its historic decision of May 17, 1954.

The *range of affection* determines the degree to which a person matures, to which he can be called democratic. The child first knows only himself. Gradually he discovers a world outside of his own body and desires—his mother, father, brothers and sisters, neighbors, and classmates. The degree of his maturation and adulthood is in direct proportion to his capacity to enlarge his horizon and make friends with all kinds of persons.

The immature personality stops early in this process; he can only identify with his own group (the in-group) and considers others (the out-group) as dangerous and hostile. This group-egotism may include the family only, or it may extend to social class, political party, or nation. In all these cases, the attachment to the in-group is frequently more an *expression of hatred for the outsider than of affection for the insider.*

By contrast, the democratic personality is always aware of his own imperfections and those of his social class, party, or nation, and this realization makes him tolerant of different people, different races, different religions, different ideas. His capacity to cooperate and love is not a rigid fixation on one particular object, but the expression of a *general capacity to cooperate, to share, to love.*

Love that is exclusively directed at one person or group is usually not love, but either masochistic self-abasement or sadistic domination. Love and cooperation in the democratic sense imply freedom, equality, and integrity, not exclusiveness and domination. When St. Paul said that there was "neither Jew nor Greek, neither bond nor free," he gave expression to a conception of human relations in which there was no in-group and no out-group, but only one humanity.

The strength of the democratic personality is proportionate to the strength of democratic institutions and practices in the society in which he lives. To the extent that persons are given leeway to develop and to act freely and spontaneously, they will experience less frustration and hatred.

Aggression is generally the *result of frustration,* although the causal relationship does not always appear immediately. Many persons are able to repress temporarily their aggressive impulses following frustration; such delays and repressions do not destroy the aggressive reaction, but merely postpone, exaggerate, and distort it. The democratic society minimizes frustration by removing its sources as much as possible. Thus, in a democracy, everybody has the right to criticize any political leader, the government, or any idea.

This *freedom of expression serves as a safety valve*, preventing resentment and hostility from being repressed and transformed into aggression and hatred. As everybody knows from his own experience, once he has told somebody off he feels better. Freedom of expression is a psychological catharsis, in which the soul keeps itself from accumulating resentment and hostility.

In contrast, a totalitarian society seems to be happy and united, and apparently there is no dissent. Yet this artificial calm builds up tremendous resources of hatred, which can often be expressed only in gossip, jokes, and other informal channels of expression. But when the lid is off, the accumulated frustrations break out into open violence.

The artificiality of the calm and uniformity in totalitarian regimes is best demonstrated by the periodic purges and blood baths that are characteristic of communist and fascist states. Thus, Lavrenti Beria, one of the top three rulers in Russia, was executed in December, 1953, for a long assortment of crimes he allegedly committed or planned to commit. A regime in which treason can reach so high up that the man in charge of the nation's secret police and internal security is killed as a spy in the pay of Wall Street is scarcely a model of internal strength.

Finally, totalitarians invariably misjudge the apparent dissensions and disagreements in a democratic society. It is precisely because such disagreements are openly expressed that there is so little smouldering hatred and hostility within a free society, and it can act unitedly and strongly in the hour of need.

It is generally agreed that the democratic personality is more tolerant, more cooperative, friendlier, and fairer than the authoritarian personality. But the question is often raised whether these human gains are not paid for by the loss of efficiency. Controlled experiments with children and adults have shown that the efficiency of a group can be raised by substituting a democratic group decision for a lecture, request, or command from the top. In industry, management is increasingly using democratic group discussions to raise efficiency. This is still a new field of experimentation, but there is certainly no evidence that the autocratically run group produces more efficient individuals.

In the field of education too, schools and colleges are trying to get away from the lecture method, by which the teacher tells the student that such and such is so and so—period. The advantage of the discussion method over lecturing is that the teacher no longer functions as a little god issuing the law from Mount Sinai but is more in the nature of an umpire who sees to it that the rules of debate are properly observed; the discussion itself has to be carried forward by the students, and whatever conclusions they arrive at are the product of their own group thinking, not of superior authority. Discussion, of course, assumes equality; superiors do not discuss with inferiors, but tell them what to do.

The *feeling of being wanted is one of the strongest driving forces of action and allegiance;* nothing can produce that feeling better than the democratic process of consultation, discussion, and

Reprinted by permission from *Saturday Review.*

"Is that the truth, Hopgood? You really like me for myself?"

free exchange of ideas. With love, greater things can be accomplished than with hatred. This old religious truth is also borne out by psychology, politics, and history.

In the last two hundred years, not a single major war has been won by the apostles of hatred and strife over the more democratic side, which would indicate that totalitarian efficiency fails even in the one field where it is supposed to be highest: war. The reason for such failure may be the tendency of the totalitarian personality to close his mind to new and changing circumstances, to adhere rigidly to fixed dogma, to aim at unrealistic objectives, or to pursue possible objectives with impossible means. Self-criticism is one of the most crucial correctives in doing any job; and although everybody is somewhat sensitive to criticism, the democratic personality can tolerate more of it than can the totalitarian.

Individual freedom and national security

The best introduction into the problem of individual liberty is still John Stuart Mill's essay *On Liberty* (1859). Mill wrote his essay at a comparatively civilized time, when there seemed to be little need for it. Yet he foresaw that illiberal forces would gain in influence, and he hoped that men would then turn to *On Liberty.* Though Mill modestly disclaimed originality other than that which "every thoughtful mind gives to its own mode of conceiving and expressing truths which are common property," the essay has grown in stature as time goes on, because many of Mill's predictions have come true, and much that he has to say is still valid today.

As Alexis de Tocqueville had done in his *Democracy in America* (1835–1840), Mill attacked the illusion that evolution of government from tyranny to democracy necessarily solves the problem of individual liberty. *Tyranny can be exercised by one, by a few, or by the majority,* and the latter is potentially the worst of all, since it commands the widest moral support, whereas oppression by one or a few is mainly physical. The power of public opinion in a democracy often exercises more restraint and repression against dissidents than a dictator exercises by physical means in a dictatorship. Protection against political tyranny is therefore not enough. It must be supplemented by protection against social tyranny, which leaves fewer means of escape, "penetrating much more deeply into the details of life, and enslaving the soul itself."

Mill sees that the natural tendency of man is not to be tolerant and open-minded, but to impose his views on others, and that lack of power is frequently the major cause of tolerating dissent. It makes little difference how numerous the dissenting minority is: "If all mankind minus one, were of one opinion, and only one person were of the contrary opinion, mankind would be no more justified in silencing that one person, than he, if he had the power, would be justified in silencing mankind."

Silencing an unorthodox opinion is not only wrong but harmful, because it robs others of an opportunity to get acquainted with ideas that may be true or partly true. "All silencing of discussion," Mill argues, "is an assumption of infallibility." Therefore Mill states that, unless *absolute freedom of opinion*—scientific, moral, political, and theological—is guaranteed, a society is not completely free.

No individual can grasp more than a fragment or portion of truth; no society can speak for all mankind; finally, whole eras are no more infallible than individuals. History is full of opinions held by one age as the last truth, only to be considered false and absurd by subsequent ages.

Just as liberty is not complete unless it is absolute, so discussion must be completely unhampered, and free discussion must not be ruled out when "pushed to an extreme," because the arguments for a case are not good unless they are good for an extreme case. Mill is aware of the argument that some opinions are so useful and important to society that they must be excluded from public discussion and criticism, but he answers that the "usefulness of an opinion is itself a matter of opinion."

Mill does not accept the "pleasant falsehood" that truth inevitably triumphs over persecution; history "teems with instances of truth put down by persecution." In the history of religion in the West, for example, there are numerous sects and churches that have been successfully suppressed, and Mill therefore concludes that "persecution has always succeeded, save where the heretics were too strong a party to be effectually persecuted."

Moreover, *the greatest harm of persecution is inflicted not on those who dissent from established beliefs, but on those who do not,* because the mental development of the latter is stifled by the fear of expressing unorthodox or dissenting views. In an atmosphere of cowed uniformity there may be a few exceptional great thinkers but not an intellectually active people. "No one can be a great thinker who does not recognize that as a thinker it is his first duty to follow his intellect to whatever conclusions it may lead."

Moreover, dogmatism robs truth of its vigor and vitality and is more likely to destroy truth than keep it alive. For its own health, truth needs to be "fully, frequently, and fearlessly" discussed. If possible at all, the opposing opinion should be expressed by someone who really believes in it. Only in the constant process of being challenged can truth grow and remain healthy. "Both teachers and learners go to sleep at their posts, as soon as there is no enemy in the field."

The necessity of the fullest expression of opinion may be based on three grounds. First, the silenced opinion may be *wholly true,* in which case its suppression is wholly unjustified. Second, the silenced opinion may be *partly true and partly false,* as most opinions tend to be, in which case "it is only by the collision of adverse opinions that the remainder of the truth has any chance of being supplied." Third, even if the silenced opinion be *wholly erroneous,* it should not be suppressed, because its very challenge of truth prevents the latter from degenerating into dogma and prejudice.

The purpose of individual liberty is personal self-development. It is the privilege of every person to interpret experience in his own way, and his moral faculties can only be brought into play when he is obliged to choose between alternatives. A person who merely follows custom and tradition makes no choice, nor does he who lets others make his decisions for him. *Different persons should be permitted to lead different lives;* the principle of liberty thus inevitably implies that of variety and diversity.

It should be noted that the progress of industrial civilization does not make it easier for men and women to remain individual personalities, because increasingly "they now read the same things, listen to the same things, go to the same places, have their hopes and fears directed to the same objects, have the same rights and liberties, and the same means of asserting them." People who do the same things tend to think the same thoughts.

This standardization has progressed enormously in the last hundred years; the radio, television, and movie industries have added new dimensions of prefabricated opinion. The number of daily papers is steadily declining in Britain and the United States (there are hundreds of cities and towns with only one daily paper) and the number of newspaper readers is constantly increasing, so that more and more people are reading fewer and fewer papers. Moreover, standardization has now reached the point where not only is identical news coverage published in thousands of papers, but even editorials, purporting to present the viewpoint of the local paper's editor, are actually "canned," prepared in a New York or Washington agency and then "farmed out" all over the country.

Mill reminds those who are willing to repress individual liberty for the sake of a strong state that the worth of a state is no more than the worth of its individual citizens. When the state "dwarfs" its men and reduces them to docile instruments, it will find that "with small men no great things can really be accomplished."

Mill is still the best guide to liberty based on reason. Yet *On Liberty* is a century old, and it cannot be expected to give clear-cut answers to the problems that baffle us today. In particular, Mill did not deal with two problems that did not exist in his day but are of paramount importance today.

First, Mill always assumed that in every debate both sides were after the truth and were honestly searching for it. Today we face a situation where totalitarian movements like fascism or communism disseminate statements which not only are false, but which the communist or fascist propagandists *know to be false*—for example, the communist stories of American germ warfare in Korea.

The second problem that did not exist in Mill's day and that has tremendous practical importance today is the phenomenon of a *revolutionary, subversive party directed from abroad.* In Mill's day, apart from a few mild anarchists or theoretical revolutionaries whom no one took seriously, there was no organized movement of a revolutionary, subversive nature. Today, revolutionary subversion is organized in powerful movements, movements that are particularly difficult to cope with because they are not homegrown but instruments of a foreign power, whose purposes alone they serve.

In the United States, the curbing of revolutionary movements by legal means is based on the Smith Act of 1940, Section 2 of which makes it unlawful for any person knowingly or willfully to "advocate, abet, advise, or teach the duty, necessity, desirability, or propriety of overthrowing or destroying any government in the United States by force or violence, or by the assassination of any officer of such government." In 1948, eleven top communist leaders were indicted for violation of the Smith Act. The trial, one of the most important political trials in American history, lasted over nine months and required almost 16,000 pages to record. Finally, the Supreme Court took up the case and decided against the communist leaders on June 4, 1951.

The main constitutional issue involved was *whether the Smith Act violated the First and Fifth Amendments.* The First Amendment provides that Congress shall make no law "abridging the freedom of speech, or of the press; or the right of the people peaceably to assemble, and to petition the government for a redress of grievances." Under the Fifth Amendment, no person "shall be deprived of life, liberty, or property, without due process of law." By a majority of six to two, the Supreme Court held the Smith Act constitutional.

A central concept in the conflicting opinions of the Court was the *clear and present danger* doctrine, as expressed by Mr. Justice Holmes in 1919: "The question in every case," Holmes wrote, "is whether the words used are used in such circumstances and are of such a nature as to create a clear and present danger that they will bring about the substantive evils that Congress has a right to prevent. It is a question of proximity and degree."

Writing for the majority in the case of the communists, Chief Justice Vinson declared that the communists *did* create a clear and present danger in recommending the overthrow of the government by force and violence. Chief Justice Vinson even went beyond the "clear and present danger" doctrine by accepting a narrower concept of *probable danger:* "In each case [courts] must ask whether the gravity of the 'evil,' discounted by its improbability, justifies such invasion of free speech as is necessary to avoid the danger." In a concurring opinion, Mr. Justice Jackson denied that the clear-and-present-danger doctrine could properly be applied to the case; otherwise communists plotting a revolutionary conspiracy would be protected during its period of incubation, and the Government could move "only after imminent action is manifest, when it would, of course, be too late."

In his dissenting opinion, Mr. Justice Black emphasized that the communist leaders were not charged with any nonverbal acts designed to overthrow the government and that the outlawry of verbal expressions of revolution constitutes a drastic qualification or complete repudiation of the clear-and-present-danger doctrine. Mr. Justice Douglas, in his dissenting opinion, concedes that "the freedom to speak is not absolute," and accepts, in general, the Holmesian principle. However, whereas Holmes left the meaning of his principle rather vague, Douglas quotes approvingly Mr. Justice Brandeis in *Whitney* v. *California* (1927) that "no danger flowing from speech can be deemed clear and present, unless the incidence of the evil apprehended is so imminent that it may befall before there is opportunity for full discussion." Following Brandeis, Douglas argues that free speech *has* destroyed communism in the United States and that it is "inconceivable" that advocates of communist revolution in the United States would have any success. Under the Brandeis doctrine, it might be one thing to preach publicly against conscription when there is ample opportunity to rebut pacifism in public debate and quite another thing to preach pacifist doctrine outside a draft board, when such opportunity to rebut does not exist.

The Brandeis doctrine was expressed much earlier by Thomas Jefferson, who was willing to "tolerate error so long as reason is left free to combat it." In his first inaugural address Jefferson said that "having banished from our land that religious intolerance under which mankind so long bled and suffered, we have yet gained little if we countenance a political intolerance as despotic, as wicked, and capable of as bitter and bloody persecutions." Going into the fundamental question of how to deal with those who advocate basic change, Jefferson had this to say: "If there be any among us who would wish to dissolve this Union or to change its republican form, let them stand undisturbed as monuments of the safety with which error of opinion may be tolerated where reason is left free to combat it."

Jefferson was willing to allow even antirepublican (or antidemocratic, as we would say today) doctrines, not only on the basis of rational argument but also because he had tremendous faith in a free America, "the strongest government on earth." It is possible that our present wavering with regard to the Jeffersonian doctrine coincides with something deeper: a loss of self-confidence in the strength of liberty and the growing fear that antidemocratic propaganda, if unchecked, might gain too many converts.

There are indications that a return to more traditional American concepts is under way. Virtually reversing its position of 1951, the Supreme Court ruled on June 17, 1957, in the case against fourteen West Coast communist leaders that a distinction must be made "between advocacy of forcible overthrow as an abstract doctrine and advocacy of action to that end," and that "mere membership or the holding of office in the Communist Party" did not constitute sufficient evidence of the intent to overthrow the government by force. While this decision did not explicitly invalidate the constitutionality of the Smith Act, it marked, at least, a return to the clear-and-present-danger doctrine that had been strongly modified, if not abandoned, in 1951. In any case, the 1957 decision of the Supreme Court re-established the traditional democratic (and American) concept under which all doctrines, including revolutionary ones, may be lawfully advocated and propagated.

In other words, the validity of democracy is no longer a taboo issue that must not be challenged.

Under the Internal Security Act of 1950 (popularly known as the McCarran Act), the Communist party was required to register with the government. In 1961, the Supreme Court held that this requirement was constitutional, but in 1964 and 1965 it effectively nullified the practical value of this position, for it ruled that neither the Communist party nor individual party members could be compelled to register, since this would be compulsory self-incrimination forbidden by the Fifth Amendment. The net effect of these (and other) decisions since 1957 has been to allow the Communist party to come out into the open more and more. In 1966, the party held its eighteenth national convention—the first since 1959. Yet despite the considerable freedom enjoyed by communists in recent years—due mainly to the lenient interpretation of existing laws by the courts and law enforcement agencies—the membership of the Communist party has remained stable at the all-time low of about ten thousand. Above all, the party has failed to make any significant progress in penetrating its three prime targets: Negroes, Mexican-Americans, and labor unions.

In the protection of traditional liberties, the judiciary has held up best in the contemporary crisis. In 1955, for example, the United States Court of Appeals upheld the "natural right" of American citizens to travel abroad, thus denying the Department of State the authority to decide arbitrarily who may undertake such travel. Since that decision, upheld in a similar case by the Supreme Court in 1958, the government can deny the issuance of a passport only after due process of law, whereas until that time it could, and did, make such vital determinations on its own discretion. Although the Fifth Amendment does not specifically mention the right to travel, the Supreme Court held in 1958 that it is part of the "liberty" protected by the Fifth Amendment against infringement without due process of law. In 1964, the Supreme Court declared unconstitutional the provision of the McCarran Act under which communists were forbidden to apply for passports. The Court ruled that the government has the right to restrict travel under special circumstances on grounds of national security but that it could not forbid all communists from traveling to all countries where passports are required. The government must show in each specific case why denial of a particular trip to a particular communist is required by considerations of national security.

In education too, the Supreme Court has had to reconcile individual liberty with national security. In 1957, the Court dealt with an important aspect of academic freedom. Professor Paul Sweezey, after lecturing at the University of New Hampshire on economics, was questioned by the state's attorney general about his political activities and beliefs. He denied the charge that he had ever been a member of the Communist party but refused to give any information about his teaching or his political opinions and associations. As a result, he was held to be in contempt by the New Hampshire Supreme Court. The United States Supreme Court decided that Professor Sweezey's conviction was invalid and added the warning that government should be "extremely reticent" to tread in the areas of academic freedom and political expression: "No one should underestimate the vital role in a democracy that is played by those who guide and train our youth. To impose any strait-jacket upon the intellectual leaders in our colleges and universities would imperil the future of our nation."

The British approach to civil liberty and loyalty

Britain no longer occupies the position of the leading great power which it held in the nineteenth century. Yet it is still the nation with the longest experience in constitutional government, or freedom under law, and its way of dealing with a basic problem of modern democracy—how to reconcile civil liberty with national security—may be of interest to other democratic nations.

The main problem posed in civil liberty is that of public policy toward the revolutionary totalitarian movements of communism and fascism. The British position is clear, unhedged by any ifs and buts: there are no legal restrictions on advocating communist or fascist doctrines or on organizing such parties. Only acts are punished. Espionage, for example, is a punishable crime, but a communist who spies for the Soviet Union is punished for the crime of spying and not for being a communist.

The definition of what constitutes an act is not always easy. Under the Public Order Act of 1937, for example, the wearing of political uniforms (generally indulged in by fascists rather than by communists) is forbidden. This prohibition, however, is based on the reasoning that the wearing of a political uniform is more than an expression of a political conviction. It is, in itself, an act of intimidation, particularly when thousands of uniformed party members march in paramilitary formation through main thoroughfares. Nearly all countries of whatever political persuasion forbid the unlawful wearing of official uniforms, since the uniform symbolizes the governmental monopoly of power and force. A private political army of uniformed men easily gives the impression to the public that it is on a par with the police and armed forces. Totalitarians in Britain may still display their political ideals in an outward manner clearly visible to the public, provided it is not done through uniforms.

The Public Order Act also forbids private political organizations to train their members in the use of firearms. After the assassination of President Kennedy in 1963, many Americans were shocked to learn how easy it is for anybody in the United States to buy guns—from mail order houses, sporting goods stores, and from a thousand and one other sources of supply. In Britain, strict control of firearms is not confined to political organizations. Weapons can be bought and owned only by holders of a special license. The unlawful possession of firearms is a serious crime. Even policemen are unarmed, on the supposition that no self-respecting criminal would think it cricket to attack an unarmed policeman with a deadly weapon.

All these restrictions lie in the area of action, and they in no way affect the teaching of revolutionary doctrines or the organizing of revolutionary parties. In Britain, there is no special legislation against communist or fascist groups, no House of Commons Committee on Un-British Activities, no Internal Security Act, no Subversive Activities Control Board, and no restrictions on the right of communists or fascists to run for public office. Both parties have put up candidates for many elections, but their miserable showing has done them more harm than if they had been prevented by law from running. The fascists, for example, have never been able to elect a single member of the House of Commons. The communists had one member in the Commons in the 1930's, and two were elected in 1945; but since that time not a single communist (out of 630 members) has been elected. Moreover, the communists not only lost in all elections since 1950, but their defeats were embarrassing and humiliating to them as a result of the extremely small communist vote. Part of this communist failure was due to a consistent policy followed by the Labor Party.

The British labor movement has at no time approved of any

cooperation with communists. In the middle 1930's, when the communists in many countries sponsored Popular Fronts and United Fronts of all antifascist forces against the Berlin-Rome-Toyko Axis, the British labor movement forbade its members to have anything to do with such efforts, on the grounds that its integrity would be jeopardized by association with communist aims. Members of the Labor Party who violated the ban by cooperating with communists in front organizations or appearing with communist speakers on the same platform were ousted from the party. At the time, the Labor Party's policy of not getting tangled up with communists was markedly different from that of antifascist parties, both socialist and nonsocialist, in other countries, and the Labor Party was attacked for being hypocritical, sanctimonious, intransigent, and dogmatic. The passage of time, however, would seem to have vindicated fully the consistent policy of British socialism to have no dealings whatsoever with communism.

In 1945, the Labor government surprised many people by allowing the fascists in Britain to reorganize as a political movement, although a number of fascists had committed treason during the war. The socialists in Britain took the view that the fascists had a right to engage in political propaganda as long as they did not violate any laws; further, they felt that the effectiveness of fascist propaganda depended rather on the common sense of the people than on prohibitory laws. Above all, British socialist leaders saw that if fascism lacks the protective coddling of extreme right-wingers and conservatives, it has no way of permeating larger groups of people.

In most other nations, the political Left fought fascism, whereas the Right concentrated on communism; the division of labor was exactly the opposite in Britain. *Fascism was destroyed by the Conservative Party* and *communism by the Labor Party*. Both major parties clearly understood that the issue of democracy versus totalitarianism must not be poisoned by partisan arguments and that it is too big an issue to be dragged into the mud of election campaigns. As a result, there are few (if any) countries in the world in which both fascism and communism are as dead and ineffectual as in Britain.

Moreover, this fight against totalitarianism was primarily carried on by the British people through their party organizations rather than through the strong arm of the government. In the United States, the House Committee on Un-American Activities and the Attorney General of the United States periodically publish lists of subversive organizations and publications for the information of law-enforcement officers as well as interested citizens. In Britain, the Labor Party issues from time to time lists of communist or communist-dominated organizations which no member of the Labor Party is permitted to join. This policing of the communist movement and its network of front-organizations by the Labor Party is probably more effective than if the same job were done by the government because it uses publicity, a weapon the communists do not like, rather than the authority of the state.

Often confused with the problem of civil liberty is that of loyalty and security. They are related but distinct. In civil liberty, the individual encounters the state as a *citizen*; in loyalty and security programs, the individual encounters the state as a *government employee.* Loyalty and security problems are thus much narrower than those of civil liberty: whereas all citizens may be affected by matters involving civil liberty, loyalty and security impinge only on a segment of the citizenry, that is, public officials. Also, whereas civil liberty pertains to a wide range of relations between the individual and the state, loyalty and security are limited to the employer-employee relation between government and the individual.

Yet, in spite of this narrower range, loyalty and security programs have aroused much interest and controversy in the last two decades. Both Britain and the United States adopted such programs in 1947, when it became clear that the hoped-for cooperation between the Soviet Union and the Western democracies did not materialize. In the American approach, every federal employee is subject to a general check before being hired. Under the McCarran Act, communists are barred from federal employment and from work in privately owned defense facilities. In "sensitive" positions (relating to national security or secret scientific research) there is a particularly stringent investigation, and the government may bar persons of doubtful background from such employment.

The British approach is different. From the very beginning of its security program in 1947, only applicants for, or holders of, sensitive positions are investigated with respect to political background or other personal traits that may make an individual unsuited for a position of high trust and responsibility. In the case of nonsensitive jobs, there is no political check at all, since in the

British view the state has no right to inquire into a person's political views if the position he holds or applies for is not related to national security. In this approach, a communist would be barred from any work—even janitorial—in the Air Ministry or the Atomic Energy Commission but could work—except on the very highest levels, where some information might be confidential—in the Ministry of Agriculture or the Ministry of Health.

The main differences between the British and the American methods of dealing with totalitarian revolutionary movements are twofold. First, the British allow less violence, preparation of violence, or intimidation than is the case in the United States, but they allow more freedom of speech, propaganda, and organization of revolutionary groups than is afforded in the United States. The greater acceptance of violence in the United States than in Britain goes beyond politics and constitutes one of the general differences between the two countries. For example, in proportion to its population Britain has only about one-tenth the number of homicides committed annually in the United States.

Second, there is a broader and more basic difference between the American and the British approaches. Since the passage of the Smith Act in 1940, a tendency has grown up in the United States, often (but not always) restrained by the Supreme Court, for government to act as a philosophical and moral teacher who determines which political ideas may be taught or may be the goal of organized groups. By contrast, the *British approach is to look at revolutionary movements from the viewpoint of the policeman on his beat.* Policemen are not philosophers or ideological experts, and their sole job is to prevent breaches of the peace here and now. If a public speaker causes a disturbance or an interference with the free flow of traffic, the policeman has the duty to restore order. He is not concerned with what the speaker says, but only with the breach of peace.

Although there has been no restraint on the freedom of speech and association of communist and fascist groups in Britain, they have been less influential than totalitarian and extremist groups in the United States, where legislative, executive, and judicial restraints have been employed for many years. It is a moot question whether the British approach, if used in the United States, would produce the same results as it has done in Britain. The British experience shows at least that in a democracy freedom can be a more effective weapon than repression in the struggle against revolutionary totalitarianism.

Reproduced by permission of the Proprietors of *Punch*.

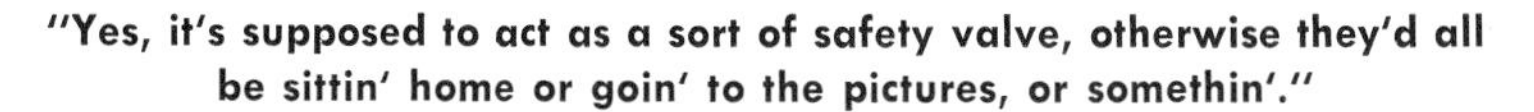

"Yes, it's supposed to act as a sort of safety valve, otherwise they'd all be sittin' home or goin' to the pictures, or somethin'."

Classical capitalism

Capitalism developed historically as part of the great movement of *rationalist individualism.* In religion, that movement produced the Reformation; in learning, the growth of the physical sciences; in human relations, the social sciences; in politics, democratic government; and in economics, the capitalist system. The concept of *capitalist civilization* is therefore a legitimate one; it suggests that capitalism is more than an economic system, that it reflects a way of life. It first developed in eighteenth-century Britain and later was transplanted to northwestern Europe and North America. A few basic traits have characterized it from the beginning.

In the capitalist system, *ownership of the means of production* (land, factories, machinery, natural resources) *is held by individuals, not by the state.* This does not exclude public ownership of natural monopolies or basic public services (post office, atomic arms), but such cases are considered the exception rather than the rule.

The bias of the capitalist civilization in favor of private ownership of the means of production is based on two considerations. First, ownership of productive property means power over the lives of other people; it is preferable that such *power* be *diffused among many property owners* rather than held by one owner, the state. Moreover, the economic power of private property owners can be curbed by the popularly elected government; were the state to own all productive property, economic and political power would coincide, and the outlook for personal economic liberty would be dim. Second, the assumption of capitalist thinking is that *technological progress* is more easily attained when each person minds his own business and has a personal incentive to do so.

The second principle of the capitalist system is that of the *market economy.* In the precapitalist era, the economy was generally local and self-sufficient; each family produced just about what it needed, supplementing its simple needs with some barter or exchange operations in a primitive local market. *Division of labor* was barely known, and each family had to do many jobs that nowadays are spread among hundreds of various crafts and specialties. Also, the type of occupation a person was in and the price he could charge for his goods and services were largely predetermined for him by custom and usage. In contrast, the market economy of the capitalist system is based on specialization of labor. Each person supplies only a very small part of his needs through his own skills and labors. The products or services are designed not for the producer's own household, but for the market.

Neither custom and usage nor the commands of a political authority determine the price in the market; this function is fulfilled by supply and demand. If prices are high, the market provides a signal that the supply of certain goods or services would be profitable; if prices are low, the market seems to say, "Try your luck in something else."

In the totalitarian economy (fascist or communist) the state, in trying to plan the whole economy, runs up against the difficulty of the limitations of the span of control. No human being can anticipate all the possible developments in an intricate economic system, encompassing many millions of persons and operated by economic decisions running daily into tens of millions.

In the capitalist market economy, each decision-maker has to watch over a much smaller area, and his span of attention and control is more limited and manageable.

The market economy is the touchstone of all economic systems. Neither communism nor fascism believes in it; in fascism, ownership of the means of production is formally still in the hands of private individuals, but this is not too important, because fascism does away with the market economy and substitutes for it the *command economy*. The state tells the individuals where to work, what jobs to choose, what to eat, what to produce, what prices to charge, and how to invest savings and profits. Communism abolishes private ownership of the means of production and the market economy. The communist economy, too, is a totalitarian command economy, in which economic decisions are made by a totalitarian state. In contrast, the market economy is an economy in which free individuals make their own economic decisions in the light of their interest, experience, and intelligence.

The tremendous political implications of the market economy have finally been recognized by socialist economists. W. Arthur Lewis, a socialist economist, examines this question in a book written for the Fabian Society, *The Principles of Economic Planning* (1949). As a socialist, Lewis is opposed to the orthodox concepts of laissez faire (as are most nonsocialist economists today).

The real issue, Lewis argues, is not between planning and no planning, but between *planning by direction* and *planning by inducement*. In the former, the government (as under fascism or communism) tries to get the right things done by direct control and regulation of output, prices, and wages. A government agent watches every step in the plan, and those workers or managers who fail to fulfill their quota are punished as traitors and saboteurs, although neglect or incapacity rather than willful disregard may have been the cause of their failure. The key mechanism in such a command economy is terror, specifically the fear of the prison or the "correctional" labor camp.

In a democratic state, the government indirectly stimulates certain economic activities through the budget, taxation, interest rates, and other policies of planning by inducement, thus avoiding the two main defects of planning by direction: bureaucratic centralization and economic inefficiency. Far from rejecting the free market as the normal mechanism of economic adjustment, Lewis holds that "our aim should be to preserve free markets wherever possible." It is also of no little interest that Lewis, in accepting the principle of the market economy, is driven to the conclusion that the nationalization of all industry is undesirable because of the usual reasons against monopoly: inefficiency, lack of initiative, and concentration of power.

Thus, the *function of the free market as a mechanism of political liberty* is now increasingly being recognized by socialists, and it gradually dawns on them that the question of ownership is less important than the question of whether economic decisions are made by free, independent individuals or corporations on the one hand, or by the state on the other.

The distinction between the command economy and the market economy thus reflects in the economic field the more basic political distinction between totalitarianism (fascism and communism) and liberalism (socialism and capitalism).

The most important specific liberties of the free market economy are the following: for the *worker*, to choose his line of work and his particular job; for the *businessman*, to choose his type of business and set it up at the place of his choice; for the *investor*, to invest his capital in whatever enterprise he chooses; finally, for the *consumer*, to buy the product he prefers.

This last freedom ("consumer sovereignty") is, in many respects, the most important of all, because it is the preference of the consumer that ultimately decides in a free market what is to be produced, at what quality, and in what quantities. In totalitarian economies, fascist or communist, consumer sovereignty is seriously curtailed. In the totalitarian economy, the state decides what is to be produced for consumption purposes and how it is to be distributed.

Another essential characteristic of the capitalist economy is *competition*. In the precapitalist economy, custom and usage dictated what goods and services were worth, and there were many persons who could not compete at all because they were excluded from certain occupations. In the capitalist economy, everybody is free to choose whatever line of work he prefers ("freedom of occupation"), and there is to be no artificial restriction or exclusion (such as on the basis of racial or religious prejudice) from any occupation or profession. Similarly, the capitalist market provides the place where goods and services are offered for sale, the quantity and quality of which are regulated by free competition. The basic assumption of the classical capitalist economy is that there is relative equality of bargaining power within, and between, buyers and sellers.

The freedom to compete in the market results from four basic capitalist freedoms: freedom of trade and occupation, freedom of contract, freedom of property, and freedom of profit-making. To the extent that any of these four freedoms is curbed, free competition is reduced.

The alternative to competition is either private monopoly or the omnipotent state. In both cases, the arbitrary determination of the prices of goods and services by a *de facto* authority (as in the case of private monopoly) or a legal authority (as in that of the state) takes the place of the free interplay of buyers and sellers, following their own choice. The economic justification of competition is that it keeps everybody—worker, businessman, investor—on his toes, constantly alert to changes in the market, and constantly on the lookout for ways to increase his efficiency and therefore that of the whole market.

In industry, *research* has become one of the keenest areas of competition. Research today means cheaper and better products tomorrow, and the vitality of competition is seen in the fact that companies are spending an increasingly larger share of their budget on research. In 1930, research expenditures in the United States amounted to $160 million; in 1966, they exceeded $24 billion. About two-thirds of this outlay is financed by the federal government, most of the rest by private industry. Research, by accelerating the rate of change in the economy, promotes competition at an early stage, long before the product or service reaches the market.

The *profit* principle is another basic principle that characterizes the capitalist system. So far, no historian has been able to show that before capitalism the profit principle was absent—the merchant in ancient Greece, for example, did not stay in business for his health.

Yet there is one tremendous difference between capitalism and precapitalist systems: the capitalist economy provides more opportunity for profit than any previous economy because it guarantees three freedoms that were not commonly found in precapitalist systems: freedom of trade and occupation, freedom of property, and freedom of contract. Obviously, where the institution of slavery exists, the slaves cannot enter the profit system. Their economic fate is determined by their social position; not possessing any of the other three basic economic freedoms, they have no access to the profit system.

In the Middle Ages, products were made by guilds and sold at prescribed prices. The profit system was thus doubly limited. Only a member of the guild could enter the process of production; furthermore, prices were defined not by freedom of contract between buyer and seller, but by the authority of custom, the church, or the state.

Even in modern states like Germany and Japan, the American occupation authorities after World War II were amazed to find how many professions and trades were virtually closed to outsiders, and they found it no easy task to induce the German and Japanese lawmakers to allow more freedom of trade and occupation.

Moreover, whenever the capitalist system is described as a profit system, it is frequently forgotten that the other side of the medal is equally important—capitalism is also a *loss* system. Although it is true to say that never have so many made so much profit as under capitalism, it is equally true that in no other system have so many lost so much as under capitalism. In American economic development, losses, bankruptcies, and failures were very heavy in the early mining, railroading, and automotive industries. In the more recent field of television, a pioneering company like the Radio Corporation of America lost many millions of dollars when it first introduced color television; the initial stages of black and white television were also loss operations.

These are not isolated instances. In a typical year, about four out of ten corporations report net losses. Out of ten business firms started in an average year, five end within two years, and eight within ten years—lack of success being the main reason.

The unparalleled opportunities of profit and loss in capitalism have one thing in common: *personal risk-taking*. Capitalism does not order anybody to take risks; it merely holds out the promise of profit to the person who is willing to take risks. Where the spirit of risk-taking is weak, investors prefer secure investments in bonds, which offer a guaranteed (and lower) return. Where the spirit of risk-taking is strong, investors prefer the common stock of corporations, which in the long run usually yield higher returns than bonds. However, if the quest for security is so strong that many investors shy away from risk investments, as so often happens in underdeveloped countries, economic stagnation is inevitable.

Stresses and strains in modern capitalism

The theory of capitalism approximated reality most closely in its classical period, roughly from the middle of the eighteenth to the end of the nineteenth century. In the twentieth century, capitalism has had to face stresses and strains—some internal, such as technological developments of industry itself; others external, such as wars.

The separation of ownership from management and financial control was made legally possible by the invention of the *corporate form of business:* each shareholder in a corporation is liable only to the extent of the shares he owns, no more and no less. In the precapitalist economy, a partnership involved full personal responsibility of each partner for the operations of the business. Partnerships tended to be relatively small, and each partner had a sense of personal involvement, financial and moral, in the business. In a big modern corporation, where fifty million or one hundred million shares are owned by more than half a million shareholders, the link between the individual shareholder and the corporation, of which he is part owner, is very tenuous. The corporation may be located thousands of miles away from most of the shareholders, and in most corporations only a small fraction of shareholders, generally less than one per cent, attend the annual meetings in which officers are elected and other important business is transacted.

Management draws up the list of officers to be elected, management presides over the elections, management explains why its proposed policy decisions should be adopted, management decides the salaries of management, management finally submits all its proposals to a vote: the vote is normally between 95 and 99 per cent in favor of management. This is a comfortable majority, as compared with average majorities of 52 to 55 per cent in political elections. "Like a stockholders' meeting" is a common phrase used to describe any perfunctorily run meeting.

In fact, whenever there is a real fight between management and a strong opposition, as there was over the New York Central Railroad in the 1950's, the controversy makes the front page. When the unusual happens and the opposition manages to acquire control, a new cycle of one-party rule starts again for an indefinitely long period. According to a recent study of 500 large corporations, the probability of a serious struggle for control in a big corporation is, on the average, once every 300 years!

The essence of the problem is simple. In government, democracy has established the principle that *those who wield power must be accountable to the public.* The people are the boss, the government their agent. Political power in a democracy must not be held for the benefit of the rulers; it is a trust, the purpose of which is to protect the interests of the people.

In the economic realm, on the other hand, a constitutional situation prevails that runs counter to the basic concept of democracy: corporation managers wield far-reaching power over stockholders and employees, and they constantly make decisions affecting the public interest without any clearly defined responsibility to the public. Whereas in a capitalist democracy political policies are arrived at through processes of consent that begin at the bottom and end at the top, in corporate business economic policies are made from the top and passed on to the bottom. The character of modern industrial organization is hierarchical, founded on discipline and obedience. Recently, however, the traditional pattern in industry has been considerably modified and made more democratic, mainly by organized labor, legislation, public opinion, and the growth in the business class of a sense of responsibility toward the community.

The more capitalism succeeds, the more it destroys—paradoxically enough—its original institutional and ideological character by collectivizing the framework of business. The first collectivists in the capitalistic era were not its critics, but the most successful cap-

Reprinted by permission from *Saturday Review.*

"And there, gentlemen, is my opinion for what it's worth."

italistic entrepreneurs—men like Andrew Carnegie, John D. Rockefeller, and Henry Ford, who created vast industrial empires.

Like other empires, industrial empires tend to become bureaucratic and conformity-minded, to follow routine and precedent, and, above all, to transform personal initiative and enterprise into impersonal rules of administrative routine. Whereas the original individual capitalists were men of bold, daring adventurousness, the bureaucratic administrators of the new, vast industrial empires tend to put security above everything else. If risk-taking was one of the most characteristic traits of original capitalists, large corporate business has tended to shy away from risk-taking investments and stick to "safe bets."

The danger is that, as business becomes bigger, the free-enterprise system may gradually become a "safe-enterprise" system.

Psychologically, there is *less difference between large-scale capitalist enterprise and large-scale socialized enterprise on the one hand than between small-scale capitalist enterprise and large-scale capitalist enterprise on the other.* It is for this reason that such defenders of capitalism as Justice Brandeis and President Wilson were afraid that the "curse of bigness" might eventually destroy not only big private enterprise, but private enterprise itself. Again, this problem of bigness is not peculiar to the economic institutions of liberal capitalism; in politics too, there is the threat of "big government" destroying the very elements that give life and color to democracy.

Who owns American business? Until recently, there were only guesses on this question, but now the facts begin to come to light. About 60 per cent of all corporate stock is owned by individuals, the rest by investment companies, insurance companies, foundations, and institutions. On the positive side, there has been a substantial growth in the number of persons owning stock: from 6.5 million in 1952 to 21 million in 1966. On the negative side, there is the fact that in 1963 fewer than 0.1 per cent of the taxpayers owned 19.5 per cent of all individually held stock, and those with incomes over $25,000 (about 1 per cent of all taxpayers) owned 48 per cent of all individually held stock. While concentration of stock ownership has been slightly declining in recent years, the present degree of concentration is high enough to suggest that the American economic system still has a long way to go before it can rightfully be called "people's capitalism."

To get some idea of the role of big business in the American economy: the 400 largest industrial corporations (manufacturing, mining, construction, trade, and services) hold over 40 per cent of the assets of all industrial corporations and nearly one-third of all industrial enterprises (incorporated and unincorporated). In manufacturing, concentration is higher: the top 200 manufacturing corporations hold 55 per cent of all manufacturing assets (corporate and noncorporate) and employ about 40 per cent of the labor force in all manufacturing enterprises. In research and development, the 50 largest corporations employ nearly half of the total scientific and technical personnel.

The phenomenon of concentration can be illustrated by a giant corporation like General Motors, the largest manufacturing company in the world. In an average year, General Motors produces about half or more of all passenger cars in the United States and is also the largest manufacturer of buses and locomotives. It employs about 3 per cent of the whole labor force in manufacturing, and its after-tax profits amount to about 5 per cent of all corporate after-tax profits. Its annual sales in the United States alone exceed the gross national product of over 100 countries.

Yet there is another side to the picture. In the first place, the small businessman has by no means disappeared from the American scene. In fact, the number of business firms has risen at a faster rate than the population. In 1900, there were 21 firms per 1,000 persons; in 1960, the figure was 26 firms per 1,000 persons. Retail trade and services have provided the largest opportunities for small business. Often, expanding big business is accompanied by a simultaneous growth of many new small businesses. For example, as people buy more cars, there are new opportunities for gas stations, garages, motels, restaurants, and all the other services and trades connected with automobile travel.

Secondly, there is *no hereditary aristocracy in big business*. Of the 100 largest industrial corporations in 1909, only 31 were among the 100 largest in 1960. Of the 10 largest corporations in 1909, only two were in the same category in 1960. Moreover, the competition is not only between individual firms in this top group; changing conditions of the economy entail keen *competition between whole industry groups*. Steel, coal mining, and textiles were relatively much more important in 1909 than in 1960, whereas the petroleum, chemical, and electrical equipment industries rose sharply in their relative importance in the top 100 corporations. This rapid change in the composition of the top group during five decades further illustrates the point that bigness is not to be identified with monopoly.

Defenders of big business maintain that a big country and a big market need big business. The very survival of the United States may depend on the productivity of big business, not only in turning out the necessary armaments and civilian goods and services but also in giving economic and military assistance to the free nations whose freedom and security are linked with those of the United States.

Individual security, too, has a better chance in big business than in small enterprises, because the former can do a better job in long-term planning of production, stability of employment, and the provision of services like pension and sickness benefits. In the field of labor-management relations, the greatest progress has been made in the mass production industries, like steel and automobiles, in which big business predominates; by contrast, labor unions have made little progress in agriculture and retailing, where the small unit prevails.

In research, too, as has been pointed out above, big business carries most of the work and responsibility. Occasionally, important inventions are still made in small laboratories; then it takes the resources and organization of larger corporations to translate the inventions into economic realities. More and more, however, industrial research is carried out by big corporations because it requires large financial resources and many years of waiting.

Concerning the impact of big business on competition, it is argued that the two are not incompatible. Big business produces a new kind of competition—internal competition. Not only is there competition between General Motors and Ford, but within General Motors itself the Chevrolet competes with the Pontiac, the Oldsmobile with the Buick. Moreover, there is competition in passenger transportation between the automobile and the railroad.

The problem of competition in the changing American economy is the key issue in *American Capitalism: The Concept of Countervailing Power* (1952), by John Kenneth Galbraith. In classical economics, competition was conceived in terms of many sellers, each with a small share of the market, and restraint of excessive private economic power was provided by competing firms on the same side of the market. Galbraith concedes that this classical model of competition has largely disappeared, since many markets have come to be dominated by a few firms and since there is frequently tacit collusion among these firms on major policy decisions. The most famous recent case of such collusion was revealed in 1961 in the successful prosecution for price-fixing of the major companies in the electrical industry.

Yet Galbraith does not conclude from the widespread disappearance of traditional competition that there is no longer any restraint of private economic power left. In fact, new restraints have taken the place of the old competitive mechanism, and these restraints—termed by Galbraith "countervailing power"—are the very product of concentration and bigness.

These new factors of restraint appear not on the same side of the market but on the opposite side, not with competitors but with customers and suppliers. The concentration of industrial enterprises not only has led to a relatively small number of sellers but also has brought about the predominant position of a few buyers. Galbraith explains the growth and expansion of retailers like Sears, Roebuck or the A&P in terms of countervailing power; by contrast, the absence of a few large firms in the housing industry has meant more traditional competition and less efficiency, since the many small enterprises in the housing industry are unable to use countervailing pressure against labor unions and suppliers of materials.

In the field of labor too, Galbraith is impressed by the fact that strong unions have developed mainly when faced by strong corporations, as in the steel, automobile, and electrical industries. In contrast, there is no major union of any consequence in the retail business or in agriculture, the closest approaches in the United States to pure competition. Galbraith concedes that countervailing power is not universally effective as a restraint on private economic power and that it fails to operate during inflation when relative scarcity of demand disappears and too many buyers compete for available goods and services. If supply is small in relation to demand, the seller need not surrender to the bargaining power of the buyer, who thus loses his capacity to function as a countervailing power.

The weakness of the concept of countervailing power lies in the fact that, though the power of the large seller may be checked by that of the large buyer, the resulting benefit need not be passed on to the consumer. Monopoly benefits may be amicably split between the large buyer and the large seller at the expense of the consumer.

In substituting the few giant competitive units of the twentieth century for the many small ones of the eighteenth, the theory of countervailing power still assumes that a socially fair market equilibrium may be obtained without the intervention of the community in defense of the public interest. In a sense, therefore, the concept of countervailing power, illuminating and provocative as it is, is essentially a sophisticated restatement of the doctrine of the self-regulating market of classical economics, imaginatively adapted to the economic facts of today.

Sources of strength of capitalist democracy

Capitalism, it has been said by a close student of the subject,

> . . . during its rule of scarce one hundred years, has created more massive and more colossal productive forces than have all preceding generations together. Subjection of nature's forces to man, machinery, application of chemistry to industry and agriculture, steam-navigation, railways, electric telegraphs, clearing of whole continents for cultivation, canalization of rivers, whole populations conjured out of the ground—what earlier century had even a presentiment that such productive forces slumbered in the lap of social labor?

The author goes on to say that capitalism "has accomplished wonders far surpassing Egyptian pyramids, Roman aqueducts, and Gothic cathedrals; it has conducted expeditions that put in the shade all former migrations of nations and crusades." This eulogy of capitalism was written, not by the research director of the National Association of Manufacturers or of the United States Chamber of Commerce, but by Karl Marx, in the *Communist Manifesto.* Few students of capitalism have been as aware as Marx of the fact that capitalism is a *revolutionary way of life,* creating a new material world as well as new intellectual and ethical values. To put the strength of capitalist democracy in one brief sentence: never before have so many had it so good. The population of the United States increased eight times between 1850 and 1960, yet its national income increased forty times (in constant dollars, to allow for changes in purchasing power). At the same time, the suffrage has been steadily broadened; education has been made available to more persons than ever before, work hours are shorter than ever before, and there is more leisure than man has known hitherto. Above all, *never before has there been so much concern with the welfare of the underprivileged classes in society.*

The abolition of slavery, education for all, health facilities on an unprecedented level, social security for everybody, the doubling of longevity within a century, the highest increase of population on record—all coincide with the development of capitalism. None of these could have been accomplished in a civilization motivated primarily by greed. Looking at precapitalist civilizations today, one is impressed by the survival of social inequalities (the caste system in India, the peon class in Latin America) that reflect a profound disregard of human dignity, an attitude that is no longer feasible in most capitalist societies.

In the fields of education, health, and welfare, more has been accomplished in capitalist societies in a spirit of service and disinterestedness than ever before in history. In the world today, the great charitable foundations are to be found primarily in the capitalist nations, particularly in the English-speaking world, not because there are no wealthy people in Asia or Latin America, but because wealthy persons in precapitalist societies rarely believe in the capitalist concept that *wealth can ultimately be justified only through service to the community.*

In the United States, there are over 7,000 private charitable foundations, with total assets of over $15 billion. The Ford Foundation alone, the largest of them all, has assets in excess of $3 billion. In 1936–1966, it spent, in the United States and abroad, well over $2 billion on education, human welfare and international aid. Yet philanthropy in the United States is not predominantly based on a few wealthy individuals or foundations. In 1966, Americans spent about $12 billion on philanthropic purposes; the bulk of this sum, about $9 billion, was contributed by individuals, the rest by philanthropic foundations and business corporations.

The United States Government and private American foundations gave India, in the years 1952–1966, over $7 billion. About half of this sum was donated as an outright gift, and the other half as loans. A large portion of the loans is repayable in rupees rather than in "hard currency" such as dollars. Since the United States returns most of these rupees to India for development purposes, the bulk of the loans are gifts in all but name. This program substantially aided India in such major areas as farming, industry, community development, education, and health. The progress in health, largely due to American assistance, has perhaps been the most dramatic. In 1953, for example, India had 75 million malaria cases, of which 1 million died. In 1962, fewer than 2,000 malaria cases were reported.

Yet this attitude is not new and is not a product of the cold war; it was practiced on a large scale long before communism existed. The Rockefeller Foundation, set up in 1913, spent over $500 million in the first forty years of its existence; most of this money was spent on education, much of it abroad. The Carnegie group (Carnegie Corporation, Carnegie Endowment, and Carnegie Foundation) has been active in the field of education and international cooperation. None of these major charitable foundations confine their benefits to American institutions or individuals; they all had their own "foreign aid" programs long before the government stepped into the picture after World War II.

Moreover, *never before has a ruling class been willing, as under capitalism, to finance the very people who seek to change the existing social system.* Reform economics need not hide, in the United States, in secret, illegal sheets, but may be taught at private and public colleges and universities endowed by large capitalist fortunes or maintained by state legislatures.

Conservatives' suspicion of social science is well founded; their frequent confusion of social science with socialism is not quite as obtuse as it may appear to the reformer, since social science, by digging up the facts, may well lead to the very social changes the conservatives fear most.

The political implications of capitalism can now be clearly seen: first, *individual risk-taking,* the desire and capacity to make decisions, to assume responsibility, to determine one's own life. Without this kind of motivation, there can be no democracy, and historically there has been no democracy without it.

Logically, it is conceivable that democracy may develop in the future without this economic background, but so far it has not happened that way. The capitalist economy developed before democratic government, but the one was bound to lead to the other. Persons who constantly faced danger, risk, and responsibility in their economic affairs were ultimately unwilling to accept authoritarian government from kings and aristocrats, and when the capitalist middle classes could not obtain their objectives peacefully, they resorted to revolution: the English civil war in the seventeenth century, and the American and French revolutions in the eighteenth century.

In fighting for itself, the capitalist middle class appealed to the principles of universal human liberty, the rights of man, and natural law. It is for this reason that democracy became an intrinsic part of capitalist civilization, and for this reason also that the greatest advances in democratic government and human liberty have so far been made in capitalist societies.

The second principle of capitalism that directly affects government is the *diffusion of decision and power.* Instead of one central authority's laying down the law of the market, thousands of little decisions hold each other in balance. Many of these decisions are based on erroneous facts and bad judgment, but such defects are preferable to the big errors made by a central authority, particularly if the central authority is subject to no political checks. Every type of democracy seeks to diffuse power by various devices in order to avoid the abuse and corruption that follow the concentration of power. By strengthening the diffusion of power in the economic area, capitalism thus supports one of the key principles of democracy.

Taking a larger, world-wide view, it should be remembered that capitalist civilization, as represented primarily by Britain in the nineteenth and the United States in the twentieth century, revolutionized the underdeveloped continents. The masses of Asia, Africa, and Latin America learned from their contact with capitalism the appreciation of more and better material things. What is less often understood is that the West also taught the underdeveloped continents the principles of the dignity of man, the right of national self-determination, and the evil of racial superiority. Gandhi, Nehru, and the other leaders of the Indian independence movement were educated in England, and it was the ideas of John Locke that taught them individual and national liberty.

Asian communism, distorted and perverted as it may appear in the light of Western democracy, owes its existence partly to Western ideas and promises that Western capitalism made but failed to carry out. Marx gathered his ideas, not in the steppes of Central Asia or Siberia, but from German philosophy, English political economy, and French revolutionary politics. The communist promise of a happier, better life for all people regardless of class or race is the original promise of capitalism; to the extent that capitalism lives up to it, communism loses its appeal. If offered a fair choice, mankind will prefer economic welfare and political freedom to economic warfare and political slavery.

Why socialism has not spread in the United States

The question is often asked why socialism has never been able to gain a strong foothold in the United States. According to socialist writers, the United States as the leading capitalist country in the world was bound to develop the "inner contradictions" out of which socialist mass movements would develop. Yet nothing of the sort has happened. Is it because socialism is European? There are strong socialist parties in Canada, Australia, New Zealand, Chile, Brazil, Japan, and other countries outside of Europe. Why the failure in the United States?

The basic reason probably lies in the fact that American capitalism—more than any other economic system in the world—has given to the people *now* much of what socialism promises them for the future. Specifically, socialism bases its appeal on two main promises: (1) *social equality* and (2) the *abolition of poverty*. Although no one will argue that American capitalism has lived up 100 per cent to these two principles, it must have done so to a very large extent, since socialist propaganda so far has had little effect.

As to the principle of equality, the Constitution of the United States and the reality of economic life keep opportunity open to anyone who looks for it. Since in public opinion polls over 80 per cent of the American people describe themselves as "middle class," it is clear that psychologically, at least, there is little class consciousness in the United States. Social mobility is very great, mainly because higher education is available to more persons than anywhere else in the world. An American has about seven times as good a chance to get a college education as has a Briton. A Negro American's chance for a college education is more than twice that of a white Briton, German, Frenchman, or Italian. The Negro minority, ten per cent of the American population and the only major group left which still lacks full social and economic equality, has nevertheless not turned to socialism or communism as the way out.

As to the second basic promise of socialism, the abolition of poverty, American capitalism has had its serious flaws, crises, and depressions. Yet when all is said and done, and although things could be better still, living standards in the United States are by far the highest in the world, and they are constantly rising. Vast resources, a single national market, and huge government spending have all contributed to the success of the American economy, quite apart from its spirit of dynamic enterprise and technological progressiveness. In contrast, where capitalism has shown itself restrictionist, timid, inefficient, and tied to a rigid class system, as in many other countries, socialism has grown up in the shadow of capitalist inefficiency and inequality.

Intelligent foreign socialists are beginning to realize that the socialist-capitalist controversy does not make much sense in the United States. Thus a leading British socialist economist, C. A. R. Crosland, writes in *The Future of Socialism* (1957), the most searching analysis of socialism in the last twenty years, that in Britain a Leftist would be a socialist, whereas in the United States he would be much less concerned "to promote social equality or material welfare, of which plenty exists already, than with reforms lying outside the field of socialist-capitalist controversy" such as civil liberties, racial equality, juvenile delinquency, and foreign policy. With respect to inequality of wealth—a key theme in traditional socialist argumentation—Crosland points out that "in the United States, property is more equally distributed than in Britain" (*The Conservative Enemy,* 1962, p. 39). In Britain in 1953, the top 3 per cent owned 49 per cent of all wealth, and the top 10 per cent owned 76 per cent; in the United States, the top 3 per cent owned 33 per cent of all wealth, and the top 10 per cent owned 56 per cent. In both top groups of wealth-holders, the figures are considerably lower in the United States than in Britain.

(Robert J. Lampman, *The Share of Top Wealth-Holders in National Wealth, 1922–1956,* 1962, p. 215.)

For generations, European socialists assumed that the absence of a strong socialist movement in the United States proved its reactionary, or at least conservative, political orientation. Now there is a growing realization in Europe that the two primary problems that socialism seeks to solve—material welfare and social equality—have been largely solved in the United States by the capitalist system, and therefore the major issues of American public life—such as civil liberties, racial equality, or foreign policy—have no relation whatsoever to the issue of socialism versus capitalism. That issue may, in fact, die out in European and other nations too, once they manage to abolish poverty and social inequality.

The new pluralistic economy

The controversy of socialism versus capitalism has also been rendered obsolete by profound structural changes in the economies of the most advanced Western nations. The public attention which the constant political tug of war over economic issues receives conceals the long-term forces that are at work.

Increased public responsibilities for social and economic welfare, for example, are not primarily the result of moral conversion or of partisan struggles between rugged individualists and do-gooders, but of increasing output of goods and services. Some of the more democratic underdeveloped nations have set up very elaborate schemes of welfare state policies—but in many cases these schemes exist on paper only, since the nations are too poor to pay for the desired welfare. By contrast, where economic levels are high enough to permit welfare policies, as in most advanced Western nations and perhaps increasingly in some communist states in the not too distant future, there is at least a realistic foundation for such schemes.

This fact may also help to explain the paradoxical phenomenon of the growing attention to the problem of poverty in the United States. As the richest nation in the world, enjoying the highest living standards and suffering from less poverty than any other country, the United States nevertheless appears to be more concerned about poverty than other, and particularly the very poor, nations. The reason behind the paradox is the fact that as the production of wealth in the United States increases, the sensitivity to the still remaining poor segments of the population also deepens, since the ultimate goal of abolishing poverty seems closer as the number of the poor goes down. In 1947, 32 per cent of Americans were poor, as compared with 18 per cent in 1964 (the poverty line for a family of four being generally defined as an annual income of under $3,000 in 1964 prices).

A second structural change of capitalism has been the relative growth of the *not-for-profit sector.* Traditional economic analysis and popular economic thinking still concentrate on the private, profit-seeking sector of the economy while neglecting the economic importance of *government* and *private nonprofit* institutions, which together constitute the not-for-profit sector of the economy. In fact, the not-for-profit sector of the economy is growing at a faster rate than the profit-seeking sector. In 1929, for example, the not-for-profit sector accounted for 12.5 per cent of the gross national product. In the late 1960's, the share rose to about 30 per cent. In 1929, employment in the not-for-profit sector was about 10 per cent of the civilian labor force. In the 1960's, employment in this sector stood at over 20 per cent of the labor force. Government in 1929 employed 7 per cent of the labor force, as compared with 15 per cent in the 1960's. The fastest growth has not been in federal government, as is commonly believed, but in state and local government.

However, the economic impact of the not-for-profit sector is even larger if one adds its indirect contribution to the economy. These indirect effects derive mainly from the goods and services it buys, such as defense contracts of the federal government or laboratory equipment bought by colleges and universities, private or public. In 1929, these indirect effects of the not-for-profit sector were responsible for about 5 per cent of the civilian labor force. In the 1960's, the share rose to about 12 per cent. Combining the more than 20 per cent of direct employment in the not-for-profit sector with the 12 per cent of indirect employment generated by it, we find that the not-for-profit sector is responsible for at least one-third of the civilian labor force. According to a pioneering study in this field, it is more likely that the not-for-profit sector of the economy directly and indirectly accounts for about 40 per cent of the labor force. (Eli Ginzberg and others, *The Pluralistic Economy,* 1965, p. 209.)

What are the reasons behind the growth of the not-for-profit sector of the economy? In the expansion of government, defense

ness. Frequently, successful men in any one of the three sectors of the economy move on to the other two. Former government officials, civilian and military, are to be found in important positions in business corporations or nonprofit foundations, and a top executive of an automobile company may become Secretary of Defense. As the number of men and women increases who have had experience in private business, private nonprofit institutions, and government, the result is likely to be a lessening of ideological rigidity, more pragmatic flexibility, and a more efficient economy.

The welfare state

The main principles of the welfare state are relatively simple: first, the recognition that every member of the community is entitled, solely because he is a human being, to a *minimum standard of living;* second, the welfare state is committed to putting *full employment* at the top of social goals to be supported by public policy.

Particularly in the United States, the adherents of the welfare state believe that free enterprise can be preserved and strengthened by full employment measures without having recourse to nationalization. Taxation properly adjusted to periods of prosperity and depression, interest rates determined by governmental decision according to economic needs, fiscal policies designed to redistribute purchasing power in harmony with the best interests of the nation, investment incentives in times of contracting business, public works for direct unemployment relief, government credits to builders or buyers of homes—these are but a few of the measures the government can adopt in stabilizing the economy without changing its foundations.

In the United States, the Great Depression of 1929–1939 undermined faith in the orthodox philosophy of laissez faire, according to which the disequilibrium of the market would eventually be restored to a new equilibrium without any interference from the outside. When the American economy reached the stage in which one out of every four employable persons found himself out of work, in which the farmer could not sell his products at reasonable prices, in which more and more business enterprises went bankrupt or were unable to pay wages to their employees or earn profits for their shareholders, something had to be done. The New Deal, starting with the first term of President Franklin D. Roosevelt in 1933, was not so much a set of premeditated philosophical principles to be superimposed upon the American people as a series of emergency measures in response to urgent practical problems.

The Agricultural Adjustment Act (May 12, 1933) attempted to help the farmer by raising farm prices to a level that would enable farmers to buy industrial products as they had been able to do in the years 1909–1914. In order to make such "parity" possible, farmers were to reduce production, in return for which they would receive higher prices (as a result of decreased supply) from the consumer and subsidies from the government. Traditionally opposed, in theory at least, to government interference, the farmers have been very content with that part of the welfare state which directly protects their interests.

The National Labor Relations Act (July 5, 1935), commonly known as the Wagner Act, established for the first time full statutory regulation of labor-management relations in the United States. In the preceding half century, the employer in the United States was free to recognize or not to recognize labor unions and to bargain or not to bargain with them. Employers frequently discharged employees for union activities, and if unions became too strong, employers would use various means to break them—company unions, private police, labor spies, lockouts, and professional strikebreakers.

The main purpose of the Wagner Act was to encourage collective bargaining between labor and management, thus substituting peaceful discussion for violence. Just as the Constitution of the United States does not prescribe the contents of statutes to be passed by Congress, but merely sets down the rules and procedures of the legislative process, the Wagner Act, too, merely created a set of rules and an atmosphere in which labor and management could talk to each other. Although the law did not, and could not, compel both sides to agree, and strikes and lockouts still remained legal, the experience of collective bargaining quickly proved that the application of democratic methods of negotiation usually leads to results beneficial to both parties.

Dissatisfaction of management with some provisions of the Wagner Act led to its replacement in 1947 by the Labor-Management Relations Act, commonly known as the Taft-Hartley Act. Though spokesmen for labor voiced deep dissatisfaction with the Taft-Hartley Act, it left the basic principle of the Wagner Act—collective bargaining—substantially unchanged.

The Social Security Act (August 14, 1935) marked another milestone in the movement for social reform in the United States. In modern industry the individual is frequently at the mercy of large impersonal forces over which he has no control. The efforts of the family, private charity, and the local community have all too frequently proved insufficient to protect the individual against the hazards of old age, disability, or unemployment. The passage of the Social Security Act marked the recognition that the community, on the local, state, and federal levels, is partly responsible for assuring its citizens of some protection against want and insecurity. Apart from its humanitarian motivation, social security also has important economic effects, since such payments provide people with a minimum purchasing power indispensable to the functioning of industry in prosperity and depression.

In a historic breakthrough, Congress in 1965 amended the Social Security Act by including health insurance for persons over 65, covering both hospitalization and doctors' bills and going into effect on July 1, 1966. Under this insurance program, popularly known as medicare, the federal government pays the entire cost of illness, apart from small basic fees paid by the insured. Although federal medicare covers only persons over 65, the federal government makes grants to state health insurance programs for families with dependent children whose income and financial resources are insufficient for necessary medical services. Numerous states quickly made use of this federal provision and set up supplementary state medicare programs. Whereas federal medicare has no means test but an age limit, state medicare programs have no age limit but a means test, since each state prescribes the income level below which it provides health insurance.

Social security—old-age pensions, survivors benefits, disability insurance, and medicare—is financed by payroll taxes levied on employers and employees. Since the government can only give what it takes, citizens are reminded that if they want higher social security benefits, the only way to get them is to work harder, produce more, and pay more. In 1966, out of a labor force of over 70 million, over 65 million were covered by social security. Most of those not covered are federal, state, and local government employees who have their own systems of social security.

Far from weakening private effort, public welfare seems to whet the appetite for more benefits to be supplied privately. For example, private pension funds have grown faster than public pension funds. Public pension funds rose from $4.5 billion in 1940 to $70 billion in 1964, but during the same period private pension funds rose from $2.4 billion to $77 billion.

In the field of education too, 1965 was a turning point in the expansion of the welfare state. Under the Elementary and Secondary Education Act of 1965, the federal government makes direct grants to individual school districts with children from low-income families. However, the criteria of eligibility are so liberal that 95 per cent of all school districts qualify. Federal aid is also available to children from private (mostly parochial) schools, although the funds are administered by public agencies. In fiscal 1967 (July 1, 1966 to June 30, 1967), over $1.5 billion were allocated for federal aid to elementary and secondary education.

In the Higher Education Act of 1965, the federal government uses a somewhat different approach. The emphasis is on a general scholarship and loan program for college students. In fiscal 1967, over 200,000 students received federal scholarships, and another 200,000 were aided through work-study programs. In addition, almost 800,000 students received government-guaranteed loans. If the student-borrower's family has an annual income of under $15,000, the federal government pays the full interest (up to six per cent) while the student is in college and pays three per cent of the interest during repayment of the loan. In all, about one out of five college students received federal aid in fiscal 1967, and the proportion is constantly rising.

The welfare state has grown in scope and cost under both Democratic and Republican national administrations. In Eisenhower's first budget year (1953), the federal government paid out $10 billion in welfare activities, or thirteen cents of every dollar spent; in his last budget year (1960), the federal government spent $25 billion on welfare, or about twenty-six cents of every federal dollar spent. In Johnson's budget for fiscal 1967, over $50 billion, or 34 cents out of every federal dollar, were allocated for social security, health, education, and welfare.

The major categories receiving social welfare benefits from federal funds in 1966 included the following: 21 million retired workers, dependents, and survivors; 7.5 million receiving state aid largely financed by federal funds; 4.5 million veterans or their survivors; 0.8 million retired federal employees; and about 1.2 million students aided by federal scholarships, interest-free or low-interest loans, and by work-study programs. These figures do not include the federally subsidized school lunch program, benefiting over 17 million children; state unemployment benefits, largely

Drawing by Alain; © 1959 The New Yorker Magazine, Inc.

"It might not be such a bad life, security-wise."

federally financed, for 5 million; and over 1 million children and youths under various anti-poverty programs, such as Head Start Project for preschool children and work-training programs for youths. Omitting these last three categories, about one out of every six Americans receives financial help from federal sources.

Yet, although the total cost of public welfare (federal, state, and local) rose from $7 billion in 1935 to $78 billion in 1965, the share of the national product spent on welfare increased only from 9.3 per cent in 1935 to 12 per cent in 1965. Social welfare cost 49 per cent of all government expenditures (federal, state, and local) in 1935, but only 42 per cent in 1965. Thus, while there has been an expansion of social welfare in terms of absolute cost, the relative cost of social welfare as a share of the national product has risen only modestly, and it has even declined as a share of all government expenditures in the period 1935–1965. Finally, the growth of the welfare state has not led to the shrinkage of local government at the expense of centralized government in Washington. Throughout the period of 1935–1965, state and local government consistently accounted for about half of all public expenditures on social welfare, the federal government paying for the other half.

One of the main mechanisms of bringing about greater equality through redistribution is *taxation.* Thus in 1962—a typical year—the top 20 per cent of consumer units in the United States received 45.5 per cent of all family personal income but paid 60.9 of all income taxes. The top 5 per cent received 19.6 per cent of all income but paid 36.1 per cent of all income taxes. By contrast, the lowest 20 per cent received 4.6 of income but paid only 1.7 per cent of income taxes. The proportionate share of the top 1 per cent of income receivers has suffered the most drastic decline. In 1929, the top 1 per cent received 14.5 per cent of total personal income, but this share was cut by about one-half after World War II. As to the top 5 per cent of income receivers, their share was 30 per cent of total personal income in 1929 but only 20 per cent in the 1960's.

Yet taxation cannot produce wealth; it can merely transfer property from one group to another. The improved material well-being of the American people in the last generation is due to increased production of goods and services. At the same time, a heightened sense of equity underlying the philosophy of the welfare state has brought about more equality in the distribution of incomes than used to prevail in the United States. Incomes have improved both absolutely (in terms of actual size) and relatively (in terms of the distribution among various groups of the population).

The income revolution is illustrated in the table below. In it,

Distribution of Families by Income Level in Constant (1964) Dollars, 1947–1964

Family Income in 1964 Dollars	Per Cent of Families	
	1947	1964
Under $5,000	62	35
$5,000-$10,000	31	43
Over $10,000	7	22
Total	100	100

Source: Statistical Abstract of the United States, 1966.

American families are divided (in terms of constant dollars) into three main groups: low-income, under $5,000 per year; middle-income, from $5,000-$10,000; and high-income, over $10,000. In 1947, 62 per cent of families were low income; in 1964, only 35 per cent, a reduction by nearly one-half. The percentage of families in the middle-income group rose from 31 per cent to 43 per cent, or by more than one-third. The proportion of high-income families more than trebled, from 7 per cent of all families in 1947 to 22 per cent in 1964. *Whereas in 1947 low-income families outnumbered middle-income and high-income families combined by about two to one, in 1964 middle-income and high-income families combined outnumbered low-income families by about the same margin of two to one.* Significantly, the number of poor families has also sharply dropped between 1947 and 1964. In 1947, 32 per cent of families had an income of under $3,000; this proportion dropped to 18 per cent in 1964. We thus see that the absolute and relative improvement of the economic status of American families has been accomplished through a process of leveling up rather than leveling down.

Another aspect of the income revolution can be seen in the relative speed by which incomes of different groups have risen in the period of 1941–1962:

Per Cent Increase in Average Income (1950 Dollars)

Rank by Size of Income	1941 to 1962
Total	59
Lowest fifth	79
Second fifth	84
Third fifth	70
Fourth fifth	62
Highest fifth	48
Top 5 per cent	30

Source: Statistical Abstract of the United States, 1965.

We see that the average income in the United States rose by 59 per cent in the period of 1941–1962 (calculated in 1950 dollars). The lowest and second fifths of income receivers did considerably better than the national average; the third and fourth fifths did slightly better; the highest fifth advanced considerably less. Most striking is the relatively slow advance of the top 5 per cent of income receivers: their increase was only 30 per cent, or about half of the national average of 59 per cent.

The income revolution can also be studied in the changing proportions of different sources of income. In 1929, 59 per cent of all personal income was derived from wages and salaries; in 1965 the percentage rose to 70. By contrast, income derived from dividends, interest, and rentals dropped from 22 per cent in 1929 to 14 per cent in 1965. This sharp drop is significant since income from dividends, interest, and rentals is primarily important to high-income groups. Income from transfer payments (public and private pensions, unemployment relief, veterans' benefits, and other types of assistance) rose from 1.6 per cent of all personal income in 1929 to 7.5 per cent in 1965. This item is mainly beneficial to the lower-income groups and further illustrates their relative advance. Taking wages, salaries, and transfer payments as one combined major category of income, we find that this item accounted for 61 per cent of all personal income in 1929, whereas the percentage rose to 77.5 in 1965.

Looking at the whole problem of income distribution in the United States, an outstanding authority in this field comes to the following conclusion: "Do the rich get a larger share of income in the United States than they do in other countries? According to the available evidence this is not the case. The United States has about the same income distribution as Denmark, Sweden, and Great Britain and a much more equal distribution than most of the other countries for which data are shown. There is no evidence that incomes are more widely distributed in any country than they are in the United States." (Herman P. Miller, *Rich Man, Poor Man,* 1964, pp. 11-13.)

Moreover, inequality within the United States is much smaller than between the United States and the rest of the world. Thus, the top 6 per cent of income receivers in the United States get about 22 per cent of total personal income. The population of the United States comprises about 6 per cent of the world's population, yet it annually produces about 33 per cent of the world's goods and services.

Just as redistribution is a way of achieving internal peace and stability within the United States, our foreign aid programs apply the same principle to the community of nations, particularly the underdeveloped countries. If the welfare state at home is cheaper than unrest and revolution, international welfare policies are cheaper than war and communist expansion.

As time goes on, the realization grows that *the welfare state is not a way of getting something for nothing*, that *every piece of welfare has to be paid for.* Since taxation in countries like England and the United States is reaching a level where there is not much left that can be obtained by soaking the rich, every increased social benefit must be paid for by increased taxation of the lower-income groups. The problem of the welfare state is becoming less and less one of philosophical principle and more and more one of actuarial calculation and specific taxation.

In the welfare state, the people agree that a high portion of their income should be spent by the government in a certain way. Experience shows that people tend to save more easily if they have committed themselves to an insurance policy or a mortgage with monthly payments than if they rely on irregular voluntary deposits in a savings account.

In the welfare state the situation is similar. The individual hands over to the state the job of saving for him in case of emergency such as disability, old age, or death. If people themselves could save for all such emergencies, much of the welfare state would be unnecessary. But the average person finds it easier to pay higher taxes every month or every year, out of which his social security is ultimately to be paid for, than to save for such eventualities in a personal savings account.

There is nothing wrong in admitting this human weakness and entrusting the state with the efficient administration of a comprehensive insurance system, as long as it is understood that the costs of such a system have to be borne largely by taxation and that therefore the financial principle behind the welfare state is *forced personal and communal saving today for the needs of tomorrow* rather than a simple method of transferring property from the rich to the poor.

Is the welfare state compatible with capitalism? When the first basic measures of the welfare state were introduced thirty years ago, the dire prediction was made that the welfare state was the first step to communism or at least to creeping socialism. Events have disproved that fear; after three decades of the welfare state, the American economy prospers more than ever before, living standards have reached an all-time high, productivity is higher than ever, people live longer and better, and there is more eco-

"Your management is proud and happy to announce that for the tenth consecutive year, despite oppressive government controls and taxation, the continuing cost-price squeeze, and unending and unreasonable wage demands, our net earnings have again topped all previous records."

nomic equality between the various income groups than in the past. Above all, the welfare state has in no way sapped the spirit of incentive and effort in the American economy; the whip of want and insecurity is not the best guide to progress, and in providing a minimum of social and economic security the welfare state has strengthened the economy as a whole. The performance of the American economy in World War II astounded the world; far from being coddled into softness and stagnation by the welfare state, it showed enormous dynamism, drive, and initiative. Since the end of World War II, the American economy has continued to grow vigorously enough to make possible a rising standard of living at home and the disbursement of over $100 billion in foreign aid to many nations throughout the world.

FOR FURTHER READING

Bell, Daniel, *The End of Ideology*. New York: Collier Books, 1963.

Berle, A. A., *The American Economic Republic*. New York: Harcourt, Brace & World, Inc., 1963.

Berlin, Isaiah, *Two Concepts of Liberty*. New York: Oxford University Press, Inc., 1959.

Beveridge, William, *Full Employment in a Free Society*. New York: W. W. Norton & Company, Inc., 1945.

Cantril, Hadley, *Human Nature and Political Systems*. New Brunswick: Rutgers University Press, 1961.

Cornuelle, Richard C., *Reclaiming the American Dream*. New York: Random House, Inc., 1965.

Dahl, Robert A. (ed.), *Political Oppositions in Western Democracies*. New Haven: Yale University Press, 1966.

De Grazia, Alfred (ed.), *Grass Roots Private Welfare*. New York: New York University Press, 1957.

Dollard, John and others, *Frustration and Aggression*. New Haven: Yale University Press (Yale Paperbacks), 1960.

Ebenstein, William, *Modern Political Thought*, 2nd ed., chaps. 2, 3, 10, 13. New York: Holt, Rinehart & Winston, Inc., 1960.

Friedman, Milton, *Capitalism and Freedom*. Chicago: University of Chicago Press (Phoenix Books), 1963.

Fromm, Erich, *The Sane Society*. New York: Holt, Rinehart & Winston, Inc., 1955.

Galbraith, John K., *American Capitalism*. Boston: Houghton Mifflin Company (Sentry Editions), 1961.

———, *The Affluent Society*. Boston: Houghton Mifflin Company, 1958.

Ginzberg, Eli and others, *The Pluralistic Economy*. New York: McGraw-Hill Book Company, 1965.

Girvetz, Harry K., *The Evolution of Liberalism*. New York: Collier Books, 1966.

Heilbroner, Robert L., *The Limits of American Capitalism*. New York: Harper & Row, Publishers, 1966.

Kaplan, A. D. H., *Big Enterprise in a Competitive System*, rev. ed. Washington, D.C.: The Brookings Institution, 1964.

Lampman, Robert J., *The Share of the Top Wealth-Holders in National Wealth, 1922-1956*. Princeton: Princeton University Press (for the National Bureau of Economic Research), 1962.

Mason, Edward S. (ed.), *The Corporation in Modern Society*. Cambridge, Mass.: Harvard University Press, 1959.

Meiklejohn, Alexander, *Political Freedom*. New York: Harper & Row, Publishers, 1960.

Miller, Herman P., *Rich Man, Poor Man.* New York: Thomas Y. Crowell Company, 1964.

Myrdal, Gunnar, *Beyond the Welfare State.* New Haven: Yale University Press (Yale Paperbacks), 1962.

Seligman, Ben B. (ed.), *Poverty as a Public Issue.* New York: Free Press, 1965.

Shonfield, Andrew, *Modern Capitalism: The Changing Balance of Public and Private Power.* New York: Oxford University Press, Inc., 1965.

Stouffer, Samuel A., *Communism, Conformity, and Civil Liberties.* Garden City, N.Y.: Doubleday & Company, Inc., 1955.

Wattenberg, Ben J. in collaboration with Richard M. Scammon, *This U.S.A.* Garden City, N.Y.: Doubleday & Company, Inc., 1965.

Democratic Socialism

Historical background

It is not easy to state when socialism first appears. Some have asserted that the ideal commonwealth in Plato's *Republic* is socialist, inasmuch as its ruling class has no property of its own and shares all things in common. Others have claimed that the Bible, particularly the Old Testament, constitutes the first socialist code, covering as it does the protection of workers, women, and the weak. The early Christians rejected the concept of "mine and thine," and practiced socialism in their everyday lives; and in the Middle Ages numerous sects and movements, mostly religious, attacked wealth and commerce as wicked and incompatible with the Christian life. Such sects frequently withdrew into isolation, living an austere existence and sharing poverty in brotherly love as a protest against the greed prevalent in the world around them.

During the Renaissance and the Reformation, there was a revival of protest against inequality based on wealth. The new arguments increasingly combined the older faith with the newer rationalism, as evidenced, for example, in Thomas More's *Utopia* (1516). In the Puritan revolution of the seventeenth century, there arose, side by side with the main movement of middle-class origin, a more radical group—called *Diggers* or *True Levelers*—that sought to attain communal ownership of land not currently in use. The movement was short-lived, but its radical protest against private landed property was not to be entirely forgotten.

Despite all such illustrations from earlier times, *socialism* as a major political force can properly be said to have originated as the *result of modern industrial capitalism.* To the extent that socialism contains within itself an element of protest against social inequality—and no movement can call itself socialist unless it expresses that kind of protest—it is as old as Western civilization itself. Both Greek and Jewish-Christian thought categorically reject the conception of wealth as the basis of the good life.

Another feature of socialism—the protest against money as the chief tie between human beings—is also not confined to the socialist tradition: many nonsocialists have voiced their disapproval of the "cash nexus." But if we look in history for something more specific and concrete than a vague protest against social injustice, we find that socialism as an effective, organized political movement is the product of the Industrial Revolution.

Just as communism has happened—and is likely to happen—only in countries *before* they have undergone the full impact of the Industrial Revolution, democratic socialism develops only in societies *after* they have experienced considerable industrialization.

Wherever industrialization has taken place in societies without deeply rooted liberal institutions, the political adjustment to the resulting tensions is likely to be either some sort of fascism (as in modern Germany, Italy, Japan, and Argentina) or communism (as in Russia and China). Because industrialization in these societies is promoted and controlled by an authoritarian state, its purpose is the power of the state, not the welfare of the individual.

In contrast, *where industrialization has occurred in relatively liberal societies* (as in northwestern Europe, North America, Australia, and New Zealand), the purpose of the economy is the welfare of the individual, and the adjustment to the inevitable tensions and conflicts of industrial capitalism assumes some form of democratic socialism or social democracy, rather than fascism or communism.

This basic distinction between the authoritarian and the liberal society can cut away a lot of confusion. Thus, the question is frequently debated whether a fascist economy is socialistic (because of the complete regulation of economic activity by the state) or capitalistic (because the means of production are left in private hands).

Such discussions are endless and insoluble because they are based on a false premise: that the basic distinction in the world's economic systems is between socialism and capitalism. In actuality, the line of division runs differently: between *free market* or *welfare economies* (which operate democratically and aim at freedom, welfare, and happiness) and *coercive* or *command economies* (which operate by command and coercion and aim at the power of the state through military expansion). Both capitalism and socialism fall into the group that is dominated by the concept of welfare economics, whereas fascism and communism fall into the second group, the command economy.

Differences among the species within each major group are important, but they are not crucial. Thus, capitalism and socialism disagree on the best method of bringing the maximum welfare to all the people; the former stresses individual property and effort, while the latter puts its faith in collective productive property and effort.

Fascism and communism do not see eye to eye in every detail on how best to operate an economy in the service of the state. Differences between fascism and communism, however, tend to fade into insignificance if it is recalled that the objective—the power of the state to wage aggressive war—is the same, and that the means—ranging from friendly pressure to slave labor and the concentration camp—are amazingly similar and frequently identical.

In some ways, of course, socialism opposes capitalism, but such opposition is the rebellion of the child against the father, not the total war of stranger against stranger. Just as the rebellious child uses arguments he has learned from his own father, socialism employs, in the controversy with its progenitor, a whole arsenal of capitalist values and attitudes, especially critical rationalism and pragmatic utilitarianism.

As to the specific problem of property, socialism inherits from capitalism one basic goal: *to preserve the unity of work and ownership.* In the seventeenth and eighteenth centuries, the early phase of modern capitalism, that unity was a reality. In the England of John Locke or the America of Thomas Jefferson, the average farm, store, or workshop was generally small enough to be owned and operated by one person or family. *Work and ownership coincided.* The chief threat to this unity came from the state, which sought to prescribe, to regulate, to snoop—in short, to play the role of an omniscient busybody in economic matters. This attitude was resented by the individual entrepreneur because he knew that he could run his own business without any unsolicited advice from pompous and self-confident state officials.

As the capitalist economy progressed, however, the individual (or single-family) form of ownership and work was gradually replaced, owing primarily to technological progress, by an economic system in which large-scale enterprise swallowed up the original capitalist-owner-manager. *As the size of industrial enterprise grew larger and larger, work became more and more socialized, collective, whereas ownership remained private.*

In seeking to restore the classical harmony between work and property, the reformer faces two alternatives—(1) the division of large-scale enterprises into small units, so that work and ownership can coincide again in one person or family, or (2) collective ownership.

The former method is feasible in agriculture, where large landed estates can be physically broken up and divided among landless farm workers, as was done in France during her Revolution in the eighteenth century, in Mexico and Guatemala during this century, and—on a smaller scale—in Italy after World War II. Whether such a breakup of large landed estates is economically sound or not is highly debatable. In many cases the productivity of dwarf farms created by agrarian reform is lower than that of the original large farm units. A reform government, however, may be willing to pay the price of lower productivity for the greater social benefit of having an independent farm class. In any case, the technology of agriculture is still simple enough so that large units can be broken up, and small units can be operated with relative efficiency.

In industry, this solution is physically out of the question. An automobile or aircraft factory cannot be divided up into 10,000 portions, each to be operated by one worker as his personal piece of property. The technological nature of modern industrial enterprise is such that there is no alternative to collective work and operation. Thus, in facing the task of reuniting work and ownership in industry, collective ownership seems to socialists the logical answer, just as the classical liberal deduced the right to individual ownership from the fact of individual work. In both systems—classical liberal capitalism and democratic socialism—there is the underlying assumption that the *right to property ultimately rests on work, effort, and industry, rather than on formal law, custom, or birth.*

John Locke, the founder of modern political and economic liberalism, based the right to property on human labor, and the value of property on the amount of labor "admixed" to nature's resources. The socialists have accepted the Lockean and capitalist rationale of labor. What has changed since Locke is simply the technological character of labor, not its ethical implications. If the logic of capitalism demands individual property for individual work, the logic of socialism demands *collective ownership* for collective work—*provided collective work is the only possible form of managerial organization.*

Where small property has survived as a technologically efficient unit, as in agriculture, the professions, the arts, and some areas of retailing, servicing, and manufacturing, socialists generally agree with adherents of capitalism that private ownership should be kept and strengthened. Thus, socialist governments have enjoyed long tenure in predominantly agrarian countries like Denmark and New Zealand because farmers in those countries have been sympathetic to the socialist program of maintaining their economic integrity and individualism by cheap credits, guaranteed parity prices, and other policies designed to protect the small farmer against the threat of domination by banks, insurance companies, and wholesalers.

Robert Owen: capitalist-socialist

The filial link between socialism and capitalism can be illustrated by the fact that the first modern socialist was a wealthy and successful capitalist. Robert Owen (1771–1858), generally regarded as the founder of British socialism, was the first to use the term "socialism." A self-made capitalist, he had made a fortune by the age of forty. He was a man of sound, practical judgment, and he could easily meet one test of experience frequently described by conservatives as essential whenever a reformer comes forth with some new scheme: "Have you ever met a payroll in your life?" Owen had. In his *A New View of Society* (1813), he describes himself as a "manufacturer for pecuniary profit."

His views were the result, not (like Marx's) of study in the British Museum, but of experience in his own industrial enterprises. Owen dedicated his book to His Royal Highness, the Prince Regent of the British Empire; he was no refugee from his own society, as were Marx and Lenin later, but a respectable, wealthy man, as English as mutton or tea. He considered drink as an incentive to crime and a main source of misery, and his list of virtues and vices would have appealed to Benjamin Franklin.

Far from looking upon capitalist Britain as a dungeon of inhumanity, he described the British constitution as being "among the best devised and most enlightened that have hitherto been established." Refusing to believe that evil can be transformed into good in a day, he advocated "progressive repeal and modification" of unjust laws and conditions; strongly rejecting the alleged blessings of revolutionary change, he felt that "the British constitution, in its present outline, is admirably adapted to effect these changes, without the evils which always accompany a coerced or ill-prepared change."

Realizing that love and fellowship cannot be conceived in hatred and born in strife, Owen appealed to "every rational man, every true friend of humanity," and he hoped for cordial cooperation and unity of action between the Government, Parliament, the Church, and the People.

Owen's rationalism also emerges from the fact that *A New View of Society* discusses one subject more than any other: *education.* Owen believed that the evils of his society were due to circumstances rather than to the depravity of man, and he was convinced that, just as crime and degradation were the result of specific social and economic conditions, education in a new environment could produce human beings endowed with rationality, habits of order, regularity, temperance, and industry.

In his own time, children of six and seven years of age were employed in factories for twelve hours a day and more, and Owen made the suggestion, bold and radical for the capitalist conscience of 1813, that a regular workday of thirteen hours from six in the morning to seven in the evening should not be imposed upon *children under twelve;* after that age "their education might be finished, and their bodies would be more competent to undergo the fatigue and exertions required of them." Human nature, Owen says, is "universally plastic," and if education is the key to make men more rational and cooperative, "the best governed state will be that which shall possess the best national system of education."

Owen in the true liberal-capitalist tradition looked to society rather than to the state for important change. A century before Keynes and Beveridge, Owen understood the crucial importance of full employment for the maintenance of a civilized society. Yet he was opposed to the dole (cash relief to the unemployed) on the ground that the "industrious, temperate, and comparatively virtuous" should not be compelled to support the "ignorant, idle, and comparatively vicious." Owen clearly saw the human aspects of unemployment; yet he did not want the state to dispense employment, but to provide an educational system good enough to equip every person with the skills wherewith to find employment in the open market.

A believer in the individualist principle of *self-help,* Owen started the cooperative movement and supported the incipient trade union organizations springing up throughout England and Scotland. For Owen, cooperation was more than selling milk to housewives; he believed that *producers' cooperatives* rather than consumers' cooperatives would establish a new social order. He sank much of his fortune in producers' cooperatives in England and spent several years and the better part of his wealth in a cooperative venture in the United States. His best-known experiment, the settlement of New Harmony in Indiana, did not succeed, but his ideas are today more important than ever.

The British experiment of nationalizing selected basic industries and services has raised the fundamental question whether the Owenite method of cooperation outside of the formal machinery of the national government is not preferable to nationalization as effected in Britain since 1945. In the British trade union movement too, the Owenite bias against the state is still strong; if the trade unions have never been overly enthusiastic about nationalization schemes, it is because they dread the growth of the state machinery and the transformation of free trade union officials, responsible to their members, into semi-government officials, responsible to the state.

Socialism and democracy

The link between democracy and socialism is the most important single element in socialist thought and policy. Looking at the history of socialism, it can be quickly seen that *successful socialist movements have grown up only in nations with strong democratic traditions,* such as Great Britain, the Scandinavian countries, Holland, Belgium, Switzerland, Australia, New Zealand and, more recently, Israel.

The reason for this parallelism is simple. Where democratic, constitutional government is generally accepted, socialists can concentrate on their program, ambitious as it may seem to some: to create more opportunity for the underprivileged classes; to end inequality based on birth rather than service; to open the horizons of education to all the people; to eliminate discriminatory practices based on sex, religion, race, or social class; to regulate and reorganize the economy for the benefit of the whole community; to maintain full employment; to provide adequate social security for the sick, unemployed, and aged; to re-plan the layout of towns and cities; to tear down the slums and build new houses; to provide medical facilities for everybody, irrespective of the size of his purse; and finally, to rebuild society on the foundation of cooperation instead of competition, incentive, and profit.

All these goals of democratic socialism have one thing in common: *to make democracy more real by broadening the application of democratic principles from the political to the nonpolitical areas of society.*

Freedom of worship and freedom of political association, historically the first liberties to be won, are still the most essential foundations of democracy. Where these foundations exist, therefore, and where democratic principles are firmly rooted in the hearts and minds of the people, socialists can concentrate on the "finer points" of democracy.

In contrast, socialist parties have fought an uphill and generally losing struggle in nations in which democracy is not a living thing, but an aspiration, a hope, an idea yet to be realized. For example, the Social Democratic Party in Germany always worked under one heavy handicap. In the Second Reich (1870–1918), political autocracy was a reality, and parliamentary institutions were a cover for the virtual dictatorship of Bismarck and then of Emperor William II. In the 1870's, Bismarck outlawed the Social Democrats as "enemies of the state," and the party leaders who escaped being jailed fled to England, other free nations in Europe, or America.

During the Weimar Republic (1919–1933), the German Social Democratic Party was paralyzed again by the insecurity of democratic institutions; the main issue of the Weimar Republic was not this or that social reform in which the socialists could take a special interest, but something much bigger: the issue of democratic government itself. Whereas, in nations with long-established democratic habits, socialists could argue over issues *within democracy*, taking the existence of democracy for granted, German socialists constantly had to argue and fight over the *issue of democracy itself*. As fascism grew in the Weimar Republic, the German socialists became more concerned with the defense of republican and democratic institutions than with problems of economic reform.

In Russia before 1917, the situation was even simpler. The despotic tsarist regime did not even make the pretense of democracy or self-government; social and economic reform by peaceful means was thus made virtually impossible, and the door for communism was opened.

World War II provides further illustrations of this point. In France, for example, the Socialist Party had become the strongest political party by 1936, far stronger than the Communist Party. During World War II, however, under the German occupation, the political environment of underground and illegal activity was much more congenial to the communists than to the socialists. Democratic socialists in a country like France function best when they can carry membership cards rather than high explosives. The type of person who joins such a party is well-meaning and stable, probably a family man, in any event a skilled worker or civil servant with a steady job. People of this kind do not readily engage in illegal, terroristic activities such as were necessary in France under German occupation in World War II.

The communists, on the other hand, attract an entirely different type of person, more fanatical, more devoted to his cause, and used to illegality and semi-illegality even in so-called normal times. What the Third French Republic (1870–1940) could never accomplish, four years of German occupation managed to do; at the end of World War II, the communists, polling about twice as many votes as the democratic socialists, emerged as the strongest single party of France. The communists remained the strongest party until the elections of November 18 and 25, 1962, in which the Gaullist party (Union for the New Republic) heavily defeated them.

In contrast, the socialist vote in *the British general election of 1966 was 210 times larger than the communist vote.* The evidence (not only from Great Britain, but also from other democratic countries with strong socialist movements) indicates that fullest civil liberty for all ideas and parties, including subversive, revolutionary organizations, seems to be the best antidote against fascism and communism, and that repression is the natural soil for the growth of revolutionary movements.

If one were to rank democratic nations today according to their respect for civil liberty, Great Britain, Norway, Denmark, Sweden,

Holland, Belgium, Australia, New Zealand, and Israel would be at the top of the list; all these countries are, or recently have been, governed by socialist administrations or by coalition cabinets with strong socialist participation.

The reasons for this parallelism are not too complex. Democratic socialists are keenly aware of the fact that without the opportunities provided by liberal, constitutional government they could not get to first base. Once in control of the government, socialists still maintain the psychology of the opposition, because they know that the possession of political power does not automatically solve the problems of social and economic organization. In other words, before socialists take over the government, they are in opposition to the government *and* to the wealthy classes; after they gain control of the government, the oppositionist psychology, directed as it is against the economic status quo, necessarily persists.

Moreover, even in the purely governmental realm, socialists tend to preserve a certain degree of caution and suspicion after they get into office, because they realize that, though they can gain control of the legislature in an election, the other sources of political power—the civil service and the judiciary—may be hostile to them.

Another factor essential to this discussion is all too frequently neglected. Examining the remarkably high state of civil liberty in nations with strong socialist movements, one tends to overlook *the high respect for civil liberty demonstrated by the opponents of socialism.* After all, if the conservative and propertied classes had shown less respect for the letter and spirit of constitutional government, the chances of socialist growth would have been very slim. From the viewpoint of dollars and cents, the conservatives' genuine acquiescence in socialism meant that they valued their faith in democracy more highly than their pocketbooks and were willing to be heavily taxed even for programs they considered undesirable or unreasonable.

It can thus be seen that both groups took a gamble: the socialists trusted their opponents not to destroy the processes of democratic government in order to protect their financial interests; the propertied classes trusted the socialists not to abuse electoral victories and to act reasonably and moderately when in office.

Where the propertied classes were unconvinced by the Biblical admonition that it is more blessed to give than to receive and were unwilling to pay an occasionally higher income tax as an insurance premium for the maintenance and stability of the social order, the natural response to distrust was more distrust. It is in this kind of political atmosphere that democratic socialism has been pushed back in Italy and France, giving way to the more radical demands of communism.

Socialism versus communism

Socialism and communism are not two of a kind, but represent two incompatible ways of thought and life, as incompatible as liberalism and totalitarianism.

There are several points of irreconcilable antagonism between socialists and communists. First, *communists* seek to bring about the end of capitalism by a single act of *revolutionary upheaval and civil war. Socialists,* on the other hand, adhere to *strict constitutional procedures;* they seek power by ballots rather than bullets, and once in office they know they are not in for keeps but are subject to being voted out in the next election.

Above all, the British Labor Party has successfully eliminated communism from its main position of influence—labor unions. *If communists are a negligible factor in Britain today, the main credit goes to the organized labor movement.* It has steadily and quietly fought them whenever and wherever they have tried to gain influence. In open elections, the communists are no menace in most democratic nations, but in labor unions the communist technique of infiltration has often been extremely effective. Because of the communist goal of revolution, it is understandable that socialist parties look upon communists as a group of troublemakers who must be kept out of unions or any other organized working-class activity. And because trade unionists have had the most intimate knowledge of communism—based on everyday contacts rather than on a study of ideology—they have generally proved themselves to be the staunchest opponents of communism in the labor movements. The purely political elements of the socialist parties have not always shown the same steadiness and vigor.

It is understandable why the communists work with such desperate energy for the control of organized labor: they know that no amount of propaganda will convert the middle and wealthier classes to communism. In contrast, the socialists have learned from elementary electoral statistics that parliamentary majorities cannot be obtained by appealing to one class only; a considerable proportion of the working class (in England about 40 pei cent) does not vote Labor, and if the Labor Party is to obtain a majority, it must appeal to other groups. The communists, prisoners of their dogmas, can only think in terms of class and class antagonisms; the socialists have learned to think in terms of parliamentary majorities.

The socialist rejection of Marxist thought applies even to the term "proletariat." As Prime Minister Harold Wilson put it: "The idea of a proletariat is nonsense. I am more interested in people as individuals than in the mass. I am interested in the family, be-

Relative Voting Strength of Socialist and Communist Parties *

(as of March 1, 1968)

Country	A: Socialist Per Cent of Total Vote	B: Communist Per Cent of Total Vote	C: Relation of A to B
Australia	47.7	0.5	95.4
Austria	44	3	14.7
Belgium	35.8	1.9	19
Canada	13.5	0.18	75
Denmark	42.3	0.7	211.5
Finland	29.8	21.2	1.4
France	15.2	21.3	0.71
Germany (West)	28.8	2.2	13
Great Britain	47.9	0.22	210
India	10.7	10	1.1
Israel	50	2.8	18
Italy	19.9	25.3	0.8
Netherlands	30	2.4	12
New Zealand	41.6	0.11	378
Norway	49.3	1.4	35.2
Sweden	47.3	5.2	9.1
Switzerland	26.7	2.6	10

* In the period 1946–1968, socialist voting strength generally remained stable. As to communist voting strength, the only major increase was in India (from 3.3% to 10%). Major declines in communist voting strength occurred in Austria (from 5.4% to 3%), Belgium (from 12.7% to 1.9%), Denmark (from 12.5% to 0.2%), France (from 28.6% to 21.3%), West Germany (from 8.4% to 2.2%), Great Britain (from 0.41% to 0.22%), Netherlands (from 10.6% to 2.4%), and Norway (from 11.9% to 1.4%). In West Germany, the Communist Party was outlawed in 1956; the figures in the table refer to the election of 1953, the last in which communists participated.

cause most happiness is family happiness. I am interested in Saturdays and Sundays and Bank Holidays." (*Manchester Guardian Weekly*, March 17, 1966.)

In the crucial issue of public ownership, the gap that separates socialists from communists is unbridgeable. Communists visualize the transition from capitalist enterprise to public ownership as sudden and complete. There is no payment for expropriated property, because communists consider that capitalist ownership of property is no better than theft. In contrast, socialists do not believe that the transition from capitalism to public ownership of the means of production can be either sudden or complete. Most socialists believe in the installment plan. Public ownership of the means of production is to be built up gradually, by installments; if one phase works, then the next will be tackled. Responsible socialists feel that they must prove pragmatically, through actual accomplishments, the usefulness and practicality of public ownership in particular industries or services.

Concerning compensation, socialists tend to share the general democratic conviction that no citizen may be deprived of his property without due process and compensation. Important as public ownership of the basic industries is to their plans, socialists consider public ownership not as an end, but as a means to an end, and a means that does not justify the violation of property rights.

There is another vital difference with regard to public ownership. Communists seek to transfer all means of production, distribution, and exchange to the state, leaving to the individual only free choice of consumer goods. Communists insist on *total nationalization*, because their dogma tells them that publicly owned property is always preferable to private enterprise.

By contrast, socialists seek to work out a set of empirical principles that will indicate in a *particular* instance whether a specific *industry or service* is to be transferred to public ownership and control. The socialists' criterion may be that the industry under examination is a monopoly (such as gas and light, telephone, and other utilities tend to become); or that the industry is sick (as the British coal industry was before its nationalization); or that the industry, although neither inefficient nor monopolistic, is of such vital importance to the national economy in peace and war that it seems socially undesirable to leave its operation in private hands (the British iron and steel industry was nationalized on these grounds).

The British Conservatives are in substantial agreement with

Labor on the first two criteria; on the third the two parties are in partial disagreement. Clearly, the irreconcilable difference of viewpoint with regard to private property is not between conservatives and socialists, but between democrats (conservatives, liberals, or socialists) and totalitarians (fascists or communists).

Philosophically and politically, the difference between communists and socialists goes to the root of things. As we saw earlier, Lenin's theory of the professional revolutionary is based on the assumption that the majority of the people (or the working class) are unable to think for themselves; that a minority, the Communist party, has the job of leading the proletariat; and that within the minority a small group of men, the professional revolutionaries, are to formulate policies and assume leadership. Thus, in Leninist theory (and in communist practice), a small minority within a minority is the ruling elite.

This elite concept is totally rejected by socialists, who believe in democracy and majority rule within their own party as much as in their own nation. Clement Attlee, British Prime Minister from 1945–1951 and leader of the Labor Party from 1935 to 1955, writes in his book *The Labour Party in Perspective* (1937) that his party's strength depends, "not on the brilliance of individuals, but on the quality of the rank and file." Attlee's own career confirms this diagnosis; brilliance was not his *forte,* and he lacked the dynamic leadership qualities of a Churchill or a Roosevelt.

Contrary to the communists, socialists believe in peaceful persuasion as the only method of promoting their program. Communists feel that it is useless to seek change by persuasion because all means of communication, education, and propaganda are biased in favor of the capitalist status quo and that freedom of the press amounts to little if one lacks the necessary funds to start a newspaper. For this reason the communists were stunned when the British Labor Party polled its electoral victory in 1945 and again in 1950, 1964, and 1966.

According to orthodox Marxism-Leninism, such victories were impossible. Since the British press was overwhelmingly in favor of the Conservative Party, how could the voters, who presumably had been reading the pro-conservative papers daily for years, vote Labor? According to Lenin, workers under capitalism are mentally enslaved to capitalist ideology and cannot therefore be peacefully converted to socialist thinking until there has been a change in the economic structure of society. Only *after* capitalism has been destroyed, Lenin argues, will the workers be able to think along anticapitalist lines, because (as Marx said) it is the conditions of man's life that determine his thinking.

To the communist, every capitalist system, whether democratic, authoritarian, or fascist, is a bourgeois dictatorship; specifically, democratic institutions in a capitalist system are considered as so much façade and hypocrisy which do not make the capitalist system any less dictatorial. Once capitalism—even liberal capitalism—is identified with dictatorship, the communist insistence on violence as the sole means of change is a logical conclusion.

Socialists, on the other hand, draw a fundamental distinction between two types of capitalist system, the political dictatorship and the liberal democracy. In a liberal democracy socialists believe in playing according to the rules of the game—provided, of course, the other side does the same.

Finally, *socialists reject the communist thesis that the choice in a democracy is between full capitalism and full collectivism.* Democratic parties do not concern themselves with bringing about the millennium at a certain date but seek to tackle issues that are comparatively manageable and to avoid definitive solutions that are irrevocable.

Socialists therefore envisage the transition from a predominantly capitalist economy (a purely capitalist economy exists and has existed only in the minds of the extreme Right and the extreme Left) to a predominantly socialist economy, not as a result of a sudden revolutionary *coup* that makes the return to private enterprise impossible, but as the result of gradual measures, none of which by itself irrevocably alters the nature of the whole economy.

Whereas the communists think in terms of three absolutes—capitalism, revolution, communist dictatorship—socialists think in terms of three *relative* concepts: a predominantly capitalist economy as the starting point, a long period of gradual change, and finally a predominantly socialized economy.

Elements of socialist thought and policy

Totalitarians of all shades have authoritative statements of doctrine, such as the *Communist Manifesto* or Hitler's *Mein Kampf*. Socialism, on the other hand, like many other liberal movements and ideas, has no bible, probably because liberals generally cannot agree on their beliefs and doctrines and are better at criticizing bibles than at writing them. Moreover, socialism has developed in different countries in accordance with different national traditions, and there has never been any central authority, such as world communism possesses in Moscow (and, to a lesser extent, Peking) to lay down a socialist party line.

Despite the absence of such authoritative statements of socialist doctrine, it is not too difficult to cull from socialist writings, and from the policies of socialist parties, the outlines of socialist thought and policy. What emerges, however, is not a consistent body of ideas and policies. It has been the main strength—and weakness—of socialism that it has had no clear-cut body of doctrine and that it has fed on contradictory sources, sources that reflect the contradictions of the societies in which socialism has developed.

The complex, and frequently self-contradictory, elements of socialist thought and policy can best be illustrated from the British socialist movement, the most influential in the world. The elements that stand out in the British movement are:

(1) religion
(2) ethical and esthetic idealism
(3) Fabian empiricism
(4) Liberalism

(1) In *The Labour Party in Perspective,* Attlee writes that "the first place in the influences that built up the Socialist movement must be given to religion. England in the nineteenth century was still a nation of Bible readers. To put the Bible into the hands of an Englishman is to do a very dangerous thing. He will find there material which may send him out as a preacher of some religious, social, or economic doctrine. The large number of religious sects in this country, and the various tenets that many of them hold, illustrates this."

The *Christian Socialist movement,* headed by two clergymen, Frederick Maurice and Charles Kingsley, reached its peak in the middle of the nineteenth century and was an important source for the later development of working-class and socialist organizations. The Christian Socialists had as their guiding principle the concept that *socialism must be Christianized, and Christianity socialized.*

George Lansbury, Attlee's predecessor as the leader of the Labor Party, writes in *My England* (1934) as follows: "Socialism, which means love, cooperation, and brotherhood in every department of human affairs, is the only outward expression of a Christian's faith.

I am firmly convinced that whether they know it or not, all who approve and accept competition and struggle against each other as the means whereby we gain our daily bread, do indeed betray and make of no effect the 'will of God.'" The late Archbishop of Canterbury, William Temple, came very close to socialism in his *Christianity and the Social Order* (1942). Temple holds that every economic system is, for good or ill, an immense educative influence and that therefore the church must be concerned with it. The church is thus bound to ask "whether that influence is one tending to develop Christian character, and if the answer is partly or wholly negative the church must do its utmost to secure a change in the economic system so that it may find in that system an ally and not an enemy."

This practical concern of Christianity was particularly strong in Victorian England, throughout the whole second half of the nineteenth century. A sense of moral seriousness and dedicated disinterestedness characterized the Victorian period, and Victorian religion, while conceding that grace and faith were essential to salvation, nevertheless emphasized conduct and *salvation by works.* Many socialist leaders of the older generation who (like Attlee and Cripps) came from upper-class homes were steeped in an atmosphere in which religion was taken seriously.

Another religious influence of profound importance in Britain was the tradition of religious dissent, of *nonconformity.* In other European states, Protestantism had resulted in freedom *of* the church in relation to Rome, but not necessarily in freedom *within* the church in matters of doctrine and church government. To the nonconformist, Protestantism meant freedom of individual conscience and the freedom to organize voluntarily in associations of like-minded believers. This principle of *voluntary association* was later translated from religion into politics, where it became the life principle of the free, democratic society.

It was in the village chapels of the eighteenth and nineteenth centuries that many local leaders of working-class organizations learned to think for themselves, as well as to conduct public meetings and administer finances. *Wherever nonconformity was strong, labor unions and cooperatives were strong;* in fact, the trade unions have been aptly called the present-day descendants of the earlier nonconformist congregations. Nonconformity supplied more than a particular religious outlook: it was also the source, in the labor movement, of the idealism, the moral dedication, and the seriousness that have characterized the movement and its leaders.

If one studies the internal organization of some nonconformist churches, one is struck by its similarity to the organization of trade unions: both are loosely federated unions of voluntary bodies freely associating with each other. The Labor Party today is also a federal union, made up of three main bodies—trade unions, cooperatives, and local constituency organizations—each of which is in turn made up of loosely federated organizations. Because the Labor Party has this federal character, its internal structure resembles more the American federal system than the much simpler and more streamlined political system of Britain itself.

The complexity of the religious root of modern socialism becomes apparent in the fact that *nonreligious, rational humanism* has also played a vital role in the evolution of socialist thought and action. Robert Owen was a rationalist and, among more modern socialist leaders in Britain, Sidney and Beatrice Webb, Harold J. Laski, G. D. H. Cole, and Hugh Gaitskell, to mention but a few, have not been much inspired by formal religious beliefs. It remains, however, of some interest that the political leaders of the labor movement, men like George Lansbury, Clement Attlee, and Sir Stafford Cripps, have more often been profoundly religious, whereas the principal intellectual figures, the men who formulate ideas rather than policies, tend to represent the *rationalist* root of socialism. Prime Minister Harold Wilson, a professional economist, comes from a background of strong religious nonconformity, and religion means a good deal to him. Although he is reluctant to express his religious feelings in public, he has often preached in nonconformist churches. His type of socialism has been called by a fellow Laborite "Methodism, not Marxism."

In the United States too, religion has played an important part in the cooperative and communal settlements established in the eighteenth and nineteenth centuries as well as in more recent socialist activities of a political and propagandistic nature. In the twentieth century, democratic socialism in the United States has been symbolized above all by Norman Thomas, who was a minister of religion before he took up the cause of socialism as his life's mission.

In contrast, religion has played a much smaller part in continental European and Latin American socialism. In England religious dissent was the bridge between religious and political unorthodoxy; in the virtual absence of nonconformity outside of the English-speaking world, however, dissent from the established social and political order has generally also included dissent from the established church, or from religion itself.

Before World War II, there were small groups of religious socialists in countries such as France and Germany, but, on the whole, socialists tended to be anticlerical or at least indifferent toward religion since most churches in continental Europe openly supported the political and economic status quo. During World War II, the heroic struggle of many priests and ministers against Nazi-fascist oppression brought about a closer understanding between churches and most socialist parties. Since then, the churches have become less committed to one particular set of social and economic theories, and the socialists have abandoned much of their earlier agnosticism and anticlericalism. Also, British socialism has proved to many socialists in other lands that socialism and religion do mix, provided the mixture is accomplished in the right spirit.

(2) *Ethical and esthetic idealism* is another source of British socialism, although its impact cannot be measured in votes and membership cards. Expressed by poets like John Ruskin and William Morris, ethical idealism was not a political or economic program, but a revolt against the squalor, drabness, and poverty of life under industrial capitalism. Developing first in England, capitalism probably produced more ugliness there than anywhere else, because English industrialists had no way of imagining what the new way of life would do to the beauty of the English countryside, no way of foreseeing the rapid disfigurement of lovely old towns and villages by slums and factory centers.

Whereas Marx approached industrial capitalism in terms of cosmic laws—the development of world history according to inevitable social laws, philosophical materialism, the law of the falling profit rate, to name but a few—Morris kept his gaze closer to the ground. He saw around him ugly household goods and furnishings, and men and women who lacked joy and beauty in their daily lives. Once, when asked in a public meeting what he thought of Marx, Morris said: "I am asked if I believe in Marx's theory of value. To speak quite frankly, I do not know what Marx's theory of value is, and I'm damned if I want to know." What Morris cared about was human beings, not this or that "system." He felt intensely that the arts must be brought back into everyday life and that people's creative impulses should be given expression in their daily life and work.

The influence of Ruskin and Morris was more negative than

positive. They showed what was wrong with a civilization—physically and morally—that was built on strife and squalor, but they did not formulate any specific program to improve the conditions to which they objected. Nevertheless, this esthetic and ethical revolt was important in preparing the intellectual environment in which socialism could later find a sympathetic response.

Ruskin and Morris were read mainly by the more educated class, which absorbed from them—as well as from Charles Dickens, Thomas Carlyle, and other writers—a groping understanding of what industrial civilization does to man, not only as a worker, but as a human being. The esthetic and ethical rebels of Victorian England undermined the self-confidence that then prevailed and fostered self-criticism; out of that doubt and self-criticism more positive socialist ideas could later be developed step by step.

In one particular field—town and country planning—the Labor Party reflects directly and explicitly the message of Ruskin and Morris. The whole concept of community planning—which is more than tearing down slums and building neat little row houses of uniform size and style—owes much to the outlook of the early pioneers of socialist thought, for whom problems of industry merged with more general problems of creating a community in which each member would have access to the means of civilized enjoyment.

(3) *Fabian empiricism* is perhaps the most characteristically *British* aspect of the British labor movement. The Fabian Society, founded in 1884, was named after a Roman general, Quintus Fabius Maximus Cunctator—the "delayer." The early motto of the society was: "For the right moment you must wait, as Fabius did; but when the right moment comes you must strike hard, or your waiting will have been vain and fruitless."

The founders and early members of the Fabian Society included George Bernard Shaw, Sidney and Beatrice Webb, H. G. Wells, and Graham Wallas. It was noteworthy that none of them came from the poorer classes and that there was a sizable proportion of writers in the group.

In Sidney Webb's historical survey of the basis of socialism, included in the *Fabian Essays* (1889), we find what is still the basic philosophy of Fabianism and, more generally, of British socialism. Webb looked upon socialism (eleven years before the foundation of the Labor Party) as an inevitable outcome of the full fruition of democracy, but he insisted that his "inevitability of gradualness" was sharply different from the Marxian inevitability of revolutionary, catastrophic change.

Webb emphasized in the *Fabian Essays* that social organization can come only bit by bit and that important "organic changes" can take place, in England at least, only under four conditions: first, such changes must be *democratic,* acceptable to a popular majority, and "prepared for in the minds of all"; second, they must be *gradual,* causing no dislocation; third, they must *not* be regarded as *immoral* by the people; fourth, they must be *constitutional and peaceful.*

Marxians on the Continent and elsewhere aimed their propaganda at the proletariat. As to the middle and upper classes, the job at hand was to liquidate them, not to convert them to socialism. Because the propaganda was thus aimed exclusively at the proletariat, it tended to be highly emotional and sloganized, taking into consideration not only the low educational level of the workers, but also the fact that they were expected to be half converted before they were ever exposed to Marxist agitation.

The Fabian Society started from the assumption that there could be *no progress toward a just social order in Britain unless the middle and upper classes could be shown the reasonableness and equity of the basic claims of socialist thought and policy.* Since government in Britain was by persuasion and consent, and since the governing classes of Britain were largely recruited from the middle and upper classes, there could be no change of policy in Britain without the preliminary consent of those classes. It was fortunate for the Fabians that they spoke the same language—literally and metaphorically—as did the governing classes and knew how to *permeate* the latter in ways which would have been closed to formal propaganda from persons outside of the same class.

The Fabian technique of permeation was based on the premise that you do not change a reasonable person through a single brilliant argument, lecture, or emotional appeal. It was the Fabian policy to work on the minds and feelings of their hearers in a slow, gradual process rather than in one sudden act of conversion, and preferably on social, informal occasions rather than on formal, official ones.

An emotional appeal to a high British civil servant, telling him that according to the Marxian dialectic the capitalist system is doomed, and that such doom will be followed by the classless proletarian society, was likely to have less effect than a casual reference at luncheon to a new government report, written by a fellow bureaucrat, on the incidence of disease and crime in slum areas. Similarly, serious discussion of a recent book by a reputable and scholarly economist on changes in the distribution of income among various social and economic groups was likely to have more effect on a conservative political leader than the shorter appeals of "Down with Capitalism" and "Long Live Proletarian Solidarity."

Permeation had also another side. The Fabians did not consider it their job to pass resolutions, make appeals to kings and parliaments, or address themselves to the masses of the people. They were interested in convincing a small group of persons, regardless of party affiliation, as long as they had two qualifications: first, they had to be persons of *continuous* influence in public life, so that the long process of permeation, if successful, would pay off; second, such persons would have to be *reasonable,* by which the Fabians meant not partisan extremists. Since such persons could be found in all political parties, the Fabians cultivated conservatives who met their qualifications as well as liberals.

This sort of Fabianism assumes a *Fabianism in reverse,* or else it would not stand a chance of success. For example, Fabians and other socialists in England religiously read *The Times,* not because they agree with its editorial viewpoint (generally conservative), but because it is "a good paper." In most other countries socialists consider the local substitute for *The Times* a source of bourgeois contamination from which they should steer clear.

The difference between the Fabian and Marxian-communist approaches can best be seen by contrasting the writings of the two groups. Marx was little interested in the minutiae of life; his *magnum opus, Das Kapital,* is an attempt to give meaning to history as a whole, and much of his thought was devoted to fundamentals of philosophy. Lenin wrote volumes and volumes on such subjects as *Materialism and Empirio-Criticism.* In contrast, over 95 per cent of all Fabian publications have been pamphlets rather than heavy tomes, and pamphlets lend themselves more to small subjects like *Municipal Milk and Public Health* (Fabian Tract No. 122) than to the future of Western civilization. The Fabian Society is rarely to be found in high intellectual altitudes, sniffing the thin air surrounding the metaphysical peaks; it is more often found "nosing about in the drains," seeking to remedy some immediate and *specific* condition.

Early in the history of the Fabian Society, Fabian Tract No. 70 (written by George Bernard Shaw) made it plain that Fabianism was no rival to existing philosophies trying to explain the whole cosmos and that it had "no distinctive opinion on the Marriage Question, Religion, Art, abstract Economics, historic Evolution, Currency, or any other subject than its own special business of practical Democracy and Socialism." This sense of practicality and concreteness is indicated by typical titles of Fabian Tracts and other pamphlets: *Liquor Licensing at Home and Abroad; Life in the Laundry; Public Control of Electrical Power and Transit; The Case for School Nurseries; The Endowment of Motherhood; The Reform of the House of Lords;* and *The British Cabinet: A Study of Its Personnel, 1909–1924.*

Two Fabian pamphlets, *Metropolitan Borough Councils: Their Constitution, Powers, and Duties,* and *Borough Councils: Their Constitution, Powers, and Duties,* were written by Clement R. Attlee in the spring of 1920, when Lenin was busy, not with the reform of borough councils, but with the destruction of states and empires.

The Fabian approach can perhaps best be shown in a simple illustration: if a slum clearance project is debated in terms of fundamental issues—such as socialism versus capitalism—agreement between advocates of the project and their opponents is unlikely. However, if the pertinent facts can be clearly brought out—the cost (in dollars and cents) of a slum area in terms of disease, crime protection, fire hazards, compared with the cost of building new houses with public assistance—the original gap has been considerably narrowed, and agreement will be likelier than it was when the argument centered on issues of apparently irreconcilable ultimate values.

The successes of Fabianism have probably stemmed chiefly from this concern with *reducing questions of principle to questions of fact.* Fabians gambled on the notion that facts do matter and that the impact of facts ultimately determines how people will think and act.

In his autobiography, *Power and Influence* (1953), Lord Beveridge has an interesting sidelight on the Fabian faith in facts. One of the greatest contributions of Sidney and Beatrice Webb was the creation of the London School of Economics and Political Science in 1895, in order to provide an adequate opportunity for the study of economics and allied subjects. The Webbs themselves chose the first four Directors of the London School. Of the four, Beveridge tells us, the first two became Conservative Members of Parliament, the third had socialist sympathies, and the fourth (Beveridge himself) was a Liberal. The Webbs, Beveridge says, "believed that the impartial study of society would further the Socialism which was their practical aim, but they were prepared to take the risk of being wrong in that belief."

The Fabian technique of trying to reduce apparently irreconcilable differences of principle to negotiable disagreements over facts is no invention or novelty but is implicit in the very nature of the democratic society. We have peace in a free society to the extent that people are willing to keep to themselves conflicting fundamentals in religion, morals, and philosophy. Separation of state and church in the United States was effected and has been maintained not because Americans are indifferent to religion, but because the framers of the Constitution felt it to be wiser to keep a fundamental issue like religion out of politics and to concentrate on issues in which people of all religions can cooperate without injury to their religious belief.

Fabianism has frequently been described as reform without resentment, social reconstruction without class war, political empiricism without dogma or fanaticism. Despite its small size (its membership never exceeded a few thousand), the Fabian Society has had an enormous impact. In the 1945 election, which led to the first Labor government based on a substantial parliamentary majority, 229 of the 394 Labor Members of Parliament were Fabians, and more than half of the Government, including Attlee (the Prime Minister from 1945–1951), was Fabian. Hugh Gaitskell, who succeeded Attlee as Leader of the Labor Party, was also a Fabian of long standing, as is Gaitskell's successor, Prime Minister Harold Wilson.

(4) *Liberalism* has become an increasingly important source of socialism, particularly since Liberal parties have dwindled to insignificance in many countries. In England, the Liberal Party has virtually disappeared and the Labor Party seems to have inherited about one-third of the estate. Temperamentally, many Liberals do not find it easy to join a socialist movement; the passion for individual liberty and individual difference is still the most distinguishing trait of the Liberal.

Apart from the tendency toward red tape and regulation for the sake of regulation, there is also in socialism a tendency toward the state, the mass, and collectivity. Both tendencies are repugnant to the true Liberal, the man who occasionally still likes to be himself and not just a number in the National Register. Yet, during the last thirty years, more and more Liberals have joined the Labor Party. Why?

In the first place, the weakness of the *British Liberal Party* is due to the fact, not that it has failed, but that *its success has made it unnecessary.* Both the Conservative Party and the Labor Party are now thoroughly committed to the Liberal principles of respect for individual freedom of worship, thought, speech, and association. Liberalism as a protest against clericalism is no longer a live issue in England (or in most other countries).

Free trade, another great ideal of nineteenth-century British Liberalism, no longer arouses passionate political interest. Both Conservatives and Laborites are committed to some form of tariff protection, and even the Liberals realize that free trade no longer has the importance it once had.

In the 1960's, the issue of free trade re-appeared in the controversy over British membership in the Common Market (France, Germany, Italy, Belgium, Holland, and Luxembourg). The division of public opinion was *within,* rather than between, the two major political parties. Liberal ideology played a less important part than the estimates of economic benefits expected from British membership.

In the question of empire too, the Liberal approach of the nineteenth century is no longer relevant, since nearly all of the empire is gone. The liquidation of the empire after World War II occurred under both Labor and Conservative governments.

The specific issues gone, many Liberals have joined the Labor Party, or vote Labor, or think of themselves as vaguely socialist. Liberalism has generally been to the Left of the Conservatives, and in a country with a two-party system, like Britain, if one wishes to stand to the Left of Conservatism, the Labor Party is now the only platform to stand on.

On issues of public ownership, the Liberal elements in the Labor Party are opposed to doctrinaire policies of nationalizing for the sake of nationalizing—*i.e.,* the Liberals in the Labor Party are generally on its Right wing, just as the Liberals in the Conservative Party are on its Left wing. The Right-wing Laborite is so close to the Left-wing Conservative in mentality, outlook, temperament, and policies that it takes a pencil of electronic sharpness to draw the line of demarcation between the two.

Liberalism has contributed much that is lasting in British socialism. Because of the Liberal influence, socialist leaders are more moderate and less doctrinaire than they might otherwise have been, and they have a deeper respect for individual liberty. Liberalism has turned the Labor Party into a national party rather than one based on class, and it has bequeathed to the Labor Party the Liberal message that there can be reform without bitterness and hatred.

Social-economic changes and reforms

The victory of the democratic nations in World War I provided a strong stimulus for the growth of socialist parties throughout the world. The war had been fought in defense of the ideals of liberty and social justice against the authoritarian imperialism of Germany and her allies, and during the war promises were made to the peoples of the major democratic belligerents that military victory would be followed by the establishment of a new social order based on greater opportunity and equality.

In England, the Labor Party reflected in its growth and development the protest against the old social order. Founded in 1900, the Labor Party polled only two seats in the Parliamentary elections of that year. By 1910 forty Laborites sat in the House of Commons, and the party had ceased to be a negligible factor. In 1918 the parliamentary representation rose to 57, and in 1922 the Labor Party obtained 142 seats out of 615, replacing the fading Liberal Party as the second strongest party in the country. In 1924, the Labor Party, though still a minority, formed a government with the tacit support of the Liberal Party, but the experiment lasted only ten months, because the Liberals finally decided that they could not go along with a socialist program.

In 1929, the Labor Party became for the first time in its history the largest single party in Britain, obtaining in the general election 288 out of 615 seats in Parliament. Although lacking an absolute majority in the House of Commons, the Labor Party formed a government that lasted until the summer of 1931. The coming of the world depression in 1929 weakened Britain economically, and the Labor government, being unable to follow socialist policies to cure the depression and unwilling to adopt conservative remedies, resigned in the summer of 1931. In the ensuing election the parliamentary representation of the Labor Party dropped to 52 out of 615, but by 1935, the last election before World War II, its strength in the House of Commons had risen again to 154. As long as the shadow of Nazi-fascist aggression hung over Britain, however, there was little chance for embarking upon a major experiment of social and economic reform.

Between 1935 and the end of the war in Europe there was no general election. In the first postwar general elections, held on July 5, 1945, the Labor Party obtained 394 out of 640 seats, with the result that for the first time in British history a Labor government was formed with a clear majority in the House of Commons. In 1950, the Labor majority fell to a bare 315 out of 625 seats, and because of the narrow margin and the resulting instability of government, a new election was held in 1951. The Labor Party lost it, as it lost the next two general elections in 1955 and 1959. In 1964, Labor staged a comeback and won the election by a narrow margin. But since its majority of three in the House of Commons proved insufficient for a stable government, Prime Minister Harold Wilson called for a new election in 1966. This time Labor won with a decisive majority of 97 Members of Parliament—not the triumphant victory of 1945, when Labor had a majority of 148 in the House of Commons, but still a clear mandate from the people to be governed by Labor for a full term of five years.

Between 1900 and 1918, the Labor Party was not officially committed to socialism, although it included, of course, many individual socialists. In 1918, when the party adopted socialism in its program, its commitment to the nationalization of industry was just about complete. But as the party learned the facts of life it changed its outlook drastically and urged nationalization only where it had been proved pragmatically that public ownership would do more for the welfare of the nation than private ownership. In the election of 1945, for example, the Labor Party did *not* enter the campaign with a program of "socialism" in the abstract but promised to nationalize specifically listed industries and services if elected to office.

In each case, it explained why nationalization was necessary. For gas and light, water, telephone and telegraph, and other utilities, the criterion of nationalization was the existence of a *natural monopoly.* On the coal industry, there was general agreement in Britain, regardless of party, that the industry was so sick and inefficient that it could not be put on its feet except through nationalization. The iron and steel industries were declared to be so *vital to the nation,* in peace and in war, that their management could not safely be subject to the decisions of private persons. The nationalization of all inland transportation, by rail, road, and air,

Reproduced by permission of the Proprietors of *Punch.*

Round the Corner.

was proposed on the ground that *wasteful competition* could best be avoided by a *coordinated scheme* of transportation owned and managed by public authorities. The Bank of England was also proposed for nationalization on the ground that its purpose was so obviously public. Finally, the election program of 1945 also promised the setting up of a National Health Service, so that the best possible health and medical facilities might be available to every person without regard to his ability to pay.

After the electoral triumph of 1945, the Labor Party methodically carried out its program. With one exception, there was little argument over nationalization. On the exception, iron and steel, the Conservatives argued that the industry was highly efficient and that the needs of the national welfare could be accommodated without nationalization.

The attitude of the British public toward nationalization was generally one of indifference. The exception was, and is, the National Health Service, because of its direct effect on the everyday life of the individual citizen. Although no one was compelled to join the National Health Service, 97 per cent of the population and 96 per cent of the doctors are in it. At first the administrative and technical difficulties in setting up the necessary machinery caused considerable delay and confusion. As the program began to hit its stride, however, adverse criticism died down. Now the National Health Service has established itself as a part of British life. The Conservative Party, like the Labor Party, is fully committed to the program. The medical profession, while not enthusiastic about it, has nevertheless publicly accepted it as essentially "sound." As to the British public, a Gallup poll in 1962 found that 89 per cent of those questioned were satisfied with the National Health Service. Discussion in Britain is no longer about the basic issue of a national health insurance program, but about ways of improving its practical operation.

The Labor government elected in 1945 also set up a comprehensive cradle-to-grave scheme of *social security*. The system provides protection against sickness, unemployment, and old age, supplemented by maternity grants, widows' pensions, and family allowances. Social security as set up by the Labor government was no invention of the Labor Party, but the culmination of several decades of social legislation enacted by Conservative and Liberal governments. A fully integrated system of social security was first proposed during World War II in the *Beveridge Report* (1942); in the middle of the war, both the Conservative Party and the Labor Party pledged themselves, if elected to office after the war, to introduce a comprehensive system of social security.

A further policy of the Labor government in the years 1945–1951 aimed at greater *social equality*. The setting up of the basic institutions of the welfare state in itself contributed to greater social equality by bringing within the reach of large sections of the population many facilities and services that hitherto had not been available to them. *Educational opportunities* on the secondary and university levels, for example, were made available to children of lower-income families. In addition, several new colleges and universities were founded in an attempt to combine British educational features with the American goal of providing higher education for the many rather than for the select few.

In 1965, the Labor government began to tackle one of the keys to social equality—the secondary school. In Britain—as in most other countries—there are two main types of secondary school: an academic type, for a small minority, that leads to college; and a vocational type, for the mass of the people, that ends at age 15. The main disadvantage of such a system is that the decision about going to college must be made at age 10 or 11 on entering a specific type of secondary school; an additional disadvantage is that the system segregates the members of different social classes at a very early age. For these reasons, the Labor government started, from 1965 onward, to adapt the British system of secondary education to the American pattern, in which most high schools combine academic with vocational education. Interestingly, Labor spokesmen for this reform often refer to the American experience; as in so many other instances, what socialists in other countries call the socialist ideal of equality is accepted in the United States as the noncontroversial American concept of equality of opportunity.

Taxation was the greatest leveler. Thus, in 1910 a person with an income of £100,000 retained, after payment of taxes, about £94,000. In 1966, the net income on £100,000 after payment of taxes had shrunk to about £17,000. Inheritance taxes took about 50 per cent of larger fortunes in 1938, and about 80 per cent after World War II. In 1938, the last normal prewar year, there were 6,600 persons in Britain whose income was over £6,000 after payment of taxes. The number of persons in that group had dwindled to 60 by 1949 but rose again to 3,000 in 1960 and to 17,700 in 1963. However, the total after-tax income of the 6,600 persons with incomes over £6,000 in 1938 was £62.2 million, or about £10,000 of average income in that group. In 1963, the total after-tax income of the 17,700 persons with incomes over £6,000 was £129.5 million, or about £8,000 of average income in that group. It should be remembered that the value of the pound was cut to one-third of its prewar purchasing power, so that the *average real income in the top group* in terms of purchasing power was only *about one-quarter* in 1963 of what it had been in 1938.

While the share of high incomes in terms of the national in-

Reproduced by permission of the Proprietors of *Punch*.

"It fought for years against rising taxation, but at last it surrendered."

come has declined in Britain, there has been a sharp increase of the middle-income groups, particularly skilled workers. The trend toward more social equality can also be seen in the fact that the proportion of the national income paid in wages and salaries increased from 60 per cent in 1938 to 70 per cent in 1965, whereas the income from dividends and interest declined considerably during the same period. All these policies have by no means brought about absolute equality, but they have gone a long way toward eliminating extremes of inequality.

Dropping much of the traditional socialist belief in nationalization, the Labor Party has come close to the Conservative Party, which in turn no longer opposes the basic principles of the welfare state. Inasmuch as both parties seem to be united on kindred principles of social policy, and because so much of the British economy depends upon factors external to it (such as prosperity in the United States), there is little room left for such differences in principle as characterized the classic nineteenth-century struggles between the Whigs and the Tories.

In the 1960's, British politics thus give the impression of ideological peace and near-uniformity. The Labor Party, in particular, is in search of a new program and set of principles that can inspire the country, for the *impulse of early socialism*—nationalization plus social security—*has been largely spent*. The very success of the welfare state has thus become the main source of socialist hesitation and stagnation.

In domestic economic policy, one of the main concerns of the Wilson cabinet since 1965 has been the defense of the pound. In pursuit of this objective, the Labor government has put financial orthodoxy—the soundness of the currency at the expense of economic expansion—above the socialist objective of full employment and rising wages at the price of inflation. Ironically, a Labor government can carry out such an orthodox and conservative policy more effectively than a Conservative government, which can be easily subjected to the charge that its financial orthodoxy merely reflects the views of bankers and coupon-clippers.

In its foreign economic policy too, the Wilson cabinet has pursued orthodox policies aimed at a more favorable balance of payments by imposing new tariffs on imports, freezing wages to make British exports more competitive in the world market, and by trimming welfare expenditures at home rather than by drastically cutting British defense expenditures and military commitments abroad. Prime Minister Wilson has thus put the international political interests of Britain as a great power above her social welfare at home.

Conservative adherence to welfare state policies and Labor adherence to financial orthodoxy make it difficult to decide which is the more reformist and which the more conservative party of the two.

On the European Continent, the Scandinavian countries have had the most impressive record of social reform, both in the interwar years and after World War II. From the early 1930's onward, the Scandinavian countries have been generally governed by socialist administrations based on parliamentary majorities, and as a result communism has been kept down to minor proportions in all three countries (Norway, Denmark, Sweden). The Scandinavian socialist movements have emphasized economic development and social security rather than nationalization, and their economic policies have been centered on fiscal measures (such as cheap money) and taxation rather than on public ownership. Full employment is a major point in Scandinavian (as in British) socialism.

One of the important lessons of the social and economic reform in Scandinavia in the last thirty years is the emphasis on *socialization rather than nationalization.* One of the most serious political weaknesses of the British program of economic change has been the tendency to substitute *state* ownership and management for private ownership, thus increasing the tendency toward governmental centralization. In contrast, the Scandinavian reform programs have experimented with other types of social ownership in lieu of private ownership.

The most significant contribution of Scandinavia to social reform is the use of the *cooperative movement* rather than the state as the agent of social and economic reform. Whereas in Britain the cooperative movement has been largely confined, as in most other countries, to retail and wholesale trading in a selected group of articles, the Scandinavians have set up cooperatives for slum clearance, health insurance, and industrial production. This Scandinavian *middle way* avoids the evils of unbridled capitalism and avoids, at the same time, the dangers of statism.

Problems of nationalization

Socialist theory and practice have undergone drastic changes on the issue of nationalization in the last fifty years. When the British Labor Party adopted a socialist platform in 1918, it demanded (in Clause IV of its revised constitution) "the common ownership of the means of production, distribution, and exchange." At that time, this formula expressed the prevailing socialist orthodoxy.

Today, not a single socialist party in the world, nor a single socialist leader of repute and responsibility, still adheres to the old formula of nationalizing *all* the means of production, distribution, and exchange. In July, 1951, the Socialist International, speaking for over thirty socialist parties throughout the world, adopted a program that specifically rejected the older doctrine of total nationalization and conceded that socialist planning is compatible with private ownership in agriculture, handicrafts, retail trade, and small and medium-sized industries.

In 1959, the German Social Democratic Party, the largest democratic socialist party on the European Continent, adopted a new program in which freedom, justice, and respect for the individual are declared as its highest values. As to nationalization, the program specifically states that "efficient small and medium-sized enterprises are to be strengthened to enable them to prevail in competition with large-scale enterprises." Only where, for natural or technical reasons, competition is impossible, does public ownership become a necessity. The following two general principles are included in the program: "Private ownership of the means of production is no longer identical with the control of power"; and "Every concentration of economic power, even in the hands of the state, harbors dangers."

In 1964, the Social Democratic Party adopted a series of new resolutions spelling out its domestic and foreign policies in detail. This time, the word "nationalization" did not even appear, so dead an issue had it become since 1959. The economic policy was summarized as follows: "Only a combination of the market economy and monetary and fiscal over-all control and welfare policy can be the solution suited for our time." This goal differs in no way from the policies pursued by middle-of-the-road parties in most democracies today, and only extreme Right-wing conservatives or doctrinaire Left-wing socialists will object to it.

Even many of those who still object to private capitalism increasingly reject nationalization as the only alternative. In his *Democratic Socialism: A New Appraisal* (1953), Norman Thomas, the leader of American socialism during the last forty years, writes that "the state under the most democratic theory and practice will become too huge, too cumbersome, if it seeks to control directly all economic activity." Thomas speaks of the *dangers of statism* inherent in total nationalization, and like most thoughtful socialists today he stresses that the alternative to private capitalism is *socialization, not nationalization.*

Freedom is inextricably linked to the *diffusion of power;* this truism has always been admitted by socialists to apply to political government. They are now finally coming around to the idea that *in the economic realm too, there can be no freedom unless there is diffusion of economic power.*

Total nationalization—even under the most democratic safeguards—is bound to lead to the all-powerful state, and such a state is a threat to liberty even if it uses its powers benevolently.

The concept of socialization, in contrast, implies the diffusion of publicly owned property. Property is owned and managed not by the state but by producer or consumer cooperatives, trade unions, churches, educational institutions, hospitals and other organizations, and these organizations derive their powers from voluntary association rather than from the sovereign authority of the state.

This approach has been successfully tried in Scandinavia as well as in Israel. In Scandinavia, most public housing has been built, not by the state, but by corporations that combine individual ownership and management with financial assistance from housing cooperatives and municipal agencies. In Scandinavia too, as mentioned earlier, cooperatives are not confined—as they are in many countries—to the retail business, but are common in the fields of manufacturing and wholesaling. In Israel, the Federation of Labor is the largest employer in the nation; it has a considerable share in the ownership and control of such basic industries as transportation, building, foundries, heavy machinery, cement, glass, and rubber. Also, a sizable proportion of Israel's agricultural production is in cooperative farm communities.

None of these solutions are final, and mistakes are constantly made, but these forms of socialization do seem to their advocates to avoid the worst evils of nationalization—monopoly and the resulting concentration of economic and political power. In a capitalist democracy, the economic power of private monopolies can at least be opposed by the political power of the state. *When the monopolist is the state itself, who will protect the citizen against the state?*

Today then, no socialist party advocates any longer that *all* industries be collectivized; nationalization is recommended only for *some* industries. How many is some? There is no clear-cut answer, but there seems to be universal acceptance among socialists of the idea that natural monopolies in the public utilities field should be publicly owned and managed. The concept of the "sick industry" (*e.g.*, the British coal industry) and the criterion of the "key industry" (*e.g.*, the British steel industry) have also been accepted as standards upon which nationalization may be based.

It appears that *nationalization lends itself best to industries or services that are highly standardized—i.e.*, where *uniform rules of administration* can be easily applied (this is the thesis of "gas and water socialism"). On the other hand, in industries that demand high adaptability to changing conditions, for example, industries which produce largely for export or industries which operate with a considerable element of risk, the case against nationalization or socialization is strong. The tendency of a bureaucratically run enterprise to put security above adventure and risk is incompatible with rapid industrial expansion. The automobile industry a generation ago and the photocopying industry today are the products, not of pre-existing giant enterprises, but of relatively small corporations that were willing to put risk capital into new products.

It remains to be proved that this same spirit of adventure, risk, and experimentation can be shown by publicly owned enterprises. After all, it is one thing to risk, and speculate with, one's own money; it is quite another thing to use the public treasury for questionable ventures.

The traditional concern of socialists has always been with *distribution* rather than *production.* The most creative contribution of socialism has, therefore, been its revision of the internal social structure of nations in the direction of equality. Many countries with strong socialist parties exhibit internal cohesion and unity, the direct result, according to socialist leaders, of a high degree of social justice based on the concept of "fair shares for all." In contrast, these leaders point out, where socialism has recently been weak, as in France and Italy, the people are torn and disunited, and there is a general feeling of frustration and resentment.

It has not been shown so far that publicly owned enterprise is any more efficient in production than private enterprise or that it has materially increased the people's standard of living. C. A. R. Crosland, a leading British economist and member of the Wilson cabinet, makes important concessions on both points. First, he admits that the performance of nationalized industries in Britain has not been conspicuously better than that of private enterprise and that nationalized industries have been plagued by "bureaucratic centralization." Speaking of living standards, he also argues that further nationalization "cannot be said to be necessary to full employment and prosperity, for these exist already." (*The New Leader,* February 29, 1960.)

From the very beginning, public enterprise has found that three specific difficulties hamper its over-all performance. First, there is the *managerial problem* of administering vast public enterprises with flexibility and initiative and at a low cost. The excessive tendency toward centralization and playing it safe is a serious matter. Moreover, it is not certain that the managerial situation will improve as nationalization continues. In the first phase of public ownership, the public corporation can draw upon managerial talent which has been trained in the tough environment of private competition, but if nationalization goes on, management of public enterprises will have to draw its top personnel from among its own ranks. It will then be seen whether persons trained and bred in the secure, sheltered atmosphere of bureaucratic monopoly will possess as great a capacity to operate large undertakings as is shown by graduates of the hard school of private, competitive business.

If the American experience can serve as a guide to managerial performance, the outlook for nationalized enterprise is uncertain. In American corporate business, industries that are near the bottom of the executive pay scale (and presumably attract less able executives) include regulated industries like insurance, savings and loan associations, banking, air transport, railroads, and public utilities. These industries are either monopolies (as in the case of the public utilities) or enjoy relatively little competition since their very existence generally depends on a governmentally granted franchise. There is relatively little product innovation in such industries, operations are often highly routinized, and seniority is a determining factor in promotions. By contrast, the industries near the top of the executive pay scale (automotive, chemical, metals manufacturing, electronics, department stores) are characterized by creativity and product innovation under the pressure of substantial competition. Promotion is less influenced by seniority, outside executive talent is more frequently brought in, and there is therefore a greater turnover of executive personnel.

In nationalized industries producing standardized goods or services (such as public utilities) the management problem may not be too serious. But in competitive industries, where flexibility and innovation are essential, nationalized industries will find it more difficult to attract top quality executives for two reasons. First, as an industry becomes nationalized, it automatically becomes monopolistic and routinized and allows for less creativity and executive initiative than are demanded under conditions of private, competitive enterprise. Second, nationalized industries—like regulated industries in a nonsocialist economy—pay lower executive salaries, and able executives prefer more challenging positions that offer better pay to more routinized work at lower pay. Since Britain is likely to remain a predominantly private enterprise economy for a long time, outstanding managerial talent will continue to move into the high-paying private, competitive sector.

The steel industry may well become a testing ground. During

its six years of office in 1945–1951, the Labor government hesitated to nationalize the steel industry, although it had committed itself to do so, because there was little public support for the measure outside of a doctrinaire, Left-wing element in the Labor Party. Before leaving office in 1951, the Labor government laid the ground-work for the nationalization of steel, but before the scheme could be put into full operation, the Conservatives came into office in 1951. They immediately returned steel to private ownership but set up a national Iron and Steel Board to protect the national interest in the industry.

When Labor returned to office in 1964, the Wilson cabinet did not dare to propose re-nationalization of steel, since the Labor majority in Parliament was only three or four, and the government preferred to play it safe. However, after Labor was returned to office in 1966 with a substantial majority of 97, it proceeded to "re-nationalize" steel. In the opinion of independent observers, this was not done for economic reasons, but in order to placate the Left-wing group in the Labor Party that insisted on nationalized steel.

The problem of management is closely connected with a second major problem. In private business, the *system of profits and losses* operates in a crude but effective way to keep efficiency at a relatively high level, and the threat of bankruptcy is always real. In a public enterprise, this system no longer operates to the same extent; if there are losses, no one goes bankrupt, and the losses of one division can be passed on to the whole enterprise. Even if the whole enterprise or industry is in the red, management can, because it has a monopoly, either increase prices or receive subsidies from general taxation.

The British government has periodically published comparative data about the commercial performance of nationalized enterprise. During the eight-year period of 1955 to 1962, for example, the annual rate of net return on net assets in private manufacturing and distribution ranged from 12 to 17 per cent. In the steel industry, the average annual net return was impressively high—14 per per cent. By contrast, the nationalized sector showed a much less impressive performance. Coal produced an average annual return of 3 per cent, electricity about 5 per cent, while railways and BOAC were heavy losers. Part of BOAC's losses was due to its decision, under government advice, to buy more costly British aircraft in order to subsidize the British aircraft industry. While private international airlines have chalked up huge profits in recent years, BOAC has managed to lose substantial sums.

Third, there is the *political difficulty*. How are public corporations to be related to the elected representatives of the people? If the public corporation is too closely supervised by parliament or congress, its management may become demoralized and lose efficiency. If parliamentary control is relaxed, on the other hand, up goes the cry that there is not much difference between the old and the new systems (since if management can do more or less as it pleases, what has nationalization changed?).

Because of all these difficulties and complexities, many leading socialists are increasingly reconciling themselves to the virtually complete elimination of nationalization from the socialist program, emphasizing the concepts of equality and welfare instead. In a Fabian Tract on *Socialism and Nationalization* (1956), Hugh Gaitskell, the late Leader of the British Labor Party, concludes that "the most vital question is how far greater social and economic

Reproduced by permission of the Proprietors of *Punch*.

"I was the Chairman of the Board until I found out about the rates for overtime."

equality can be achieved without more nationalization and public ownership." After the electoral defeat of 1959, Gaitskell went even further by publicly advocating that the Labor Party eliminate from its constitution Clause IV (which demands the common ownership of the means of production, distribution, and exchange).

A prominent spokesman of the right wing in the Labor Party and Minister of Defense in the Wilson Cabinet, Denis Healey, goes even beyond Gaitskell. A generation ago, American writers like A. A. Berle said that in the American capitalist enterprise the real power is in the hands of professional managers rather than of the shareholders who legally own it. This viewpoint is now increasingly recognized by socialists as being equally applicable to publicly owned enterprise. "Industrial power in every large, developed economy now rests with a managerial class which is responsible to no one. The form of ownership is irrelevant. State control over nationalized industries is as difficult as share-holder control over private firms." (Denis Healey, *The New Leader,* August 17, 1957.) For a high-ranking socialist to say that the form of ownership is irrelevant marks a basic change of outlook.

More important than what socialist leaders and thinkers have said is the fact that most voters have clearly and repeatedly expressed their opposition to further nationalization. In the 1950's and 1960's, numerous polls were taken on this question, some by independent polling organizations and others by Labor organizations. In every instance, from 65 to 80 per cent of the voters have opposed further nationalization; more seriously, even among Labor Party supporters the number of those who favor further nationalization is generally only one-third to one-half of those who oppose it.

In the elections of 1964 and 1966, the Labor campaign therefore barely mentioned public ownership and concentrated on the topic of economic growth as Britain's No. 1 problem. Taking his cue from the successful Kennedy campaign in 1960, Harold Wilson stressed the need for Britain to "move forward," to get out of the lethargy and stagnation which, according to him, were the result of thirteen years of Conservative rule. In particular, Wilson promised that a Labor government would increase and strengthen higher education and scientific research and that the new opportunities in research would stop the "brain drain," or the emigration of British scientists to other countries, mainly to the United States. In his devotion to scientific growth Wilson went even so far as to say that "if there was one word I would use to identify modern Socialism it was 'science'." (*The Relevance of British Socialism,* 1964, p. 41.) While Wilson also promised social welfare improvements in the campaigns of 1964 and 1966, the emphasis clearly shifted from accelerated social justice to accelerated economic growth. Because the rate of British economic growth since the 1950's has fallen way behind that of Western Europe, Japan, the United States, and numerous other countries, nationalization, whether commercially a success or a failure, has proved itself wholly irrelevant to the problem of British economic growth. By staking its future, at least for the next decade or two, on this issue rather than on the outmoded side issue of nationalization, the Labor Party is aware of the fact that it will be judged by the people in the light of its record on restoring Britain to a position of economic excellence and leadership.

More recently, surveys in various parts of the world (including Western Europe and Britain) have shown that about two-thirds of those polled reject both capitalism, if capitalism means the exploitation of the many by the wealthy few, and socialism, if socialism means government ownership of the economy. Two-thirds of the interviewees favored social welfare and private property. More specifically, 70 per cent of those polled stated that socialism meant to them "social welfare" rather than "government ownership." (Ralph K. White, *Foreign Affairs,* January 1966, p. 225.)

A leader of the Labor Party, Douglas Jay, has succinctly stated the reason why democratic socialist movements have swung away from nationalization toward the welfare state, economic security, and social justice: "Modern experience has proved that although governments are not always very efficient at producing goods, they are highly efficient at redistributing income and wealth." ("The Future of British Socialism," *New Politics,* Winter 1963, p. 97.)

The impasse of socialism today

Socialists today find themselves bewildered and uncertain of the future. For over half a century, the socialist movement was almost entirely devoted to propaganda and organization outside the framework of governmental responsibility. Now that so much of the socialist program has been realized, however, socialism faces a fate similar to that of organized political Liberalism.

Just as political Liberalism has passed away largely because some of the causes it championed have died a natural death while others have been solved by conservatives and socialists along liberal lines, socialism too may gradually pass away, as far as its original program is concerned, even though political parties with the socialist label may continue for a long time.

In the field of international politics, the main weakness of socialists has been the *failure to understand the role of power.* This intellectual failure was based on an admirable emotion: the desire to remove power from the society of nations and establish a world commonwealth based on peace and justice. Desirable as this goal may be, however, specific international problems cannot be solved by it or any other abstraction. Moreover, the practical realities of national economic planning have frequently given socialist foreign policies a strong element of *isolationism,* which is in sharp contrast with the traditional socialist slogan of international brotherhood.

Thus the foreign policy of the Labor government during the years 1945–1951 was discouraging to all those, in Europe and America, who believed that Britain would be the natural leader in a movement for a united Europe. In fairness to the Labor government, however, it should be noted that the Conservative government that followed it vacillated for years on the issue of joining the Common Market. Britain finally applied but was turned down by the opposition of France led by de Gaulle. Yet this French attitude in 1963 would have been ineffective if Britain's commitment to European unity had been less half-hearted and less hedged with ifs and buts. The division of public opinion in Britain on the Common Market was not based on party. Although the Conservative Party, as a whole, was a little more receptive to the idea of European integration than was the Labor Party, the main line of division was within each of the two major parties. It is, therefore, at least conceivable that when British public opinion more vigorously embraces the idea of European unity, a Labor government may well lead Britain into the Common Market, just as a Conservative government almost did in 1963.

Since its return to office in 1964 and 1966, the Labor government has cautiously moved toward entry into the Common Market, but its caution reflected, not any doctrinaire commitments to socialist ideology, but national pride and sensitivity after the debacle of 1963. One the issue of Vietnam, Britain under Labor proved one of the few major powers supporting the United States. In the words of the independent (but more often conservative) *Economist,* Prime Minister Wilson "has rightly (and, against the

"I'm happy to tell you, Your Majesty, that de Gaulle has allowed us to join the Common Market on only one ··· er ··· trifling condition"

Cummings in The Daily Express, London.

feelings of half of his party, courageously) underwritten American policy in Vietnam. He has been closer to the Americans than Sir Winston Churchill and Sir Anthony Eden were in the Vietnam crisis of 1954" (February 26, 1966).

In Norway, the socialists have been in favor of a strong alliance with the North Atlantic treaty powers, whereas in Sweden the socialist government has been in favor of neutrality and avoiding advance commitments. In the Middle East, the socialist-dominated government of Israel is strongly associated with the United States and her allies, but India's government, though strongly pro-socialist, is trying to maintain "non-alignment" between East and West. All these policies have little to do with socialism and are based primarily on national interests, attitudes, and traditions.

In sum, therefore, it can be said that from the viewpoint of ideology the pacifist heritage of socialism has frequently paralyzed its ability to solve international problems realistically and that, taking the picture as a whole, the foreign policies of socialist governments in recent years have been no better and no worse than those of nonsocialist governments in the same countries. The quality of a particular government depended on how intelligent and far-sighted that government was, rather than on whether it was socialist, liberal, or conservative.

In July, 1951, the Socialist International was re-established. At its first congress, over thirty socialist parties committed themselves to support the rearmament of their countries for collective defense against communist aggression. Meeting again in June, 1962, in Oslo, the Socialist International rejected the idea that the democratic nations should disarm unilaterally. As to the causes of the cold war, the Socialist International stated that the "East-West rivalry has largely been imposed upon an unwilling world by the communist leaders." These resolutions, an expression of realism and common sense rather than of socialism as such, are primarily of interest as reflecting a definite change of socialist outlook on the nature of war.

A generation ago, socialists looked upon capitalism as *the* cause of war and upon universal socialism as the only guarantee for peace. From experience with both fascist and communist imperialism, socialists have learned that war is a much more complex problem and that the forces of imperialism can be tied to any system of economic organization.

The present difficulties of the economic program of socialism are not likely to be resolved so soon. One great objective of socialism, the *welfare state*—i.e., the responsibility of the community for a minimum standard of social and economic security for every person—*is no longer a monopoly of socialist parties.* All other parties in democratic nations, with the exception of ultraconservative diehards, are also in favor of the welfare state. Some parties are more warmly for it than others, and some parties recommend more benefits than others; but, as a general principle, the welfare state (in the minimum sense) is accepted by reasonable persons in all parties and is no longer a matter of partisan controversy.

The concept of the welfare state no longer requires a separate political party. In fact, much of the welfare state in England was historically the work of the Conservative Party, and the limits of the welfare state are increasingly set by the ability to pay for its benefits rather than by differences of ideology.

The very fact that after two generations of socialist propaganda and accomplishment the main principles of the welfare state have been accepted by all parties in democratic states has created a real dilemma for the future of socialism. If it keeps on trying to convert the converted, it will lose the old fire and enthusiasm that made it a distinctive movement in the Western world in the last three generations. If its leaders are unable to formulate a new program, adapted to the needs of the last third of the twentieth century, the party may simply settle down to a fixed position slightly to the Left of the conservative parties, separated from the latter not by a basically different economic or political philosophy, but simply by its own concentration on translating the conception of the welfare state into a reality at the earliest possible moment.

Socialism in underdeveloped countries

The distinction between socialism and communism is of particular importance in the underdeveloped countries. The overriding political fact in poor nations is the desire to attain rapid economic growth. Without such economic progress, the newly emerging nations feel, there can be no genuine political independence or international leadership. Domestically, rapid economic growth is the only means of satisfying the yearning of the people for better living standards, health, and education.

The history of the last two centuries has shown two methods of rapid economic development: first, that of the most advanced Western nations (northwestern and central Europe, North America, and Australia and New Zealand), in which the free market was the main instrument of producing rapid economic growth. While it is true that government greatly aided this process (tariffs for infant industries; land grants for railways and educational institutions; legislatures, executives, and courts favoring the employer rather than the employee), it is still true that private initiative and capital were primarily responsible for the economic progress of the Western nations in the last two centuries. Without any government-sponsored five- or ten-year plans, private individuals decided how available resources—labor, capital, land, raw materials—were to be used, and individual consumers decided how much of their income was to be consumed and how much saved.

Economic growth in these Western nations was greatly favored by factors that are largely absent in underdeveloped nations today: a stable government, a fairly efficient civil service, relatively high levels of education, means of transportation and communication (highways, canals), and—perhaps most important of all—a considerable level of technological and entrepreneurial skill and initiative. Some nations—such as Great Britain, the Scandinavian countries, or the United States—even had the good fortune of having developed political institutions of free government before rapid economic expansion took place. As Alexis de Tocqueville noted in his *Democracy in America* (1835), "democracy is favorable to the growth of manufacturing, and it increases without limit the numbers of the manufacturing classes." His prophecy has come true. Equality of opportunity, the rule of law, the right to pursue happiness—these are but a few principles of democracy which have been favorable to economic expansion.

The second historically proved method of rapid economic growth has been through totalitarian communism. In this method, the state owns the means of production and sets an over-all goal—such as a five-year plan—of what is to be produced and how the available resources of labor, land, and capital are to be employed. The freedom of the consumer, worker, and producer is replaced by the dictate of the state. Because the communist state possesses totalitarian power, it can generally ensure that the plan is translated into reality. This may take a few decades, and millions of people may pay with their lives, but eventually a modern industrial economy does develop at a rapid pace. It is important to note that no nation has so far freely chosen the path of communist economic development: communism has either been imposed by internal revolution or civil war (Russia, China, Yugoslavia, Cuba) or by external armed force (the communist states in Eastern Europe, and North Vietnam and North Korea in the Far East). Every nation that has been subjected to communism by internal force was characterized by economic backwardness, low levels of education, corruption or inefficiency in the public service, and traditions of authoritarian government.

In facing the problem of economic development, underdeveloped nations today generally do not wish to imitate either the Western capitalist process of development or the communist path of complete state planning and ownership based on political terror. Nearly every underdeveloped nation likes to think that its economic and social problems can be solved through methods which are different from both Western capitalism and Soviet or Chinese communism. The label which is attached to this "third way" is that of socialism. In the context of underdeveloped countries socialism means many things to those who profess it.

First, socialism in the underdeveloped world stands for the ideal of social justice. In underdeveloped countries, the differences between the rich and the poor are proportionately greater than in the wealthier countries. Socialism, then, stands for the commitment to raise the poor masses to a higher level and to narrow the gap between the thin upper class of the privileged and the vast mass of the dispossessed. Socialism means more welfare services for the poor, more schools for the uneducated, and more human dignity for the traditionally underprivileged. Where tribal organization of society is still alive, socialism is but a new term for traditional tribal loyalty and solidarity. Thus, African socialism is defined by a leading Tanzanian statesman as follows: "The foundation, and the objective, of African Socialism is the Extended Family. The true African Socialist does not look on one class of men as his brethren and another as his natural enemies. He does not form an alliance with the 'brethren' for the extermination of the 'non-brethren.' He rather regards all men as his brethren—as members of his ever extending Family." (Julius K. Nyerere, *"Ujamaa": The Basis of African Socialism,* 1962, p. 8.)

When attacked for betraying socialism by encouraging private foreign investments in India's fertilizer industry, essential to its increased production of food, Prime Minister Indira Gandhi affirmed her government's commitment to both socialism and democracy in a nationwide address on April 24, 1966. Then she gave her definition of socialism: "What we all want is a better life, with more food, employment, and opportunity in conditions of economic justice, equality, and with individual freedom."

Second, the term socialism in underdeveloped countries often stands for the ideal of human brotherhood and world peace through law. As a result, socialists in underdeveloped nations frequently advocate nonalignment between the two sides in the cold war. Even where, as in India, the reality of Red Chinese invasion has made nonalignment a pure ideal or illusion, socialists still cling to it as a hope for the future. In Africa, the view is held that the world is divided, not between capitalist and communist countries, but between rich and poor countries, and the poor countries "should be very careful not to allow themselves to be used as the 'tools' of any of the rich countries of the world," whether such rich countries are capitalist or communist. (Paul E. Sigmund, ed., *The Ideologies of the Developing Nations,* 1963, p. 208.)

The third meaning of socialism in underdeveloped countries is the commitment to planning. Because underdeveloped countries look upon economic growth with a sense of urgency, they feel that the functioning of the free market may not ensure the kind of rapid economic expansion and growth that are called for. Some basic elements of a modern economy—highways, means of transportation, hospitals, low-cost housing, schools—cannot, in the very nature of things, attract private enterprise, since they are the framework within which private enterprise and profits can be generated but which in themselves usually do not create such profits. Also, there is the kind of basic enterprise, such as the manufacture of steel, for which there is either not enough private capital available or which cannot hope to compete with foreign established enterprises. Only the state can build the foundations of a modern economy (highways and the like), and only the state can assume the risks of profitless enterprise over a number of years, if such enterprise is necessary for the economy as a whole. In 1963, for example, India had five steel plants, of which three were state-owned. With a population of over 460 million, India produced only 5.6 million tons of steel in 1962, as compared with nearly 100 million tons produced in the United States. Yet even at her low level of development, India needed in 1963 at least 10 million tons of steel. As a step toward this goal, she asked American aid for the building of a sixth steel plant, to be state-owned, which would eventually produce about 4 million tons of steel. After several years of negotiation, the United States finally turned India down, largely because the projected plant would be state-owned. Indian businessmen, opposed to socialism as a general principle, publicly regretted the American position, because, in the words of the Indian Chamber of Commerce, the American refusal "could also hurt the private sector of Indian industry, which is badly in need of more steel." (*The New York Times*, September 8, 1963.)

Shortly after India was turned down by the United States, Communist Russia offered to build the needed steel mill—one of the great Soviet propaganda triumphs of the decade. Although India is anticommunist in her domestic policy and has a predominantly private property economy, the Soviet Union was able to overcome dogmatic ideological inhibitions more effectively than was the United States. Yet the ideological gulf between India and the Soviet Union is much wider than that between India and the United States.

The need for planning, to which all underdeveloped countries are committed, does not imply over-all, or even large-scale nationalization of the means of production. Here, India again provides a good illustration, as she is committed to the general idea of socialism. If planning can be measured by the extent to which a country's gross national product is controlled and disposed of by the government, we find that the figure is close to 30 per cent for the United States (on the federal, state, and local levels) but only 13-14 per cent for India. Where rapid development was necessary in the United States—as recently in atomic energy, jet aircraft, supersonic planes, space technology—the planning and financing have come almost entirely from the government, since in each of these areas the initial job was too big, too costly, and too profitless for private enterprise or initiative. What atomic energy or space technology in their beginning stages are for the United States, steel or railroads may be for India or any other underdeveloped country.

In the economic field, socialism in underdeveloped countries thus means an economic structure in which some industries are completely private (such as farming, handicrafts, small business), in which others have both a private and a public sector (as in heavy industry), and finally, in which the public sector dominates (transportation, public utilities). While this is the general meaning of socialism in the economic sphere in underdeveloped areas, the practical application varies in different countries. In general, it can be said that nationalization has gone furthest where political democracy is weak or nonexistent, as in Egypt, Algeria, or Burma. Where constitutional government is a reality (as in the Philippines, India, Israel, Chile), private enterprise is encouraged or at least tolerated.

Thus, we see that the meaning of socialism in underdeveloped countries differs from that in the wealthier countries, because the historical situation is different. In the West, socialism has meant, not how to industrialize a backward country, but how to distribute the fruits of a wealthy society in a more equitable way. As a result, the concept of the welfare state has virtually absorbed the idea of socialism. By contrast, socialism in underdeveloped countries is confronted with the task, not so much of distributing the fruits of an industrial economy which hardly exists, but to build an industrial economy, so as to raise the economic and intellectual level of the masses of the people. For the same reason, while socialism in Western countries has generally developed best within a framework of established constitutional government (as in Britain or Scandinavia), socialism in underdeveloped countries frequently develops within a tradition in which authoritarian rule by foreign imperialists or by native power-holders has been the rule. It is therefore to be expected that socialism in some underdeveloped countries will show a greater tolerance for authoritarian practices than has generally been true of Western socialism.

Yet, in the final analysis, socialism in the underdeveloped countries tries to imitate neither the Western capitalist pattern *in toto* nor the communist totalitarian pattern. From communism, the underdeveloped nations (regardless of their commitment to socialism) have borrowed the idea that economic development can be planned, and in some cases must be planned, by the state. However, the peoples of the underdeveloped countries, particularly the leaders among them (India, Nigeria, Mexico, Brazil), have decided that they want planning without the totalitarian police state of communism. As to the capitalist West, the underdeveloped countries, and especially the socialist elements in them, greatly admire its technological efficiency and spirit of progress, as exemplified in particular by the United States. Nonetheless, the great disparities of wealth as produced by the relatively freely functioning capitalist economies of the West seem a less worthy object of imitation in underdeveloped countries. The most important aspect of Western nations that appeals to underdeveloped nations is the political idea of self-government based on the rule of law. Whether the underdeveloped nations will be able to merge, under their concept of socialism, the Western political idea of liberty with the economic concept of planning, largely borrowed from the practice of communism, still remains to be seen. If the underdeveloped nations should fail in their attempted synthesis of constitutional government and economic planning (including partial government ownership of industry), there is the possibility that they (or some, at least) may consider constitutional government expendable, but not rapid economic development through full-fledged planning and public ownership of industry.

FOR FURTHER READING

Attlee, Clement R., *As It Happened.* New York: The Viking Press, Inc., 1954.

Buber, Martin, *Paths in Utopia.* Boston: Beacon Press, Inc. (Beacon Paperbacks), 1960.

Caute, David, *The Left in Europe Since 1789.* New York: McGraw-Hill Book Company, 1966.

Cole, G. D. H., *A History of Socialist Thought,* 5 vols. New York: St. Martin's Press, Inc., 1953–1960.

Cole, Margaret, *The Story of Fabian Socialism.* Stanford: Stanford University Press, 1962.

Crosland, C. A. R., *The Future of Socialism.* New York: The Macmillan Company, 1957.

———, *The Conservative Enemy: A Program of Radical Reform for the 1960s.* New York: Schocken Books, 1962.

Crossman, R. H. S., *The Politics of Socialism.* New York: Atheneum Publishers, 1965.

Datta, Amlankusum, *Socialism, Democracy, and Industrialization.* London: George Allen & Unwin, 1962.

Ebenstein, William, *Great Political Thinkers,* 3rd ed., chap. 24. New York: Holt, Rinehart & Winston, Inc., 1960.

———, *Modern Political Thought,* 2nd ed., chap. 11. New York: Holt, Rinehart & Winston, Inc., 1960.

———, *Political Thought in Perspective,* chap. 21. New York: McGraw-Hill Book Company (McGraw-Hill Paperbacks), 1963.

Egbert, Donald D. and Stow Persons (eds.), *Socialism and American Life,* 2 vols. Princeton, N.J.: Princeton University Press, 1952.

Fisher, Margaret W. and Joan V. Bondurant, *Indian Approaches to a Socialist Society.* Berkeley, Calif.: University of California Press, 1956.

Fried, Albert and Ronald Sanders (eds.), *Socialist Thought: A Documentary History.* Garden City, N.Y.: Doubleday & Company, Inc. (Anchor Books), 1964.

Friedland, William H. and Carl G. Rosberg (eds.), *African Socialism.* Stanford: Stanford University Press, 1964.

Gaitskell, Hugh, *Socialism and Nationalization.* London: Fabian Society, 1956.

Hayek, Friedrich A., *The Road to Serfdom.* Chicago: University of Chicago Press (Phoenix Books), 1960.

Heilbroner, Robert L., *The Great Ascent: The Struggle for Economic Development in Our Time.* New York: Harper & Row, Publishers (Harper Torchbooks), 1963.

Lewis, W. Arthur, *The Principles of Economic Planning.* Washington, D.C.: Public Affairs Press, 1949.

———, *Development Planning: The Essentials of Economic Policy.* New York: Harper & Row, Publishers, 1966.

Man, Henri de, *The Psychology of Socialism.* London: George Allen & Unwin, 1928.

Mises, Ludwig von, *Socialism.* New Haven: Yale University Press, 1951.

Morgan, H. Wayne (ed.), *American Socialism: 1900–1960.* Englewood Cliffs, N.J.: Prentice-Hall, Inc., 1964.

Morris, William D., *The Christian Origins of Social Revolt.* New York: The Macmillan Company, 1959.

Nyerere, Julius K., *"Ujamaa": The Basis of African Socialism.* Dar Es Salaam, Tanzania: (no publisher given), 1962.

Pigou, A. C., *Socialism Versus Capitalism.* New York: The Macmillan Company, 1937.

Rostow, W. W., *The Stages of Economic Growth: A Non-Communist Manifesto.* New York: Cambridge University Press, 1960.

Schapiro, J. Salwyn, *Movements of Social Dissent in Modern Europe.* Princeton, N.J.: D. Van Nostrand Co., Inc. (Anvil Books), 1962.

Schumpeter, Joseph A., *Capitalism, Socialism, and Democracy.* New York: Harper & Row, Publishers (Harper Torchbooks), 1962.

Sigmund, Paul E. (ed.), *The Ideologies of the Developing Nations.* New York: Frederick A. Praeger, Inc. (Praeger Paperbacks), 1963.

Thomas, Norman, *Socialism Re-Examined.* New York: W. W. Norton & Company, Inc., 1963.

Tinbergen, Jan, *Central Planning.* New Haven: Yale University Press, 1964.

Ward, Barbara, *India and the West.* New York: W. W. Norton & Company, Inc., 1961.

Wilson, Harold, *Purpose in Politics.* Boston: Houghton Mifflin Company, 1964.

Index

Index

A

B

C

H

I

J

K

L

M

S

T

U

V

W

Y